Ruby on Rails Web Mashup Projects

A step-by-step tutorial to building web mashups

Chang Sau Sheong

[PACKT]
PUBLISHING

BIRMINGHAM - MUMBAI

Ruby on Rails Web Mashup Projects

A step-by-step tutorial to building web mashups

First published: April 2008

Production Reference: 1160408

Published by Packt Publishing Ltd.
32 Lincoln Road
Olton
Birmingham, B27 6PA, UK.

ISBN 978-1-847193-93-3

www.packtpub.com

Cover Image by Raghuram Ashok (raghuram@iiitb.ac.in)

Credits

Author

Chang Sau Sheong

Reviewer

Walt Stoneburner

Senior Acquisition Editor

Douglas Paterson

Development Editor

Nikhil Bangera

Technical Editor

James Lumsden

Editorial Team Leader

Mithil Kulkarni

Project Manager

Abhijeet Deobhakta

Project Coordinators

Aboli Mendhe

Lata Basantani

Indexer

Monica Ajmera

Proofreader

Chris Smith

Production Coordinator

Shantanu Zagade

Cover Work

Shantanu Zagade

About the Author

Chang Sau Sheong has more than 12 years experience in software application development and has spent much of his career in Web and Internet-based applications. He has a wide range of experience in banking payment-related as well as Internet-based e-commerce software. Currently he is the Director of Software Development of a 50+ strong software development team in Welcome Real-time, a multi-national payment/loyalty software company based in France and Singapore.

Sau Sheong frequently writes for technical magazines and journals including Java Report, Java World, and Dr. Dobb's Journal. He also contributes to open-source projects in various technologies including smart cards, Ruby, and Java. His interests revolve mainly around technology and software development. He has done programming in Java/Java EE, C, C++, PHP, Python, Perl, Smalltalk, Erlang, Ruby/Ruby on Rails, various smart card platforms, and also worked on various databases. He has a wide range of experience in banking payment-related as well as Internet-based e-commerce software.

Sau Sheong hails from tropical Malaysia but has spent most of his adult and working life in sunny Singapore, where he shares his spare time enthusiastically writing software and equally playing Nintendo Wii with his wife and son. He has a Bachelor's degree in Computer Engineering, a Master's degree in Commercial Law, and is a certified international arbitrator.

Acknowledgements

Firstly, many thanks to Douglas Peterson, Nikhil Bangera, Walt Stoneburner, and James Lumsden who patiently guided me through my first book. I would also like to thank the following people from the Singapore Ruby Brigade who contributed comments and reviews on this book as well as general support: Peter Bohm, Chew Choon Keat, Herryanto Siatono, Johan Gozali, Jeffrey Lim, Wong Keng Onn, and many others from the 'last Thursday of the month' sessions. Grateful thanks also to Mech, Watt, and Simon for their good support and general cheerleading in Rails and non-Rails related matters. Special thanks to Sebastien Guillaud and all those people in Welcome Real-time who believed that I can run software development center, write a book, and go home in time to tutor my son.

Final thanks to the love of my life, Wooi Ying, who suffered my erratic 'nightlife' huddling in front of my laptop, creating software and writing this book, and also to Kai Wen for just being my son.

About the Reviewer

Walt Stoneburner is a software architect with over 20 years of commercial application development and consulting experience. Fringe passions involve quality assurance, configuration management, and security. If cornered, he may actually admit to liking statistics and authoring documentation as well.

He's easily amused by programming language design, collaborative applications, and ASCII art. Self-described as a closet geek, Walt also evaluates software products and consumer electronics, draws cartoons, produces photography, writes humor pieces, performs sleight of hand, enjoys game design, and can occasionally be found on ham radio.

Walt may be reached directly via email at wls@wwco.com. He publishes a tech and humor blog called the Walt-O-Matic at http://www.wwco.com/~wls/blog/. Rumors suggest that some of his strange videography may be found on iTunes.

Currently he is employed at Business & Engineering Systems Corporation as a lead engineer developing advanced software solutions for knowledge management.

Other book reviews and contributions include *AntiPatterns and Patterns in Software Configuration Management* (ISBN 978-0-471-32929-9, p. xi) and *Exploiting Software: How to Break Code* (ISBN 978-0-201-78695-8, p. xxxiii).

Table of Contents

Preface

A web mashup is a new type of web application that uses data and services from one or more external sources to build entirely new and different web applications. Web mashups usually mash up data and services that are available on the Internet—freely, commercially, or through other partnership agreements. The external sources that a mashup uses are known as mashup APIs.

This book shows you how to write web mashups using Ruby on Rails—the new web application development framework. The book has seven real-world projects—the format of each project is similar, with a statement of the project, discussion of the main protocols involved, an overview of the API, and then complete code for building the project. You will be led methodically through concrete steps to build the mashup, with asides to explain the theory behind the code.

What This Book Covers

The first chapter introduces the concepts of web mashups to the reader and provides a general introduction to the benefits and pitfalls of using web mashups as stand-alone applications or as part of existing web applications.

The first project is a mashup plugin into an existing web application that allows users to find the location of the closest facility from a particular geographic location based on a specified search radius. The location is mapped and displayed on Google Maps.

The second project is another mashup plugin. This plugin allows users to send messages to their own list of recipients, people who are previously unknown to the website, on behalf of the website. The project uses Google Spreadsheets and EditGrid to aggregate the information, and Clickatell and Interfax to send SMS messages and faxes respectively.

The third project describes a mashup plugin that allows you to track the sales ranking and customer reviews of a particular product from Amazon.com. The main API used is the Amazon E-Commerce Service (ECS).

The fourth project shows you how to create a full-fledged Facebook application that allows a user to perform some of the functions and features of a job board. This mashup uses Facebook, Google Maps, Daylife, Technorati and Indeed.com APIs.

The fifth project shows you how to create a full web mashup application that allows users to view information on a location. This is the chapter that uses the most mashup APIs, including Google Maps, FUTEF, WebserviceX, Yahoo! geocoding services, WeatherBug, Kayak, GeoNames, Flickr, and Hostip.info.

The sixth project describes a mashup plugin that allows an online event ticketing application to receive payment through Paypal, send SMS receipts, and add event records in the customer's Google Calendar account. The APIs used are Google Calendar, PayPal, and Clickatell.

The final project shows a complex mashup plugin used for making corporate expense claims. It allows an employee to submit expense claims in Google Docs and Spreadsheets, attaching the claims form and the supporting receipts. His or her manager, also using Google Docs and Spreadsheets, then approves the expense claims and the approved claims are retrieved by the mashup and used to reimburse the employee through PayPal. It uses the PayPal APIs and various Google APIs.

Conventions

In this book, you will find a number of styles of text that distinguish between different kinds of information. Here are some examples of these styles, and an explanation of their meaning.

There are three styles for code. Code words in text are shown as follows: "This will copy the necessary files to your RAILS_ROOT/vendor/plugins folder and run the install.rb script."

A block of code will be set as follows:

```
class Kiosk < ActiveRecord::Base
  def address
  "#{self.street}, #{self.city}, #{self.state}, #{self.zipcode}"
  end
```

When we wish to draw your attention to a particular part of a code block, the relevant lines or items will be made bold:

```
begin
kiosks.each { |kiosk|
loc = MultiGeocoder.geocode(kiosk.address)
kiosk.lat = loc.lat
```

Any command-line input and output is written as follows:

```
$./script/plugin install svn://rubyforge.org/var/svn/geokit/trunk
```

New terms and **important words** are introduced in a bold-type font. Words that you see on the screen, in menus or dialog boxes for example, appear in our text like this: "clicking the **Next** button moves you to the next screen".

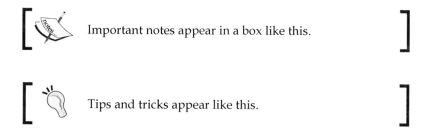

Important notes appear in a box like this.

Tips and tricks appear like this.

Reader Feedback

Feedback from our readers is always welcome. Let us know what you think about this book, what you liked or may have disliked. Reader feedback is important for us to develop titles that you really get the most out of.

To send us general feedback, simply drop an email to feedback@packtpub.com, making sure to mention the book title in the subject of your message.

If there is a book that you need and would like to see us publish, please send us a note in the **SUGGEST A TITLE** form on www.packtpub.com or email suggest@packtpub.com.

If there is a topic that you have expertise in and you are interested in either writing or contributing to a book, see our author guide on www.packtpub.com/authors.

Customer Support

Now that you are the proud owner of a Packt book, we have a number of things to help you to get the most from your purchase.

Downloading the Example Code for the Book

Visit `http://www.packtpub.com/files/code/3933_Code.zip` to directly download the example code.

The downloadable files contain instructions on how to use them.

Errata

Although we have taken every care to ensure the accuracy of our contents, mistakes do happen. If you find a mistake in one of our books — maybe a mistake in text or code — we would be grateful if you would report this to us. By doing this you can save other readers from frustration, and help to improve subsequent versions of this book. If you find any errata, report them by visiting `http://www.packtpub.com/support`, selecting your book, clicking on the **let us know** link, and entering the details of your errata. Once your errata are verified, your submission will be accepted and the errata will be added to the list of existing errata. The existing errata can be viewed by selecting your title from `http://www.packtpub.com/support`.

Questions

You can contact us at `questions@packtpub.com` if you are having a problem with some aspect of the book, and we will do our best to address it.

1

Introduction to Web Mashups

Web mashups

Welcome to the world of web mashups! A web mashup is a new type of web application that uses data and services from one or more external sources (usually from the Internet) to build entirely new and different web applications. This book shows you how to write web mashups using Ruby on Rails—the new web application development framework.

The idea of taking data and services from various places and making them available in a single application is not new. Data feeds such as RSS and ATOM feeds have been around for a while, making information available for anyone to re-use in another application. Screen scraping was a commonly used older technology that takes content directly from another application's display. Portals where different data and services were aggregated into portlets and displayed on the portal were popular during the dot-com era. What's so different about web mashups?

The answer is that while older data and service aggregation technologies aggregate and integrate in a fashion, a true web mashup creates a completely different and new function out of the existing content and services, driving different purposes and objectives.

The word **mashup** itself comes from the world of hip-hop music, where two or more songs are mixed together to form a new song. Web mashups are primarily web applications (though it is not a strict requirement). Web mashups also usually mash up data and services that are available on the Internet—freely, commercially or through other partnership agreements. The external sources that a mashup uses are known as mashup APIs.

Ruby and Ruby on Rails

Ruby is a dynamic, object-oriented programming language that is highly suitable for integrating various pieces of data and software together:

- Ruby is designed for programmer productivity and can be used to quickly develop maintainable pieces of software.

- Ruby is interpreted in real time, meaning that whatever is coded can be executed immediately without compilation.

- Ruby has a significant number of libraries that can be easily re-used through the gem packaging mechanism.

Ruby on Rails is an open-source full stack web application framework built on Ruby. Ruby on Rails follows two basic guiding principles—Convention over Configuration and Don't Repeat Yourself (DRY).

Convention over Configuration is a programming design that favors following a certain set of programming conventions instead of configuring an application framework. Certain commonly used configurations (by convention and not by rule) are pre-set and the framework just works if you follow those conventions. For example in Ruby on Rails, the convention states that a controller for a model object `Book` will be called `BookController` and all view pages relating to that controller will be kept in a folder called `book`.

DRY is a principle that focuses on reducing information duplication by keeping any piece of knowledge in a system in only one place. For example, in ActiveRecord (a major component of Ruby on Rails), schema information doesn't need to be duplicated in complex XML configuration files but is derived from the database schema itself. If the schema changes, the model changes accordingly, without the need to make changes in other parts of the system.

All this translates into a highly productive development framework in which web applications can be developed, deployed, and maintained easily. This framework, coupled with the fact that it uses Ruby, makes it an excellent platform for developing web mashups.

For more in-depth discussion into Ruby's capabilities I would recommend you look at *Programming Ruby: The Pragmatic Programmer's Guide* by Dave Thomas, Chad Fowler, and Andy Hunt as well as *The Ruby Way, Second Edition: Solutions and Techniques in Ruby Programming* by Hal Fulton.

The recommended reading for Ruby on Rails is *Agile Web Development with Rails, Second Edition* by Dave Thomas and David Heinemeier Hansson.

A note of caution here — this book is written with Rails 1.2.x in mind and the projects and examples in this book follows this version. There is no significant change in the projects though, if you choose to use Rails 2.x instead. As of writing, Rails does not work with Ruby 1.9. If you're a complete beginner with Ruby and Ruby on Rails I would recommend you flip through the books mentioned in the information box opposite before plunging into this one.

Types of web mashups

There are some existing classifications of mashups in various literatures available on this subject though none are authoritative. In many cases, web mashups are categorized according to their functionality; for example, some define data mashups, photo and video mashups, news mashups, and business mashups. However, in this book, I classify web mashups by how they are used in building an application. From this perspective, we can see two broad types of web mashups:

- A fully standalone mashup application.
- An embedded mashup plugin.

A **mashup application** is a web mashup that provides a complete set of functions for the user. This means a mashup application is the entire purpose of the system. For example, a mashup might take data from Flickr, the photo storage and sharing application and mash it up with Google Maps, the online mapping application to display photos that come from a particular geographical area. By themselves, neither Flickr nor Google Maps are able to provide these features. However, this mashup's functionalities only come from combining both APIs; the web application cannot exist without the APIs. The functionality of the mashup is a synergistic product of creative usage of APIs from both sources.

A **mashup plugin**, on the other hand, only provides part of the functionality of an existing web application. For example a leave (time off work) submission and approval application's core functionality is to allow users to submit and approve leave as part of an HR process. A mashup plugin can be embedded into this application to allow an employee to apply optionally for leave through an online calendar and send a text message to the manager to alert him or her. The data from the online calendar is passed to the core application and also the text messaging APIs to enhance the value of the core application. However, the leave submission and approval application can still exist and its core functionality is not reduced without the mashup plugin.

The difference might not be apparent at first glance, but the thinking behind the mashups and their creation can be quite different. Mashup plugins are usually created to supplement an existing application that is probably not a mashup. They are a means of providing more services and data to the user of the application. Mashup applications, on the other hand, are created mashups in the first place and all the functionalities are derived from the mashup APIs they source from.

This has an interesting implication in developing web mashups. While many still regard web mashups as interesting technology toys and probably the latest buzzword alongside AJAX and Web 2.0, this classification of web mashups allow us to see mashups not just as Web 2.0 startup applications but potential value-added services for our existing applications. While mashup applications are an exciting and growing phenomenon on the Internet, mashup plugins will probably provide the most practical way of using mashups immediately within an existing environment.

What can I do with web mashups?

So what is in it for *you?* I assume you are a programmer, either professional or amateur, looking perhaps to extend your repertoire of skills and capabilities to develop and maintain software more easily, better, and faster.

Web mashups represent a new way of developing software and along with any new development techniques come opportunities and risks. Here's an example of what you can do with mashups:

- Create a platform for a new breed of applications
- Provide access to a large set of external data and service sources
- Innovate and create extra value for your existing applications quickly
- Save on development and maintenance
- Leverage on common or widely available external applications and integrate them into your application

As a new breed of applications

Web mashups are a new breed of web applications (Wikipedia defines a mashup as a web application hybrid). While most prominent web mashups use publicly available APIs like Google Maps, Amazon ECS, and so on, this is not the only way to do mashups. Significant innovation can be achieved with further aggregation and hybridization of code and data from publicly available APIs, with private data as well as private applications.

The idea behind web mashups is creativity and innovation in new data and services, not just aggregation of existing ones, which most of the older technologies focus on. In comparison with portals, web mashups differ because portals aggregate and dish out content and applications in discrete packages, whereas mashups integrate the data and services together and serve them out as a single application.

An example of this is that while a portal will happily display a map of your current location, your address book, and today's astrology readings in 3 different portlet windows, a mashup will display the astrology readings of 10 of your friends who are closest to you, in an online map occupying the whole browser space.

This integrated and mashed up approach to programming can provide much insight into the way we program applications.

Access large sets of external sources

There are an increasing number of applications on the Internet providing an amazing variety of data and services as APIs or data sets for mashups. A quick check on the Programmable Web (`http://www.programmableweb.com`), which hosts a directory listing mashup APIs as well as mashup applications, shows up service APIs ranging from social networks to sending snail mail through the Internet. You can also get tons of data from hotel bookings to government spending data.

With the wealth of these external data sources, you can build amazing new applications that bring these data and services into meaningful new services. While mashups are not the only way to consume large sets of external sources of data and services, they are probably the most creative. Buzzword aside, anytime you take data or services from another application, you're already doing a mashup.

Innovate and create extra value for your application

If you have an existing application already, web mashups can allow you to innovate and create new value to your application by grafting new functionality through the external sources. For example, if you run a reservation application, you can alert your user through text messages from an SMS mashup API, add the date of reservation into his or her Google Calendar account through Google Calendar APIs, and show the location of the venue on Yahoo Maps.

Save on development and maintenance

Using mashups you can build new functions much faster and save on the development and maintenance effort. For example, if you are the developer of a facilities reservation system you don't want to spend time mastering the development of a text message sending component, which you normally would have to do if you wanted to have that feature.

Besides development, you can also reduce the maintenance of a feature that is outside your core domain. While this is often critical for startups, it is equally important for larger organizations that want to focus on their core domain. In the example given earlier, you don't want to spend time developing and maintaining a text-messaging component—you'll want to leave it to the text-messaging experts to do their job.

Leverage on and integrate common and widely available external applications

Besides saving on effort, instead of doing it yourself—you might want to leverage on common and popular applications to do the work for you. Effort aside, such applications already have a widespread user base that is familiar with the functionality. You can tap these users to extend your own user base and use the features of these applications to give an easily recognizable interface for your users.

For example, if you want online calendaring features, you wouldn't want to redevelop another Google Calendar. Instead, you would mash up Google Calendar APIs into your application and use their interface to provide something more familiar to your users.

Things to watch out for when doing web mashups

With all the exciting talk on mashups, it's important to realize that, as with any new technology and way of programming, the road is usually fraught with dangers. Rightly the map around mashups should have bright neon lights flashing 'Here Be Dragons'. Here are some possible problems (but not all) you might face when developing web mashups:

- Unreliable external APIs
- Commercial dependency on third party data and services
- Losing your users to external source providers

Unreliable external APIs

One of the most common complaints you will encounter as you develop web mashups is that you are highly, if not totally, dependent of the reliability of the mashup APIs you use. The two critical aspects of a web application—availability and response time—are not under your control, especially from sources that are provided freely to you.

Unfortunately at this point in time there is no viable way of resolving this completely. The only way of ensuring full availability and response time that meets your own requirements is to not have external dependencies at all. This is not possible of course, because web mashups are all about using external data and services.

However there are a number of ways to work around this issue:

- Do not use mashups for mission-critical services. If the service is mission critical for you or your user, don't use mashups or at least not those that fail to guarantee certain availability and response time.

- Have an agreement (normally commercial) with your external mashup API provider that provides back-to-back service agreements with your own services. For example, if you promise 98% uptime, make sure you have an agreement with your provider that also agrees to 98% uptime.

- Design your mashup to have graceful error handling. This could range from a user-friendly error page to a caching system for data feeds and even a standby secondary service provider. For example, if you have a mashup that sends text messages to your users, you can do a mashup with more than one provider—if a provider fails you, quickly switch to another.

This issue is generally more difficult to accept in mashup applications because should core functionality of the system be compromised, it is difficult to proceed. In any case, catering and planning for backup or alternatives in case of an external source breakdown is a must for all mashups if you intend to go into production.

Commercial dependency

This problem is related to the first. Besides being dependent on the external APIs for functionality, the larger issue could be that the provider of the external API changes its service partially or completely. This could range from the provider being shut down altogether, to the provider changing its business model or commercial terms and it becoming no longer viable to continue with that provider anymore. Even simpler issues like changes in API parameters and accessibility can potentially cause service outage.

For example, a free service could start to charge a fee (or increase its existing fees) and you can no longer afford to include it in your mashup. Sometimes the service itself is no longer sustainable because of licensing issues or the company behind the service abandons its business model in pursuit of another revenue source.

This problem is more acute in areas where the provider is the only one around. Again, planning for alternatives is important if you intend to go into production because this problem can potentially kill your mashup altogether. Some possible defenses against this risk:

- Avoid using mashups in cases where there is only a single provider.
- Plan for backups and be alert to the happenings of the external providers you're using. Keep an active lookout for API changes as well as news on the company providing your sources. For example, if an online mapping provider is being bought by Google and you use either Google Maps or the online mapping provider's sources you should be wary that either one or both services are likely to change.
- Be aware of the competition available to the providers you're using and design your mashup for easy switching. For example, if you need an online map make sure you're familiar with more than just Google Maps and design your system to be able to switch to another online mapping service easily.

Losing your users

Another problem might not be related to reliability or availability at all. If your mashup becomes commercially interesting, it is sometimes quite easy for your external source API provider to extend their existing functionality to include yours and you to be left with an 800-pound gorilla in your backyard. A related risk is for your users to decide that if they are already using the external provider anyway, they might as well switch over to it completely and bypass your mashup altogether.

Again both risks are more likely for mashup applications since a mashup application's main value is in the creative combination of the external sources. Mashup plugins are less likely to encounter this because your main application already has functionality that should be different from external APIs (or else you might want to ask yourself why you're doing it!).

The main defense against such risks is to continually innovate and possibly include more APIs. A mashup application that combines two APIs creatively is more likely to be made irrelevant than a mashup application that combines three, four, five or more APIs and uses them in a creative way that none of your external providers can match by themselves. Remember that your main advantage in creating a mashup application is that you are able to be the best of breed by combining the best aspects and features of various providers to create a unique service for your users.

At the end of the day, although there are significant risks in creating web mashups, there are always ways of mitigating them. Ultimately it's up to you to decide if the risks are worth taking compared to the services you're providing in your mashup.

How this book works

The approach I use in this book is pragmatic and direct and tends to be hands-on. If you're not a practicing programmer, you might want to dust off your programming books and read them again!

There are seven mashup projects in this book, with one chapter per project. Each chapter has the following sections:

- What does it do?
- Domain background
- Requirements overview
- Design
- Mashup APIs on the menu
- What we will be doing
- Summary

Each chapter explains the technical (and some domain) aspects of what the project does in increasing levels of difficulty and complexity. The first few chapters will be on simpler mashups and we gradually move on to more complex ones. Also, as you progress with the chapters there are more assumptions made on your abilities to understand how mashups work. For example, the first few chapters describe how you can get accounts in the various mashup APIs but subsequent ones dispense with this altogether, assuming that you can navigate your way to registering for your own account.

The chapters tend to have less theory and more discussion on background technology while focusing more on a step-by-step guide in building the project in the chapter. The chapters also tend to be standalone though there are occasionally some references back to earlier chapters for some background technology; so feel free to explore them in any sequence you like.

The following explains each subsequent chapter's structure, section by section.

What does it do?

This section gives a brief summary of the mashup's functions and objectives. This is normally just a paragraph or two.

Domain background

What follows after the summary of objectives is a description of the domain background of the mashup's functions. For example, in Chapter 5 we will be discussing how we can create a job board mashup. The domain background section of the chapter gives a simple introduction to job boards, what they are and what they do.

Requirements overview

This section provides an overview of the requirements of the mashup we will be creating in the chapter. It lists the requirements and objectives to meet in building the project in the chapter.

Design

This section describes how we will be building the project, the rationale behind the design, and how we approach the creation of the mashup.

Mashup APIs on the menu

This is a major section in the chapter, and it describes the list of mashup APIs that we will be using to create the mashup. In the first few chapters we will also describe how we register for the mashup APIs at the external sources. Later chapters will dispense with this. All of the APIs are either freely available or have trial accounts where you have limited access to the APIs.

This section also describes the various libraries we will be using to build the mashups. This includes open-source libraries as well as libraries included in the standard Ruby distribution. Whenever necessary there will be some discussion on the theory behind the libraries and how they work.

What we will be doing

This section is the bulk of the chapter and goes through the step-by-step creation of the project. All necessary code is shown and major steps are described in detail. Each major step is explained in its own sub-section. In some cases additional information is given to explain why certain aspects of the code are written that way.

This section starts with the creation of a Ruby on Rails project and ends with a final completion of the whole project. Most projects are coded in a straightforward manner without much optimization. In some cases I will even go some way out to code the project in a way that a more advanced Rubyist might find not following the 'Ruby Way'. This is intentional as the purpose of the book is to focus on web mashups and not on Ruby or Ruby on Rails, and the code should normally be very readable by any programmer, even those less familiar with Ruby.

Summary

The chapter is finally wrapped up in a short summary that describes what we have done in the chapter.

Ready?

So much for the brief introduction to web mashups! While some of the caveats in this chapter sound scary, ultimately web mashups are a brave new world altogether, and an exciting one for programmers.

It's time to jump into the projects, so let's begin and have fun!

2

'Find closest' mashup plugin

What does it do?

This mashup plugin allows your Rails website or application to have an additional feature that allows your users to find the location of the closest facility from a particular geographic location based on a specified search radius. This mashup plugin integrates with your existing website that has a database of locations of the facilities.

Building a kiosk locator feature for your site

Your company has just deployed 500 multi-purpose payment kiosks around the country, cash cows for the milking. Another 500 more are on the way, promising to bring in the big bucks for all the hardworking employees in the company. Naturally your boss wants as many people as possible to know about them and use them. The problem is that while the marketing machine churns away on the marvels and benefits of the kiosks, the customers need to know where they are located to use them. He commands you:

> "*Find a way to show our users where the nearest kiosks to him are, and directions to reach them!*"

What you have is a database of all the 500 locations where the kiosks are located, by their full address. What can you do?

Requirements overview

Quickly gathering your wits, you penned down the following quick requirements:

1. Each customer who comes to your site needs to be able to find the closest kiosk to his or her current location.

2. He or she might also want to know the closest kiosk to any location.

3. You want to let the users determine the radius of the search.

4. Finding the locations of the closest kiosks, you need to show him how to reach them.

5. You have 500 kiosks now, (and you need to show where they are) but another 500 will be coming, in 10s and 20s, so the location of the kiosks need to be specified during the entry of the kiosks. You want to put all of these on some kind of map.

Sounds difficult? Only if you didn't know about web mashups!

Design

The design for this first project is rather simple. We will build a simple database application using Rails and create a main Kiosk class in which to store the kiosk information including its address, longitude, and latitude information. After populating the database with the kiosk information and address, we will use a geolocation service to discover its longitude and latitude. We store the information in the same table. Next, we will take the kiosk information and mash it up with Google Maps and display the kiosks as pushpins on the online map and place its information inside an info box attached to each pushpin.

Mashup APIs on the menu

In this chapter we will be using the following services to create a 'find closest' mashup plugin:

*   Google Maps APIs including geocoding services
*   Yahoo geocoding services (part of Yahoo Maps APIs)
*   Geocoder.us geocoding services
*   Geocoder.ca geocoding services
*   Hostip.info

Google Maps

Google Maps is a free web-based mapping service provided by Google. It provides a map that can be navigated by dragging the mouse across it and zoomed in and out using the mouse wheel or a zoom bar. It has three forms of views—map, satellite and a hybrid of map and satellite. Google Maps is coded almost entirely in JavaScript and XML and Google provides a free JavaScript API library that allows developers to integrate Google Maps into their own applications. Google Maps APIs also provide geocoding capabilities, that is, they able to convert addresses to longitude and latitude coordinates.

We will be using two parts of Google Maps:

- Firstly to geocode addresses as part of GeoKit's APIs
- Secondly to display the found kiosk on a customized Google Maps map

Yahoo Maps

Yahoo Maps is a free mapping service provided by Yahoo. Much like Google Maps it also provides a map that is navigable in a similar way and also provides an extensive set of APIs. Yahoo's mapping APIs range from simply including the map directly from the Yahoo Maps website, to Flash APIs and JavaScript APIs. Yahoo Maps also provides geocoding services. We will be using Yahoo Maps geocoding services as part of GeoKit's API to geocode addresses.

Geocoder.us

Geocoder.us is a website that provides free geocoding of addresses and intersections in the United States. It relies on `Geo::Coder::US`, a Perl module available for download from the CPAN and derives its data from the TIGER/Line data set, public-domain data from the US Census Bureau. Its reliability is higher in urban areas but lower in the other parts of the country. We will be using Geocoder.us as part of GeoKit's API to geocode addresses.

Geocoder.ca

Geocoder.ca is a website that provides free geocoding of addresses in the United States and Canada. Like Geocoder.us. it uses data from TIGER/Line but in addition, draws data from GeoBase, the Canadian government-related initiative that provides geospatial information on Canadian territories. We will be using Geocoder.ca as part of GeoKit's API to geocode addresses.

Hostip.info

Hostip.info is a website that provides free geocoding of IP addresses. Hostip.info offers an HTTP-based API as well as its entire database for integration at no cost. We will be using Hostip.info as part of GeoKit's API to geocode IP addresses.

GeoKit

GeoKit is a Rails plugin that enables you to build location-based applications. For this chapter we will be using GeoKit for its geocoding capabilities in two ways:

- To determine the longitude and latitude coordinates of the kiosk from its given address
- To determine the longitude and latitude coordinates of the user from his or her IP address

GeoKit is a plugin to your Rails application so installing it means more or less copying the source files from the GeoKit Subversion repository and running through an installation script that adds certain default parameters in your environment.rb file.

To install the GeoKit, go to your Rails application folder and execute this at the command line:

```
$./script/plugin install svn://rubyforge.org/var/svn/geokit/trunk
```

This will copy the necessary files to your RAILS_ROOT/vendor/plugins folder and run the install.rb script.

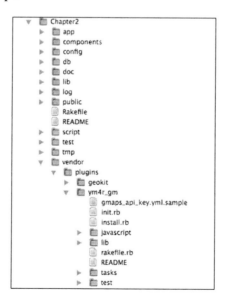

Configuring GeoKit

After installing GeoKit you will need to configure it properly to allow it to work. GeoKit allows you to use a few sets of geocoding APIs, including Yahoo, Google, Geocoder.us, and Geocoder.ca.

These geocoding providers can be used directly or through a cascading failover sequence. Using Yahoo or Google requires you to register for an API key but they are free. Geocoder.us is also free under certain terms and conditions but both Geocoder.us and Geocoder.ca have commercial accounts. In this chapter I will briefly go through how to get an application ID from Yahoo and a Google Maps API key from Google.

Getting an application ID from Yahoo

Yahoo's application ID is needed for any Yahoo web service API calls. You can use the same application ID for all services in the same application or multiple applications or one application ID per service.

To get the Yahoo application ID, go to `https://developer.yahoo.com/wsregapp/index.php` and provide the necessary information. Note that for this application you don't need user authentication. Once you click on submit, you will be provided an application ID.

Getting a Google Maps API key from Google

To use Google Maps you will need to have a Google Maps API key. Go to `http://www.google.com/apis/maps/signup.html`. After reading the terms and conditions you will be asked to give a website URL that will use the Google Maps API.

For geocoding purposes, this is not important (anything will do) but to display Google Maps on a website, this is important because Google Maps will not display if the URL doesn't match. However all is not lost if you have provided the wrong URL at first; you can create any number of API keys from Google.

Configuring evironment.rb

Now that you have a Yahoo application ID and a Google Maps API key, go to `environment.rb` under the `RAILS_ROOT/config` folder. Installing GeoKit should have added the following to your `environment.rb` file:

```
# Include your application configuration below
# These defaults are
used in GeoKit::Mappable.distance_to and in acts_as_mappable
GeoKit::default_units = :miles
```

```
GeoKit::default_formula = :sphere
# This is the timeout value in seconds to be used for calls to the
geocoder web
# services. For no timeout at all, comment out the setting. The
timeout unit is in seconds.
# GeoKit::Geocoders::timeout = 3
# These settings are used if web service calls must be routed through
a proxy.
# These setting can be nil if not needed, otherwise, addr and port
must be filled in at a minimum. If the proxy requires authentication,
the username and password can be provided as well.
GeoKit::Geocoders::proxy_addr = nil
GeoKit::Geocoders::proxy_port = nil
GeoKit::Geocoders::proxy_user = nil
GeoKit::Geocoders::proxy_pass = nil
# This is your yahoo application key for the Yahoo Geocoder
# See http://developer.yahoo.com/faq/index.html#appid and
http://developer.yahoo.com/maps/rest/V1/geocode.html
```

GeoKit::Geocoders::yahoo = <YOUR YAHOO APP ID>

```
# This is your Google Maps geocoder key.
# See http://www.google.com/apis/maps/signup.html and
http://www.google.com/apis/maps/documentation/#Geocoding_Examples
```

GeoKit::Geocoders::google = <YOUR GOOGLE MAPS KEY>

```
# This is your username and password for geocoder.us
# To use the free service, the value can be set to nil or false. For
usage tied to an account, the value should be set to
username:password.
# See http://geocoder.us and
http://geocoder.us/user/signup
GeoKit::Geocoders::geocoder_us = false
# This is your authorization key for geocoder.ca.
# To use the free service, the value can be set to nil or false. For
usage tied to an account, set the value to the key obtained from
Geocoder.ca
# See http://geocoder.ca and
http://geocoder.ca/?register=1
GeoKit::Geocoders::geocoder_ca = false
# This is the order in which the geocoders are called in a failover
scenario
# If you only want to use a single geocoder, put a single symbol in
the array.
# Valid symbols are :google, :yahoo, :us, and :ca
# Be aware that there are Terms of Use restrictions on how you can
use the various geocoders. Make sure you read up on relevant Terms of
Use for each geocoder you are going to use.
```

GeoKit::Geocoders::provider_order = [:google,:yahoo]

Go to the lines where you are asked to put in the Yahoo and Google keys and change the values accordingly. Make sure the keys are within apostrophes.

Then go to the provider order and put in the order you want (the first will be tried; if that fails it will go to the next until all are exhausted):

```
GeoKit::Geocoders::provider_order = [:google,:yahoo]
```

This completes the configuration of GeoKit.

YM4R/GM

YM4R/GM is another Rails plugin, one that facilitates the use of Google Maps APIs. We will be using YM4R/GM to display the kiosk locations on a customized Google Map. This API essentially wraps around the Google Maps APIs but also provides additional features to make it easier to use from Ruby. To install it, go to your Rails application folder and execute this at the command line:

```
$./script/plugin install svn://rubyforge.org/var/svn/ym4r/Plugins/GM/
trunk/ym4r_gm
```

During the installation, the JavaScript files found in the `RAILS_ROOT/vendors/plugin/javascript` folder will be copied to the `RAILS_ROOT/public/javascripts` folder.

A `gmaps_api_key.yml` file is also created in the `RAILS_ROOT/config` folder. This file is a YAML representation of a hash, like the `database.yml` file in which you can set up a test, development, and production environment. This is where you will put in your Google Maps API key (in addition to the `environment.rb` you have changed earlier).

For your local testing you will not need to change the values but once you deploy this in production on an Internet site you will need to put in a real value according to your domain.

What we will be doing

As this project is a mashup plugin, normally you would already have an existing Rails application you want to add this to. However for the purpose of this chapter, I show how the mashup can be created on a fresh project. This is what we will be doing:

- Create a new Rails project
- Install the Rails plugins (GeoKit and YM4R/GM) that will use the various mashup APIs

- Configure the database access and create the database
- Create the standard scaffolding
- Populate the longitude and latitude of the kiosks
- Create the find feature
- Display the found kiosk locations on Google Maps

Creating a new Rails project

This is the easiest part:

```
$rails Chapter2
```

This will create a new blank Rails project.

Installing the Rails plugins that will use the various mashup APIs

In this mashup plugin we'll need to use GeoKit, a Ruby geocoding library created by Bill Eisenhauer and Andre Lewis, and YM4R/GM — a Ruby Google Maps mapping API created by Guilhem Vellut. Install them according to the instructions given in the section above.

Next, we need to create the database that we will be using.

Configuring database access and creating the database

Assuming that you already know how database migration works in Rails, generate a migration using the migration generator:

```
$./script/generate migration create_kiosks
```

This will create a file `001_create_kiosks.rb` file in the `RAILS_ROOT/db/migrate` folder. Ensure the file has the following information:

```
class CreateKiosks < ActiveRecord::Migration
  def self.up
    create_table :kiosks do |t|
      t.column :name, :string
      t.column :street, :string
      t.column :city, :string
      t.column :state, :string
```

```
        t.column :zipcode, :string
        t.column :lng,  :float
        t.column :lat,  :float
      end
  end
    def self.down
        drop_table :kiosks
  end
  end
```

GeoKit specifies that the two columns must be named `lat` and `lng`. These two columns are critical to calculating the closest kiosks to a specific location.

Now that you have the migration script, run it to create the Kiosk table in your `RAILS_ROOT` folder:

Now that you have the migration script, run migrate to create the Kiosk table in your `RAILS_ROOT` folder:

$rake db:migrate

This should create the database and populate the kiosks table with a set of data. If it doesn't work please check if you have created a database schema with your favorite relational database. The database schema should be named `chapter2_development`. If this name displeases you somehow, you can change it in the `RAILS_ROOT/config/database.yml` file.

Creating scaffolding for the project

You should have the tables and data set up by now so the next step is to create a simple scaffold for the project. Run the following in your `RAILS_ROOT` folder:

$./script/generate scaffold Kiosk

This will generate the Kiosk controller and views as well as the Kiosk model. This is the data model for Kiosk, in the `kiosk.rb` file. This is found in `RAILS_ROOT/app/models/`.

```
  class Kiosk < ActiveRecord::Base
    def address
      "#{self.street}, #{self.city}, #{self.state}, #{self.zipcode}"
    end
  end
```

Just add in the `address` convenience method to have quick access to the full address of the kiosk. This will be used later for the display in the info box.

Populating kiosk locations with longitude and latitude information

Before we begin geolocating the kiosks, we need to put physical addresses to them. We need to put in the street, city, state, and zipcode information for each of the kiosks. After this, we will need to geolocate them and add their longitude and latitude information. This information is the crux of the entire plugin as it allows you to find the closest kiosks.

In addition you will need to modify the kiosk creation screens to add in the longitude and latitude information when the database entry is created.

Populate the database with sample data

In the source code bundle you will find a migration file named `002_populate_kiosks.rb` that will populate some test data (admittedly less than 500 kiosks) into the system. We will use this data to test our plugin. Place the file in `RAILS_ROOT/db/migrate` and then run:

```
$rake db:migrate
```

Alternatively you can have some fun entering your own kiosk addresses into the database directly, or find a nice list of addresses you can use to populate the database by any other means.

Note that we need to create the static scaffold first before populating the database using the migration script above. This is because the migration script uses the `Kiosk` class to create the records in the database. You should realize by now that migration scripts are also Ruby scripts.

Bulk adding of longitude and latitude

One of the very useful tools in Ruby, also used frequently in Rails, is **rake**. Rake is a simple make utility with rake scripts that are entirely written in Ruby. Rails has a number of rake scripts distributed along with its installation, which you can find out using this command:

```
$rake --tasks
```

Rails rake tasks are very useful because you can access the Rails environment, including libraries and ActiveRecord objects directly in the rake script. You can create your own customized rake task by putting your rake script into the RAILS_ROOT/lib/tasks folder.

We will use rake to add longitude and latitude information to the kiosks records that are already created in the database.

Create an add_kiosk_coordinates.rake file with the following code:

```
namespace :Chapter2 do
  desc 'Update kiosks with longitude and latitude information'
  task :add_kiosk_coordinates => :environment do
    include GeoKit::Geocoders

    kiosks = Kiosk.find(:all)
    begin
      kiosks.each { |kiosk|
        loc = MultiGeocoder.geocode(kiosk.address)

        kiosk.lat = loc.lat
        kiosk.lng = loc.lng
        kiosk.update
        puts "updated kiosk #{kiosk.name} #{kiosk.address} =>
                                [#{loc.lat}, #{loc.lng}]"

      }
    rescue
      puts $!
    end
  end
end
```

In this rake script you first include the Geocoders module that is the main tool for discovering the coordinate information. Then for each kiosk, you find its longitude and latitude and update the kiosk record.

Run the script from the console in the RAILS_ROOT folder:

`$rake Chapter2:add_kiosk_coordinates`

Depending on your network connection (running this rake script will of course require you to be connected to the Internet) it might take some time. Run it over a long lunch break or overnight and check the next day to make sure all records have a longitude and latitude entry. This should provide your mashup with the longitude and latitude coordinates of each kiosk. However your mileage may differ depending on the location of the kiosk and the ability of the geocoding API to derive the coordinates from the addresses.

Adding longitude and latitude during kiosk creation entry

Assuming that you have a `kiosks_controller.rb` already in place (it would be generated automatically along with the rest of the scaffolding), you need to add in a few lines very similar to the ones above to allow the kiosk created to have longitude and latitude information.

First, include the geocoders by adding GeoKit after the controller definition, in `kiosks_controller.rb`.

```
class KiosksController < ApplicationController
include GeoKit::Geocoders
```

Next, add in the highlighted lines in the `create` method of the controller.

```
def create
  @kiosk = Kiosk.new(params[:kiosk])
  loc = MultiGeocoder.geocode(@kiosk.address)
  @kiosk.lat = loc.lat
  @kiosk.lng = loc.lng
  if @kiosk.save
    flash[:notice] = 'Kiosk was successfully created.'
    redirect_to :action => 'list'
  else
    render :action => 'new'
  end
end
```

Finally, modify the `update` method in the controller to update the correct longitude and latitude information if the kiosk location changes.

```
def update
  @kiosk = Kiosk.find(params[:id])
  address = "#{params[:kiosk][:street]}, #{params[:kiosk][:city]},
#{params[:kiosk][:state]}"
  loc = MultiGeocoder.geocode(address)
  params[:kiosk][:lat] = loc.lat
  params[:kiosk][:lng] = loc.lng
  if @kiosk.update_attributes(params[:kiosk])
    flash[:notice] = 'Kiosk was successfully updated.'
    redirect_to :action => 'show', :id => @kiosk
  else
    render :action => 'edit'
  end
end
```

Creating the find closest feature

Now that you have the kiosk data ready, it's time to go down to the meat of the code. What you'll be creating is a search page. This page will have a text field for the user to enter the location from which a number of kiosks closest to it will be displayed. However, to be user-friendly, the initial location of the user is guessed and displayed on the text field.

Create a `search` action in your controller (called `search.rhtml`, and place it in `RAILS_ROOT/app/views/kiosks/`) to find your current location from the IP address retrieved from your user.

```
def search
  loc = IpGeocoder.geocode(request.remote_ip)
  @location = []
  @location << loc.street_address << loc.city << loc.country_code
end
```

The `remote_ip` method of the Rails-provided request object returns the originating IP address, which is used by GeoKit to guess the location from Hostip.info. The location is then used by `search.rhtml` to display the guessed location.

Note that if you're running this locally, i.e. if you are browsing the application from your PC to a locally running server (for example, off your PC as well), you will not get anything. To overcome this, you can use a dynamic DNS service to point an Internet domain name to the public IP address that is assigned to your PC by your ISP. You will usually need to install a small application on your PC that will automatically update the DNS entry whenever your ISP-assigned IP address changes. There are many freely available dynamic DNS services on the Internet.

When accessing this application, use the hostname given by the dynamic DNS service instead of using localhost. Remember that if you're running through an internal firewall you need to open up the port you're starting up your server with. If you have a router to your ISP you might need to allow port forwarding.

This is a technique you will use subsequently in Chapters 5 and 6.

Create a `search.rhtml` file and place it in the `RAILS_ROOT/app/view/kiosks` folder with the following code:

```
<h1>Enter source location</h1>
Enter a source location and a radius to search for the closest kiosk.
<% form_tag :action => 'find_closest' do %>
<%= text_field_tag 'location', @location.compact.join(',')  %>
<%= select_tag 'radius', options_for_select({'5 miles' => 5, '10
miles' => 10, '15 miles' => 15}, 5) %>
<%= submit_tag 'find' %>
<% end %>
```

Here you're asking for the kiosks closest to a specific location that are within a certain mile radius. We will be using this information later on to limit the search radius.

After that, mix-in the `ActsAsMappable` module into the Kiosk model in `kiosk.rb`.

```
class Kiosk < ActiveRecord::Base
  acts_as_mappable
end
```

This will add in a calculated column called (by default) `distance`, which you can use in your condition and order options. One thing to note here is that the `ActsAsMappable` module uses database-specific code for some of its functions, which are only available in MySQL and PostgresSQL.

Next, create the `find_closest` action to determine the location of nearest kiosks.

```
def find_closest
  @location = MultiGeocoder.geocode(params[:location])
  if @location.success
    @kiosks = Kiosk.find(:all,
              :origin => [@location.lat, @location.lng],
              :conditions => "distance < #{params[:radius]}",
              :order=>'distance')
  end
end
```

The `ActsAsMappable` module mixed in also overrides the find method to include an originating location, either based on a geocode-able string or a 2-element array containing the longitude/latitude information. The returned result is a collection of kiosks that are found with the given parameters.

Finally create a simple `find_closest.rhtml` view template (and place it in the `RAILS_ROOT/app/view/kiosks/` folder) to display the kiosks that are retrieved. We'll add in the complex stuff later on.

```
<h1><%= h @kiosks.size %> kiosks found within your search radius</h1>
<ol>
<% @kiosks.each do |kiosk| %>
<li><%= kiosk.name%><br/></li>
<% end %>
</ol>
```

Do a quick trial run and see if it works.

$./script/server

Then go to `http://localhost:3000/kiosks/search`. If you have some data, put in a nearby location (e.g. from our source data: San Francisco) and click on 'find'. You should be able to retrieve some nearby kiosks.

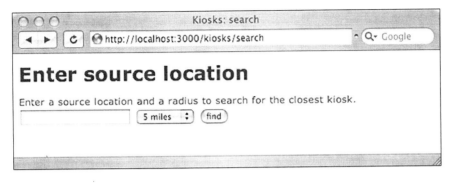

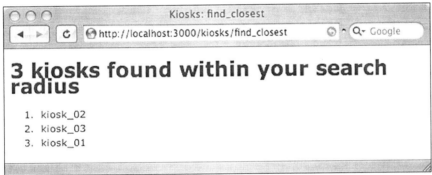

Displaying kiosks on Google Maps

Now that you know where the kiosks are located, it's time to show them on Google Maps. For this we'll be using the YM4R/GM plugin. If you haven't installed this plugin yet, it's time to go back and install it.

To add display to Google Maps, you will need to change the `find_closest` action as well as the `find_closest` view template. First, add the `find_closest` action in the `kiosks_controller.rb`:

```ruby
def find_closest
  @location = MultiGeocoder.geocode(params[:location])
  if @location.success
    @kiosks = Kiosk.find(:all,
            :origin => [@location.lat, @location.lng],
            :conditions => ["distance < ?", params[:radius]],
            :order=>'distance')
  @map = GMap.new("map_div")
```

```
@map.control_init(:large_map => true, :map_type => true)
# create marker for the source location
@map.icon_global_init( GIcon.new(:image =>
        "http://www.google.com/mapfiles/ms/icons/red-pushpin.png",
                        :shadow => "http://www.google.com/
                                    mapfiles/shadow50.png",
                        :icon_size => GSize.new(32,32),
                        :shadow_size => GSize.new(37,32),
                        :icon_anchor => GPoint.new(9,32),
                        :info_window_anchor => GPoint.new(9,2),
                        :info_shadow_anchor =>
                                    GPoint.new(18,25)),
            "icon_source")
icon_source = Variable.new("icon_source")
source = GMarker.new([@location.lat, @location.lng],
        :title => 'Source',
        :info_window => "You searched for kiosks
            <br>#{params[:radius]} miles around this source",
        :icon => icon_source)
@map.overlay_init(source)
# create markers one for each location found
markers = []
@kiosks.each { |kiosk|
    info = <<EOS
<em>#{kiosk.name}</em><br/>
#{kiosk.distance_from(@location).round} miles away<br/>
<a href="http://maps.google.com/maps?saddr=#{u(@location.to_
geocodeable_s)}&daddr=#{u(kiosk.address)}>directions here from
source</a>
EOS
    markers << GMarker.new([kiosk.lat, kiosk.lng], :title =>
kiosk.name, :info_window => info)
    }
    @map.overlay_global_init(GMarkerGroup.new(true, markers),"kiosk_
markers")
    # zoom to the source
    @map.center_zoom_init([@location.lat, @location.lng], 12)
  end

end
```

Google Maps API is a JavaScript library and YM4R/GM code is a library that creates JavaScript scripts to interact and manipulate the Google Maps API. Almost all classes in the library correspond with an equivalent Google Maps API class, so it is important that you are also familiar with the Google Maps API. The online documentation comes in very useful here so you might want to open up the Google Maps reference documentation (`http://www.google.com/apis/maps/documentation/reference.html`) as you are coding.

Let's go over the code closely.

The first line creates a `GMap` object that is placed inside a `<div>` tag with the id `map_div` while the second line sets some control options.

```
@map = GMap.new("map_div")
@map.control_init(:large_map => true, :map_type => true)
```

The next few lines then create a `GMarker` object from the source location that the user entered that uses a specific icon to show it then overlays it on the map. There are several options you can play around with here involving setting the image to be shown as the marker. For this chapter I used a red-colored pushpin from Google Maps itself but you can use any image instead. You can also set the text information window that is displayed when you click on the marker. The text can be in HTML so you can add in other information including images, formatting, and so on.

```
# create marker for the source location
@map.icon_global_init( GIcon.new(:image =>
        "http://www.google.com/mapfiles/ms/icons/red-pushpin.png",
                        :shadow => "http://www.google.com/
                                    mapfiles/shadow50.png",
                        :icon_size => GSize.new(32,32),
                        :shadow_size => GSize.new(37,32),
                        :icon_anchor => GPoint.new(9,32),
                        :info_window_anchor => GPoint.new(9,2),
                        :info_shadow_anchor =>
                        GPoint.new(18,25)), "icon_source")
icon_source = Variable.new("icon_source")
source = GMarker.new([@location.lat, @location.lng],
        :title => 'Source',
        :info_window => "You searched for kiosks
            <br>#{params[:radius]} miles around this source",
        :icon => icon_source)
@map.overlay_init(source)
```

The lines of code after that go through each of the located kiosks and create a `GMarker` object then overlay it on the map too. For each kiosk location, we put in an info window that describes the distance away from the source location and a link that shows the directions to get from the source to this kiosk. This link goes back to Google and will provide the user with instructions to navigate from the source location to the marked location.

Note that you need to URL encode the location/address strings of the source and kiosks, so you need to include `ERB::Util` as well (along with `GeoKit::Geocoders`). This is the `u()` method. In `kiosks_controller.rb`, add:

```
include ERB::Util
```

then add the following (beneath the code entered above):

```
      # create markers one for each location found
      markers = []
      @kiosks.each
      { |kiosk|
        info = <<EOS
<em>#{kiosk.name}</em><br/>
#{kiosk.distance_from(@location).round} miles away<br/>
<a href="http://maps.google.com/maps?saddr=#{u(@location.
to_geocodeable_s)}&daddr=#{u(kiosk.address)}>directions here from
source</a>
EOS
        markers << GMarker.new([kiosk.lat, kiosk.lng],
              :title => kiosk.name, :info_window => info)
      }
      @map.overlay_global_init(GMarkerGroup.new(true, markers),
                                      "kiosk_markers")
```

Finally the last line zooms in and centers on the source location.

```
      # zoom to the source
      @map.center_zoom_init([@location.lat, @location.lng], 12)
```

Now let's look at how the view template is modified to display Google Maps. The bulk of the work has already been done by YM4R/GM so you need only to include a few lines.

```
<h1><%= h @kiosks.size %> kiosks found within your search radius</h1>
<ol>
<% @kiosks.each do |kiosk| %>
<li><%= kiosk.name%><br/></li>
<% end %>
</ol>
```

```
<%= GMap.header %>
<%= javascript_include_tag("markerGroup") %>
<%= @map.to_html%>
<%= @map.div(:width => 500, :height => 450)%>
```

Gmap.header creates the header information for the map, including YM4R/GM and Google Maps API JavaScript files. We are also using GMarkerGroups so we need to include the GMarkerGroup JavaScript libraries. Next, we need to initialize the map by calling map.to_html. Finally we'll need to have a div tag that is the same as the one passed to the GMap constructor in the controller (map_div). This is done by calling the div method of the GMap object. To size the map correctly we will also need to pass on its dimensions (height and width here).

And you're ready to roll! Although the page doesn't display the best layout, you can spice things up by adding the necessary stylesheets to make the view more presentable.

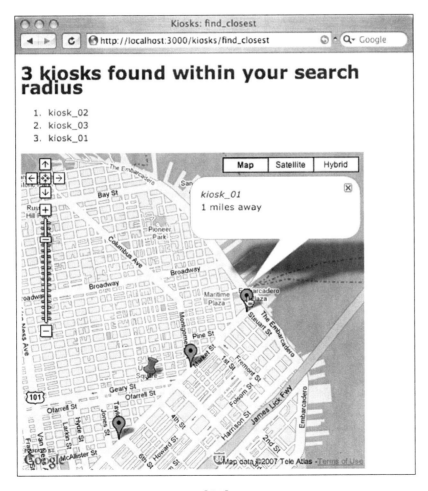

Summary

What we've learned in this chapter is to create a mashup with Ruby on Rails on a number of mapping and geocoding providers including Yahoo, Google, geocoder. us, geocoder.ca, and hostip.info. We learned to create a mashup that gives us a map of the closest kiosks to a particular location, given an existing database of kiosks that have location addresses. This is just an introduction to the synergistic value that mashups bring to the table, creating value that was not available in individual APIs. When they are all put together, you have a useful feature for your website.

3
Proxy mailing list mashup plugin

What does it do?

This mashup plugin allows your Rails website or application to have a proxy mailing list feature that includes email, SMS messages, and fax. A normal mailing list allows a website to send their messages to its list of visitors or users. A proxy mailing list allows a third-party user to send the messages to their own list of recipients, people who are previously unknown to the website, on behalf of the website.

Building a proxy mailing list feature for your website

Your boss calls you in to discuss a new feature for your company's website. There is a new marketing initiative for your company's products. You have been chosen to build in a new feature for the marketing folks on the 14th floor that allows them to send out regular email marketing messages to clients and potential clients. You dutifully write down the requirements for this mailing list feature:

- Import contacts from a spreadsheet containing the name of the client or potential client into an internal database
- Allow internal marketing users to define email campaign messages
- Send email messages to the clients and potential clients at regular intervals

Doesn't look too hard! You walked away confidently.

The next day your boss calls you in again. Oh surprise – there is a new requirement. After some meetings, the marketing people decided that sending email messages is not enough, now they want to send SMS messages and send faxes as well. Because your clients are scattered around the world, the SMS messages and faxes also need to be sent around the world! Sighing expectedly, you write down the additional new requirements:

- Allow internal marketing users to define SMS and fax messages
- Send SMS messages to clients and potential clients
- Send faxes to clients and potential clients
- Messages need to be sent worldwide

You should have known better than to expect finalized requirements from the first meeting!

You were still figuring out how to send SMS messages the next day when your boss called for an emergency meeting with you. With a sinking feeling you walked into his room.

The marketing people originally wanted to consolidate the contacts data from your company's resellers around the world into an spreadsheet file, which is used to feed into the website. However because of data privacy (and you suspect, other commercial) issues, the resellers now refuse to give your company the contacts data directly. Instead, the marketing people have struck a deal to let the resellers send the marketing messages by themselves through your website. Worse, you are no longer allowed to store any contacts information in your database.

You're stuck now! You don't have the contacts data and now you need to let the resellers send the marketing messages? How can you do it?

Requirements overview

You consolidated the following (hopefully final now) set of requirements:

1. Allow internal marketing users to define email, SMS, and fax messages in a template
2. Allow the external resellers to customize the pre-defined marketing messages according to their list of contacts
3. Send email, SMS, and fax messages to the clients and potential clients around the world on a regular basis
4. You cannot store any contacts information

Mashups to the rescue!

Design

Let's see how we can use Rails and some mashup magic to build this new feature for your website.

Define messages

Create a simple Rails web application that allows the marketing user to construct message templates that contain the messages to be sent via email, SMS text messaging, and fax. This template can be used later as the basis for sending various messages to the recipients of the marketing blitz.

Get contacts and customized message data

We need to get the reseller's contact information without storing it in our database. To do this, we need to get the resellers to define or import their contacts into an online spreadsheet. After that, the resellers need to export the spreadsheet in a data format that is suitable for extraction and processing by our website. For this chapter, we will show how this can be done through Google Spreadsheet and EditGrid, two popular online spreadsheets. The reseller will upload his or her contacts from his or her spreadsheet into Google Spreadsheet or EditGrid, and then publish a link to this spreadsheet. Subsequently the reseller will select a message template and create a message-sending job by providing this link to his or her contacts.

Send messages

The number of contacts provided by each reseller is normally high, so it is unrealistic to send the messages interactively (that is, to send the message on the click of a button in the user interface and wait for a response that indicates that the messages all sent). There are two alternatives for sending messages in a non-interactive way. One method is to create a threaded job that is separate from the main process and run it in the background when the reseller clicks on the send button. The other method is to create jobs that are stored in the database and retrieved separately by another process at regular intervals to be processed independently. I have chosen to use the second method of executing the send-message tasks in this chapter, as it is the simpler of the two.

Emails can be done easily through ActionMailer, with messages captured from the message template. However, SMS and fax messages are more complex. Let's go through some basic background knowledge on these types of messages before coming up with the strategies on sending them.

Sending SMS messages

SMS or Short Message Service is a technology that enables the sending and receiving of messages between mobile phones. SMS was part of the GSM (Global System for Mobile Communications) standards at the beginning but was later ported to technologies like CDMA and TDMA. SMS is very popular and widely used as it is supported by all GSM mobile phones.

When an SMS message is sent from a mobile phone, it will reach an SMSC in the GSM network. The SMSC then forwards the SMS message towards the destination, passing through one or more network elements, including other SMSCs. If the recipient is unavailable (for example, when the mobile phone is switched off), the SMSC will store the SMS message and forward it when the recipient is available.

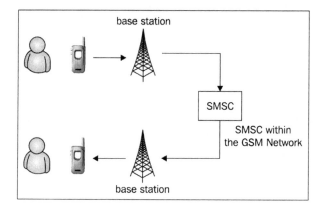

An SMSC normally belongs to a single network. For SMSes to reach mobile phones in different GSM networks, an SMS gateway is used to bridge between SMSCs in different networks.

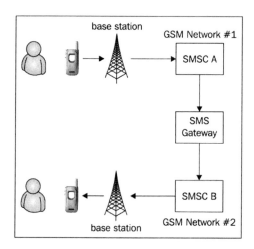

SMS gateways are also used to act as a concentrator that can access multiple SMSCs. This allows applications that send SMSes to channel their messages through a single gateway to multiple SMSCs without the need to connect to each SMSC individually. This is the model many bulk SMS providers (including Clickatell, the provider we're using in this chapter) use.

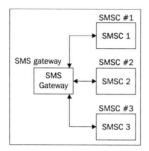

One SMS message can contain at most 140 bytes of data, so one SMS message can contain up to:

- 160 characters if the default GSM 7-bit character (ASCII) encoding is used
- 140 characters if 8-bit character encoding is used
- 70 characters if 16-bit Unicode UCS2 character encoding is used

Besides text, SMS messages can also carry binary data like ringtones, pictures, operator logos, wallpapers, animations, VCards, and WAP configurations to a mobile phone. However, such uses are vendor-specific and are not as widely supported as text-based SMS.

Probably the best way to send SMS messages in bulk is through a bulk SMS provider. A provider with wide global coverage will also allow us to send SMS messages around the world. As most bulk SMS providers also provide APIs for developers, this ties in nicely with our requirements to send SMSes to a large number of people globally. Clickatell, the SMS provider we're using in this chapter provides a bulk SMS gateway and numerous APIs to connect to it.

Sending fax messages

Fax or facsimile is a telecommunications technology used to transfer copies of documents over the telephone network. Fax is most commonly used to send documents between two fax machines connected to a telephone line. A fax machine is a three-in-one machine, with a scanner, a modem, and a printer rolled into one. The scanner extracts an image of the document in digital form, the modem sends it across to the other fax machine via the telephone network, while the printer reproduces it on the other end, and vice versa. However Internet-based faxing services and multi-function printers are fast replacing the traditional standalone fax machines.

Various Internet fax services now provide email and API services for users to send faxes directly from a file, removing the need for scanning and sending via a telephone network. The best way to programmatically send faxes would be through a fax service provider and for this chapter we will be using Interfax and sending faxes through an XML-RPC-based web service.

Mashup APIs on the menu

After reviewing the strategy and determining the best way to design for the requirements, we have established the following mashup APIs that we will use for this chapter:

- Google Spreadsheet and/or EditGrid for the user to store and share the contacts information
- Clickatell to send SMS messages
- Interfax to send faxes

The APIs in this chapter have free developer trial accounts so you can experiment with them a bit. However, the APIs we are using in this chapter are not free for full commercial use and they have some restrictions on their usage.

We will not be using any specific Ruby libraries for this mashup as the APIs we use doesn't require them. Instead we will be using standard Ruby libraries that are available out of the box from any Ruby installation, in particular the `Net::HTTP` module, which allows us to connect to XML-RPC web services and REST-based HTTP APIs. We will also use the built-in CSV module to simplify conversion of CSV formatted data into arrays.

Let's run through these online APIs as well as the `Net::HTTP` module.

Google Spreadsheets

Google Spreadsheets (`http://docs.google.com`) is an online spreadsheet service offered by Google as part of its Google Docs and Spreadsheets offering. Google Docs and Spreadsheets is a Web-based word processor and spreadsheet application that allows users to create and edit documents and spreadsheets online while collaborating in real-time with other users. Google Docs and Spreadsheets combine the features of two services, Writely and Spreadsheets.

Users can create the spreadsheet online or upload spreadsheets of various formats including CSV, Excel, and OpenDocument (.ods for spreadsheets). There is a limit to each spreadsheet, which is 10,000 rows, 256 columns, or 100,000 cells, whichever limit is reached first. When importing spreadsheets, the import file cannot be larger than 1MB in size. Users are also able to export their documents in various output formats, which include CSV, Excel, OpenDocument, PDF, and so on. Google Spreadsheets is free, and any Google user can get it as part of the package.

Google Spreadsheets has its own API, which uses part of the Google Data APIs. This API requires user account authentication to access information on private spreadsheets. However for this chapter we will not be using access-controlled data in Google Spreadsheets and only the published spreadsheets in a comma delimited (CSV) format.

EditGrid

EditGrid is a free online spreadsheet service with paid subscription for commercial/enterprise users. EditGrid allows users to create an online spreadsheet or import spreadsheets in various formats including CSV, Excel, and OpenDocument. Users are also able to export their documents in various output formats, which include CSV, Excel, OpenDocument, PDF, and so on.

You will need to register for a free personal account, which requires only a login user name and a password: http://www.editgrid.com.

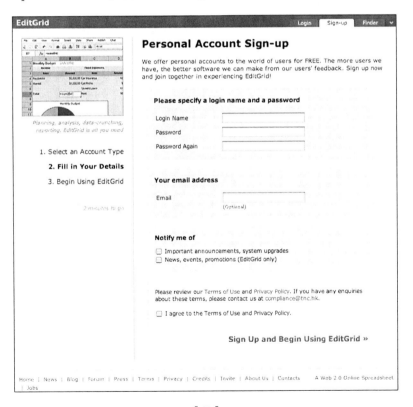

As with Google Spreadsheets, we will not use any of the private APIs but opt to access the publicly available published spreadsheet in a CSV format.

Clickatell

Clickatell (`http://www.clickatell.com`) is a bulk SMS provider that provides SMS messaging services and gateway for over 600 networks in almost 200 countries for outbound messages, and 100 countries for inbound (two-way) messaging. Clickatell allows developers to connect to its SMS gateway via various connectivity options including HTTP/S, SMTP (email to SMS), XML, SMPP (Short Message Peer to Peer protocol), FTP (file upload for SMS), and a COM object API. This provides applications with the ability to send SMSes globally, bypassing the need to hook up to local SMS providers individually.

Clickatell provides a trial account with 10 credits to allow developers to have a head start in trying out its services. To create a trial account, go to `https://www.clickatell.com/central/user/client/step1.php`.

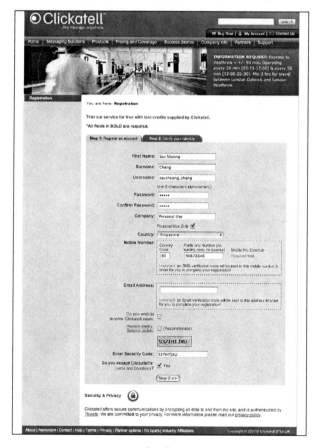

Fill in the account creation form. You will be required to provide a mobile number. This is important as in Step 2 a confirmation code is sent to your mobile number, before a trial account is provided.

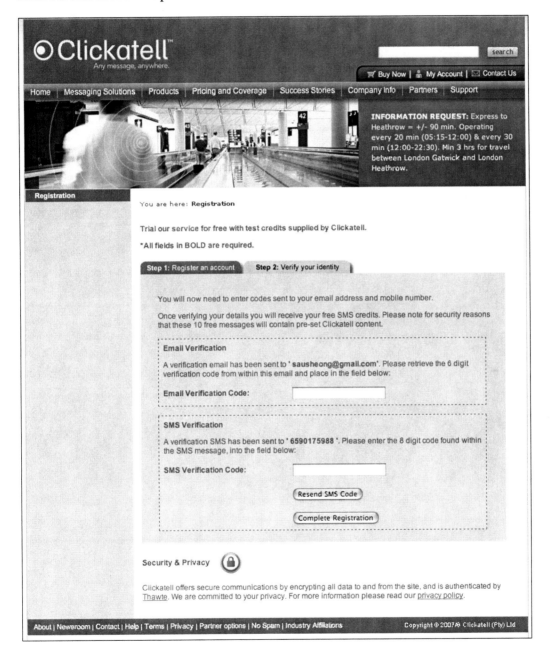

After entering your confirmation code from both your email and mobile phones, you will be presented with the homepage of your account.

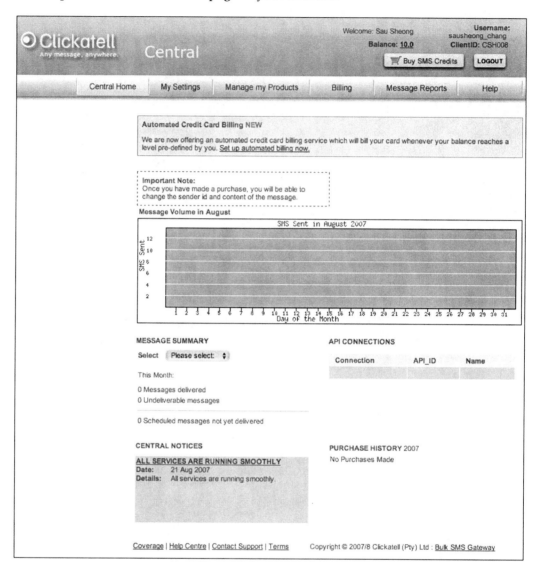

Notice the balance you have at the top of the screen. This is number of credits you have been given for the trial account. If you run out you can click on a conveniently located button to buy more credits through various payment methods. Take note of the Client ID provided, you will need it when you log into the Clickatell management console. To allow for access to an HTTP API, click on the **Manage My Products** link.

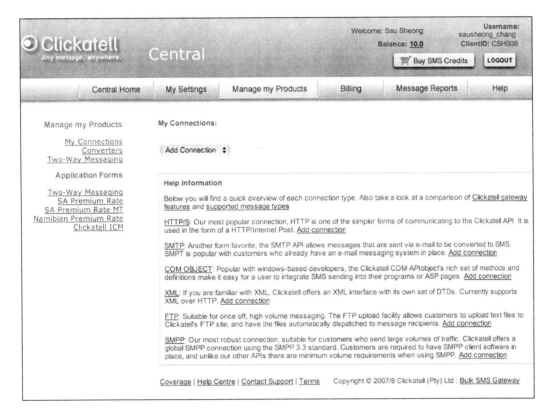

Then from the drop-down list, select **HTTP**.

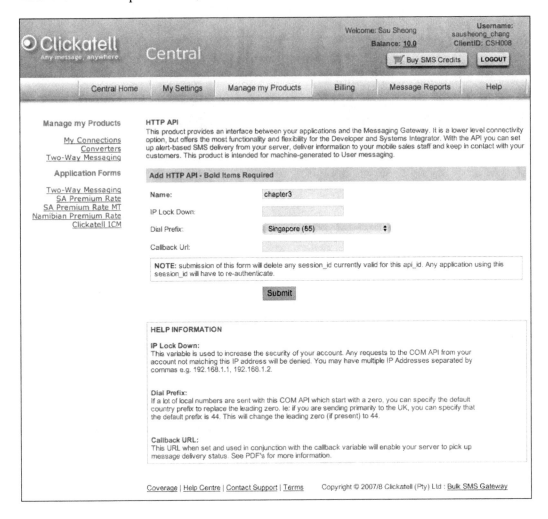

Select an appropriate name for this API. Optionally you can set the Dial Prefix if you are sending a lot of SMSes to a particular country. You can also set a Callback (to be explained in a later section) for Clickatell to call when reporting the status of the sent message. You can also specify that only a particular IP address, or set of IP addresses, can access this API. When you're done, click on the **Submit** button.

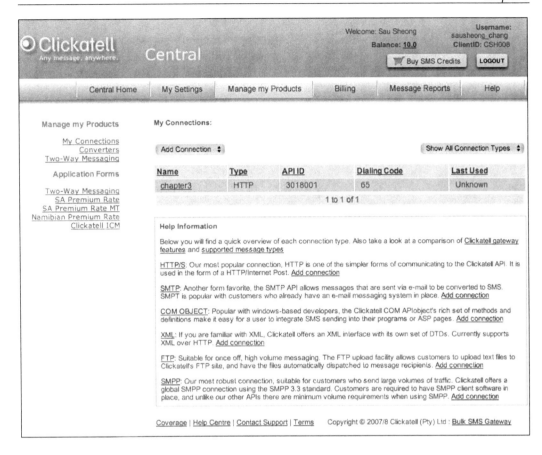

Take note of the API ID given here. We will need it when trying to access the HTTP API from our mashup.

Interfax

Interfax is a fax service provider that has coverage in a large number of countries. Interfax provides a number of API interfaces to its fax server including web services, COM object API, and an email interface. Interfax also provides reports on faxes that are sent or received through its servers. With Interfax, an application is able to send text faxes, faxes from base-64 encoded binary documents like PDF documents, Excel spreadsheets, and Word documents as well as receive faxes as TIF formatted images.

Interfax provides a free trial account for developers but faxes sent from this trial account will only reach a single fixed fax number. To be able to send to any other fax numbers you need to subscribe to its commercial account. To sign up for its free trial account, go to `http://www.interfax.net/Scripts/Reg_BP.asp` and fill in the account creation form.

After creating the account, you will be given $10 for faxing pages and a business partner ID. The business partner ID is not needed for sending faxes.

Net::HTTP

Ruby comes with a standard library for managing HTTP connections. While it is not very sophisticated, it provides the essential and basic capabilities for an application to connect to web applications through HTTP.

A basic HTTP `Get` command in `Net::HTTP` goes like this:

```
require 'net/http'
response = Net::HTTP.get_response(URI.parse
          ('http://www.packtpub.com'))
puts response.body
```

This sends an HTTP `Get` to Packt Publishing's website and returns what the web server delivers through that URL as a `Net::HTTPResponse` object.

A basic HTTP `Post` command in Net:HTTP goes like this:

```
require 'net/http'
response = Net::HTTP.post_form(URI.parse
          ('http://search.yahoo.com/search'),
                              {'p'=>'mashups'})
puts response.body
```

This code sends an HTTP Post to Yahoo's search engine with the parameter 'mashups' and it returns whatever search results are served from Yahoo, as a `Net::HTTPResponse` object.

To react according to the returned `Net::HTTPResponse` object, we need to inspect this object more closely. `Net::HTTPResponse` is actually the parent object of a hierarchy of HTTP response statuses. In order to check the status of the sent command, we can run the response object through a case loop to check the actual subclass and respond accordingly.

```
require 'net/http'
response = Net::HTTP.post_form(URI.parse
          ('http://search.yahoo.com/search'), {'p'=>'mashups'})
  case response
  when Net::HTTPSuccess
    puts response.body
  else
    puts response.error!
  end
```

This code indicates that if the response object is of the class Net::HTTPSuccess (HTTP code 2xx) it will print out the response body, otherwise it will just print out the error code.

We will be using Net::HTTP extensively in this chapter. In later chapters we will introduce another built-in Ruby package that performs a similar function.

What we will be doing

Although this is a mashup plugin, meaning it is normally added to an existing Rails application, we will be creating a new project to show how it can be used. This is the process flow of the mashup:

- The marketing user will create a marketing message template with the email, SMS, and fax messages.
- The reseller selects the message template to send and provides a link to the list of contacts to send the message to, then creates a message-sending job.
- At regular intervals, the system will check for pending jobs, process them and send all messages to the respective contacts.

This is what we will be doing in the next few pages to implement this mashup:

- Create a Rails project
- Configure the database access and create the database
- Create the standard scaffolding
- Allow the marketing users to create the message templates
- Allow the reseller to provide contacts data through a remote link
- Create the rake script to send messages at regular intervals

This mashup's main processing is not in the web application itself. The Rails web application is used to get input from the various parties i.e. the message template from the marketing user and the contacts data from the external reseller. As explained earlier, the actual processing and sending of the messages is done outside of the web application in the rake script. The rake script is triggered periodically by a scheduler like cron in Unix or at in Windows.

Creating a new Rails project

As before, creating the Rails project is the easiest part.

`$rails Chapter3`

This will create a new blank Rails project.

Configuring the database access and creating the database

The Rails web application is basic and the database needed to support it is simple as well. Change the necessary environment configuration file (development.rb for a development environment) to configure access to the database. Then generate a migration file to create the database:

$./script/generate migration create_templates_and_jobs

This will create a file 001_create_templates_and_jobs.rb in the RAILS_ROOT/db/ migrate folder. Ensure it has the following code:

```
class CreateTemplatesAndJobs < ActiveRecord::Migration
  def self.up
    create_table :message_templates do |t|
      t.column 'name', :string
      t.column 'sms_body', :text, :limit => 160
      t.column 'email_body', :text
      t.column 'fax_body', :text
    end
    create_table :jobs do |t|
      t.column 'message_template_id', :integer
      t.column 'contacts_url', :string
      t.column 'status', :string, :default => 'pending'
    end
  end
  def self.down
    drop_table :message_templates
    drop_table :jobs
  end
end
```

Now that we have the migration scripts, run migrate to create the tables:

$rake db:migrate

This should create the database tables needed. The data model in this mashup is quite simple. The MessageTemplate is the model of the message templates created by the marketing people, while each Job is created by the reseller.

Creating standard scaffolding

Next, create the standard scaffolding for the tables we've just created:

$./script/generate scaffold MessageTemplate

and:

$./script/generate scaffold Job

This will create the standard controllers, views, and models for the two classes. Next, change `MessageTemplate` and `Job` (both located in `RAILS_ROOT/app/models/`) to reflect their relationship:

```
class MessageTemplate < ActiveRecord::Base
  has_many :jobs
end
class Job < ActiveRecord::Base
  belongs_to :message_template
end
```

Allowing the marketing people to create the message templates

The standard scaffolding should already allow the creation of the message templates though we might want to do it up a bit if we are giving it to our marketing users! For testing purposes, go to: `http://localhost:3000/message_templates/list` and create some sample marketing messages for each type of message. Remember that SMS messages should be short and succinct and each message is up to a maximum of 160 characters (when using standard ASCII characters).

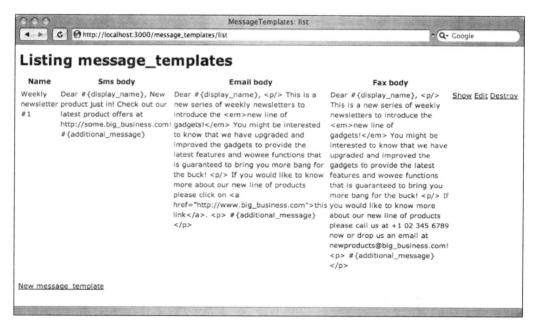

Note that in the example above, we have put in some Ruby-like variables in the messages such as `display_name`. We'll see how this is used in the coming sections.

Allowing the reseller to provide contacts data through a remote link

Next we need to let the reseller provide the contacts to our mashup. The general strategy is to allow the reseller to create message-sending 'jobs' that have the links to the contacts information. The reseller will select the message template to use and provide a link, so a simple job creation form can do this. The scaffold should have most of the code already in place, so just modify the `_form.rhtml` partial (`RAILS_ROOT/app/views/jobs/`) to link `Job` to `MessageTemplate`.

```
<%= error_messages_for 'job' %>
<!--[form:job]-->

<p><label for="job_message_template">Message template</label><br/>
<%= select('job', 'message_template_id', MessageTemplate.find(:all).
collect {|t| [ t.name, t.id ] })%></p>
<p><label for="job_contacts_url">Contacts url</label><br/>
<%= text_field 'job', 'contacts_url', :size => 100 %></p>
<!--[eoform:job]-->
```

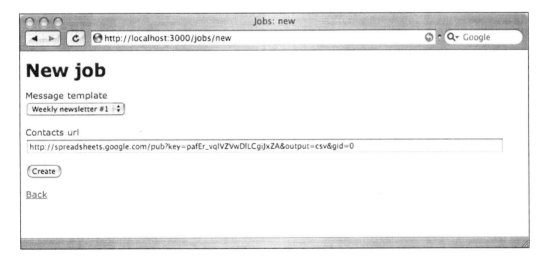

Open: `http://localhost:3000/jobs/new` and put in the spreadsheet URL (see below).

The link we are providing here is for Google Spreadsheets but it should be similar for EditGrid. Note that the URL is a link to the CSV format of the spreadsheet and not to the main document.

Uploading to and publishing from Google Spreadsheets

Before going into how this link is generated, let's first see from the reseller's perspective how he or she will upload his or her list of contacts to the Google Spreadsheet. Log into Google and go to `http://docs.google.com`.

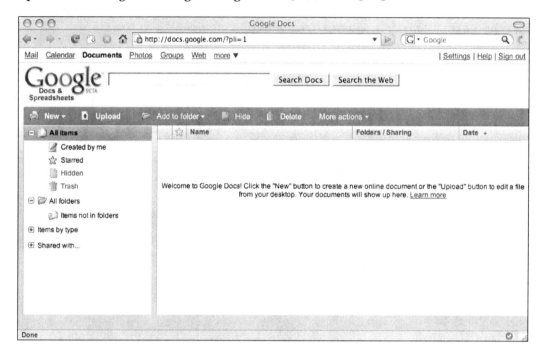

Click on the **Upload** link on the main page and follow the instructions on the page to upload a spreadsheet.

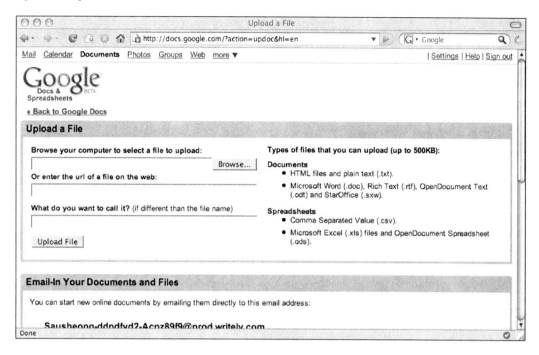

The spreadsheet that the reseller uploads must have the following columns in the following order:

- Display name
- Additional text (for the marketing messages)
- Email address
- Mobile number (for SMS messages)
- Fax number

All the columns are optional but the display name should be there at the very least, otherwise the marketing message will have no addressee! If there is a value under the email column, an email will be sent, if there is a value under the mobile column, an SMS will be sent, and if there is a value under the fax column, a fax will be sent.

Now that the spreadsheet is loaded up in Google Spreadsheets, the reseller can proceed to generate the link that publishes the contacts in CSV format. To generate this format, go to the document page of the Google Spreadsheet. Then click on the **publish** tab at the top right of the screen on the document page.

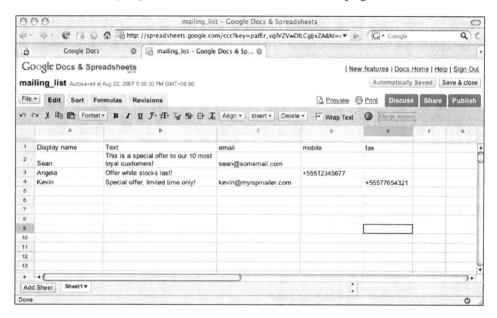

An options pane will be opened to the right of the screen. Click on the **Publish now** button.

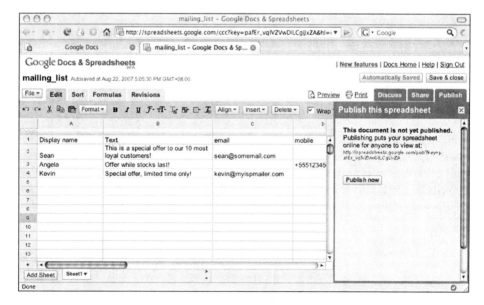

The document is now published. For additional publishing options, including the option for CSV format, click on the **More publishing options** link at the bottom of the options pane.

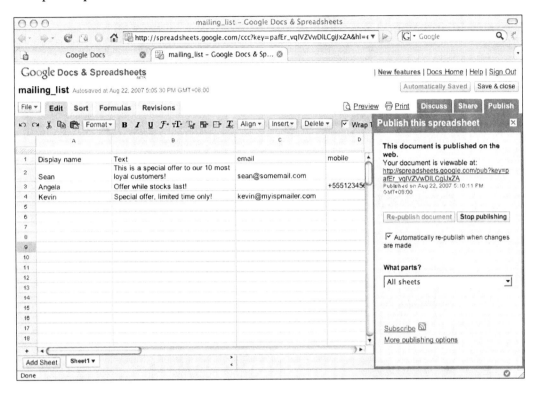

The reseller will then see a new pop-up window with several drop-down select fields. Choose **CSV** in the file format select field, and click on the **Generate URL** button. The reseller will be presented with a URL at the bottom of the window. This is the link we will ask the resellers to enter in order to retrieve the contacts and other information.

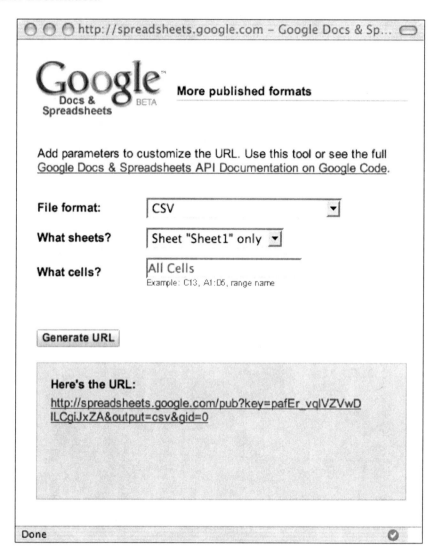

Uploading to and publishing from EditGrid

Uploading to and publishing from EditGrid is almost the same. After logging into EditGrid, the reseller will be presented with his or her workspace.

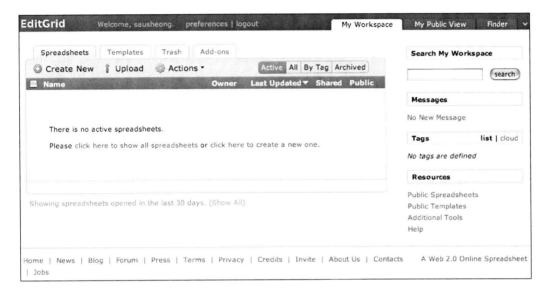

Click on the **Upload** button to upload a spreadsheet. The format of the spreadsheet should be the same as the one described above in the Google Spreadsheets section. The reseller needs to set the permission to *public read-only* to allow our mashup to read the contact information.

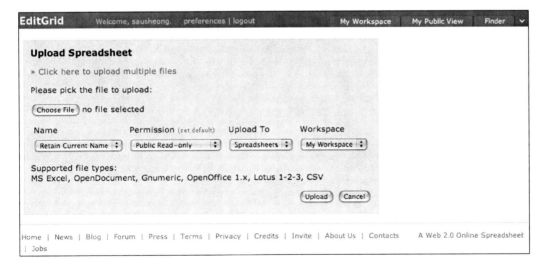

When the information has been uploaded into the spreadsheet, click on **File** in the menu bar and select the **Permalinks** menu item. Permalinks are permanent links on EditGrid. EditGrid provides permanent links support to allow you to access their spreadsheets through easy-to-understand URLs.

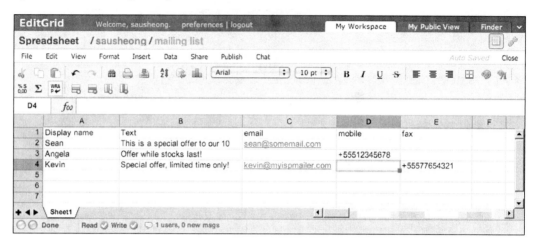

The reseller will see a list of formats in which data from this spreadsheet can be exported. The reseller needs to choose the **CSV** format link and use that as the link to provide as the input in the job creation screen. Make a record of the CSV link.

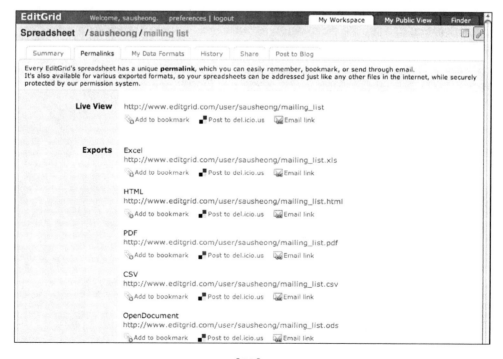

Creating the rake script to send messages at regular intervals

This is where the main action starts. As explained in Chapter 2, rake is a build program much like make, but one built with Ruby syntax. Rake is integrated and used extensively in Rails for various tasks including database migration (we used db:migrate earlier on in this chapter). We will be using rake to run a processing script that will get the data from the remote site and send the messages.

Create a rake script named process_jobs.rake in the RAILS_ROOT/lib/tasks folder:

```
require 'net/http'
require 'csv'
require 'soap/wsdlDriver'
namespace :chapter3 do
  # Clickatell credentials
  $clickatell_api_id = <your Clickatell API ID>
  $clickatell_login = <your Clickatell user name>
  $clickatell_password = <your Clickatell password>
  # Interfax credentials
  $interfax_login = <your Interfax user name>
  $interfax_password = <your Interfax password>
  $interfax_driver = SOAP::WSDLDriverFactory.new('http://ws.interfax.
net/dfs.asmx?WSDL').create_rpc_driver
  desc "Activated regularly by AT or cronjob to process all jobs"
  task(:process_jobs => :environment) do
    $clickatell_session_id = get_clickatell_session
    begin
      pending_jobs = Job.find_all_by_status 'pending'
      if pending_jobs.size > 0
        puts "#{pending_jobs.size} jobs pending processing ..."
      else
        puts "All jobs has been processed!"
      end

      pending_jobs.each { |job|
        # parse and get contacts data
        contacts_data = []
        csv = parse_data(job.contacts_url)
        puts "Found #{csv.size} contacts for this job!"

        csv.each { |line|
          contact = {}
          contact[:display_name] = line[0]
          contact[:additional_message] = line[1]
```

```ruby
        contact[:email] = line[2]
        contact[:mobile_no] = line[3]
        contact[:fax_no] = line[4]
        contacts_data << contact
    }

    contacts_data.each { |contact|
      # send email
      if !contact[:email].nil?
        t1 = Time.now
        sent = Mailer.deliver_mail(job.message_template, contact)
        t2 = Time.now
        if sent
          puts "Email sent to #{contact[:display_name]}
                              in #{(t2 - t1)} seconds"
        end
      end

      # send sms
      if !contact[:mobile_no].nil?
        t1 = Time.now
        sent = send_sms(job.message_template, contact)
        t2 = Time.now
        if sent
          puts "SMS sent to #{contact[:display_name]}
                            in #{(t2 - t1)} seconds"
        end
      end

      # send fax
      if !contact[:fax_no].nil?
        t1 = Time.now
        sent = send_fax(job.message_template, contact)
        t2 = Time.now
        if sent
          puts "Fax sent to #{contact[:display_name]}
                            in #{(t2 - t1)} seconds"
        end
      end
    }
    job.status = 'processed'
    job.save!
  }
rescue
  puts "Error during sending messages : #{$!}"
end
```

```
end
# -- end of main task --

# send fax through Interfax
def send_fax(template, contact)
  $interfax_driver.SendCharFax(
        :Username => $interfax_login,
        :Password => $interfax_password,
        :FaxNumber => contact[:fax_no],
        :Data => template.message_body(:fax, contact))
end

# send SMS through Clickatell
def send_sms(template, contact)
  begin
    res = Net::HTTP.post_form(URI.parse(
      'http://api.clickatell.com/http/sendmsg'),
    {'session_id' => $clickatell_session_id,
     'cliMsgId' => template.id,
     'to'=>contact[:mobile_no],
     'from' => 'Chapter 3',
     'text' => template.message_body(:sms, contact),
     'callback' => '3',
     'deliv_ack' => '1',
     'req_feat' => '8192' })

    case res
    when Net::HTTPSuccess, Net::HTTPRedirection
      puts "Successfully sent message to #{contact[:display_name]}"
      return true
    else
      puts res.error!
      return false
    end
    rescue
    puts "## Cannot send sms to #{contact[:display_name]}! : #{$!}"
  end
end

# get the clickatell session needed to send SMS messages
def get_clickatell_session
  res = Net::HTTP.post_form(URI.parse(
        'http://api.clickatell.com/http/auth'),
    {'api_id' => $clickatell_api_id,
     'user'=> $clickatell_login,
     'password' => $clickatell_password})
```

```
    case res
    when Net::HTTPSuccess, Net::HTTPRedirection
      return res.body.split(': ')[1]
    else
      puts res.error!
    end
  end

  # parse data from a CSV file published by Google Spreadsheet
  def parse_data(url)
    res = Net::HTTP.get_response(URI.parse(url))
    case res
    when Net::HTTPSuccess, Net::HTTPRedirection
      csv = CSV.parse(res.body)
      header = csv.shift
      return csv
    else
      puts res.error!
    end


  end
end
```

We will go through this script part by part. First, we will be using the Net::HTTP,
CSV, and SOAP packages that are default in our Ruby installation so we will require
them at the top of the file.

```
namespace :chapter3 do
  # Clickatell credentials
  $clickatell_api_id = <your Clickatell API ID>
  $clickatell_login = <your Clickatell user name>
  $clickatell_password = <your Clickatell password>

  # Interfax credentials
  $interfax_login = <your Interfax user name>
  $interfax_password = <your Interfax password>
  $interfax_driver = SOAP::WSDLDriverFactory.new('http://ws.interfax.
net/dfs.asmx?WSDL').create_rpc_driver
```

The Web Services Description Language (WSDL) is an XML-based language
used to describe web services. WSDL is often used together with SOAP to define
web services as in the case of Clickatell and Interfax. A web service consuming
application (such as our mashup) reads the WSDL to find out what is available from
the web service and how to access it. From there we can generate the proxies that we
use to access the web service as if it were a call to a local object.

Preset your global credentials for Clickatell and Interfax. We should have gotten these credentials when we registered for the developer accounts earlier on. The last line of this section creates a SOAP client to communicate with Interfax. The constructor for `WSDLDriverFactory` takes in a WSDL file provided by Interfax and creates the necessary local proxy. We will be using this proxy to send our fax.

```ruby
desc "Activated regularly by AT or cronjob to process all jobs"
task(:process_jobs => :environment) do
  $clickatell_session_id = get_clickatell_session
  begin
   pending_jobs = Job.find_all_by_status 'pending'
    if pending_jobs.size > 0
      puts "#{pending_jobs.size} jobs pending processing ..."
    else
      puts "All jobs has been processed!"
    end
    pending_jobs.each
    { |job|
      # parse and get contacts data
      contacts_data = []
      csv = parse_data(job.contacts_url)
      puts "Found #{csv.size} contacts for this job!"
      csv.each
      { |line|
        contact = {}
        contact[:display_name] = line[0]
        contact[:additional_message] = line[1]
        contact[:email] = line[2]
        contact[:mobile_no] = line[3]
        contact[:fax_no] = line[4]
        contacts_data << contact
      }

      contacts_data.each
      { |contact|
        # send email
        if !contact[:email].nil?
          t1 = Time.now
          sent = Mailer.deliver_mail(job.message_template, contact)
          t2 = Time.now
          if sent
            puts "Email sent to #{contact[:display_name]}
                                in #{(t2 - t1)} seconds"
          end
        end
```

```
      # send sms
      if !contact[:mobile_no].nil?
        t1 = Time.now
        sent = send_sms(job.message_template, contact)
        t2 = Time.now
        if sent
          puts "SMS sent to #{contact[:display_name]}
                          in #{(t2 - t1)} seconds"
        end
      end

      # send fax
      if !contact[:fax_no].nil?
        t1 = Time.now
        sent = send_fax(job.message_template, contact)
        t2 = Time.now
        if sent
          puts "Fax sent to #{contact[:display_name]}
                          in #{(t2 - t1)} seconds"
        end
      end
    }
    job.status = 'processed'
    job.save!
  }
  rescue
  puts "Error during sending messages : #{$!}"
  end
end
# -- end of main task --
```

We start off the processing run by getting a Clickatell session:

```
$clickatell_session_id = get_clickatell_session
```

This session is needed by Clickatell to identify that we are an authorized user to send SMS messages. Next, we get all pending jobs in the system and for each pending job:

```
pending_jobs = Job.find_all_by_status 'pending'
```

we get the contacts URL and parse it:

```
csv = parse_data(job.contacts_url)
```

Remember that the contacts URL is actually a link to a CSV file published from an online spreadsheet. Parsing it returns an Array of Arrays that has the title row truncated. We will take this Array of Arrays and create an Array of Hashes to make the code simpler to read:

```
csv.each { |line|
        contact = {}
        contact[:display_name] = line[0]
        contact[:additional_message] = line[1]
        contact[:email] = line[2]
        contact[:mobile_no] = line[3]
        contact[:fax_no] = line[4]
        contacts_data << contact
    }
```

This is our list of contacts!

Now that we have the contacts data, we iterate through each one of them to send the messages. We run the contact through three if loops (one for each of the communications methods) to see if there is any contact information in that row. We will send the message if there is, that is, if there is an email given we will send the email message:

```
sent = Mailer.deliver_mail(job.message_template, contact)
```

If there is a mobile number given we will send the SMS message:

```
sent = send_sms(job.message_template, contact)
```

If there is a fax number given, we will send the fax:

```
sent = send_fax(job.message_template, contact)
```

This is the main loop for this script; let's see how we can extract the contacts information from the online spreadsheet and the send methods for each of the communications channels next.

Parsing data from the online spreadsheet

We extract the data from the online spreadsheet (either Google Spreadsheets or EditGrid) through the link that is given by the reseller in the job. To do this we use Net::HTTP to send an HTTP Get to the server, which should return a plaintext CSV string embedded within the response object.

```
# parse data from a CSV file published by Google Spreadsheets or
EditGrid
def parse_data(url)
```

```
      res = Net::HTTP.get_response(URI.parse(url))
      case res
      when Net::HTTPSuccess, Net::HTTPRedirection
        csv = CSV.parse(res.body)
        header = csv.shift
        return csv
      else
        puts res.error!
      end
    end
```

Next, we use the CSV module (also built into Ruby) to parse the CSV string into an Array of Arrays. We also remove the header so that we get only data in the returned Array object.

Sending a fax with Interfax

Sending the fax through Interfax is relatively simple. Using the local proxy we have created from the WSDL provided by Interfax, we need only call any of the provided methods. In this example we will use SendCharFax, which sends a text message to the recipient.

```
    # send fax through Interfax
    def send_fax(template, contact)
      $interfax_driver.SendCharFax(
            :Username => $interfax_login,
            :Password => $interfax_password,
            :FaxNumber => contact[:fax_no],
            :Data => template.message_body(:fax, contact))
    end
```

The username and password parameters are self-explanatory. The faxnumber submitted, however, needs to be in the international notation. The format is: + <Country-Code><AreaCode><Local number>. For example: A number in New York, NY, USA will look like: +12123456789, where:

+ is a constant;
1 is the USA country code;
212 is New York area code;
3456789 is the local number.

The data in this case is the text fax message stored in the message template.

The SendCharFax web service is a basic one that only sends text messages. Normally this is not realistic, as this will only send an ugly string message to the recipient.

To improve on this, we can use either `Sendfax` or `SendfaxEx_2` to send files as faxes. We can send files with types including Word documents, Excel spreadsheets, Acrobat documents, or HTML-formatted text. To do this we can get the marketing user to upload a document to the database, which can then be sent to the contacts (we will skip this to keep this chapter simple). Check out the Interfax developer site at `http://www.interfax.net/en/dev/webservice/reference.html` to get the details of the various web services that are provided by Interfax.

Sending an SMS through Clickatell

Sending an SMS through Clickatell is only slightly more complicated. We will need to get a session key from Clickatell first by logging in and presenting our credentials, and then use this session key to send the SMS messages.

```
# get the clickatell session needed to send SMS messages
  def get_clickatell_session
    res = Net::HTTP.post_form(URI.parse(
                              'http://api.clickatell.com/http/auth'),
    {'api_id' => $clickatell_api_id,
     'user'=> $clickatell_login,
     'password' => $clickatell_password})
    case res
    when Net::HTTPSuccess, Net::HTTPRedirection
      return res.body.split(': ')[1]
    else
      puts res.error!
    end
  end
```

Clickatell provides many different ways for developers to access its services, but for this chapter we will be using its HTTP APIs. To use the HTTP APIs we use the Net::HTTP package to send an HTTP Post command to `http://api.clickatell.com/http/auth` with the various credentials as part of a Post form in the request body to get a session key. Note that we need to provide an API ID to Clickatell—this is the number we get from Clickatell when we register as a developer for that set of API services (see section above). The session ID is retrieved then stored in a global variable for use when we send the messages.

```
# send SMS through Clickatell
  def send_sms(template, contact)
    begin
      res = Net::HTTP.post_form(URI.parse(
            'http://api.clickatell.com/http/sendmsg'),
        {'session_id' => $clickatell_session_id,
         'cliMsgId' => template.id,
```

```
            'to'=> contact[:mobile_no],
            'from' => 'Chapter 3',
            'text' => template.message_body(:sms, contact),
            'callback' => '3',
            'deliv_ack' => '1',
            'req_feat' => '8192' })
    case res
    when Net::HTTPSuccess, Net::HTTPRedirection
      puts "Successfully sent message to #{contact[:display_name]}"
      return true
    else
      puts res.error!
      return false
    end
  rescue
    puts "## Cannot send sms to #{contact[:display_name]}! : #{$!}"
  end
end
```

We also use Net::HTTP to send the SMS messages through the Clickatell SMS gateway by sending an HTTP Post request to `http://api.clickatell.com/http/sendmsg` with a set of parameters.

The Client Message ID or `CliMsgId` is a parameter that's set by the external application (in our case it is our application), which Clickatell uses to group messages sent by different applications. Clickatell does not use it internally and we can use up to 32 alphanumeric characters though we cannot have any spaces in it.

The `To` parameter is the mobile number we wish to send to. As with Interfax, we need to provide the full international number, together with country and area codes. However, unlike for Interfax we should not use '+' or leading 0's.

The `From` field is an alphanumeric field. Normally when sent through a mobile phone, the `From` parameter is populated with the mobile number of the sender. However Clickatell allows us to use any 11 character alphanumeric string or an international format mobile number that is between 1 and 16 characters.

The `Text` parameter contains the text message. To send Unicode characters (for example, for a Chinese text message) we need to set the 'Unicode' parameter to '1'. For Unicode messages, the text message limit is 70 Unicode characters per message. SMS messages are limited to 160 characters for normal ASCII characters. If we wish to send messages longer than 160 characters, we will need to set the `concat` parameter to '1', '2', '3' or N number of messages to send. Clickatell does not automatically do this for us, so we will need to check the length of the characters in the message and set this accordingly.

The `callback`, `deliv_ack`, and `req_feat` parameters are linked in usage. SMS messages are sent asynchronously if called by HTTP (since HTTP is a connectionless protocol). This means we have no idea if the SMS message really gets to the mobile user.

Clickatell uses the `callback` parameter to inform our mashup of the status of the message. If callback is set to '0', no statuses are reported, if it is set to '1', only intermediate statuses are sent, if it is set to '2', only final statuses are sent and if it is set to '3', both intermediate and final statuses are sent.

Clickatell uses an HTTP `Get` command to call a URL that we set in the user interface to inform us of the status of the sent message and will return the client message ID (`CliMsgId`), `To`, `From`, `api_id`, and `timestamp` parameters for our application to identify the message sent. For the rake script earlier, we specified that we do not want to get the status of the message but under production conditions we should create a simple action for Clickatell to call.

The delivery acknowledgement parameter (`deliv_ack`) is closely related to the callback parameter. If it is set to '0', Clickatell will not report the delivery status to the handset, but only to the SMS upstream gateway. If it is set to '1', Clickatell will report the delivery status to the final handset itself. However delivery acknowledgement is not a guaranteed service as not all upstream gateways report delivery acknowledgements to the handset.

The requested features parameter (`req_feat`) is related to the delivery acknowledgement and callback features. By default Clickatell will send messages by best effort. However, if we set certain constraints in the requested features parameter, Clickatell will drop those messages that do not fit the requested features.

Hex value Decimal Feature Description

Hex Value	Decimal	Feature	Description
0x0001	1	FEAT_TEXT	Text—set by default.
0x0002	2	FEAT_8BIT	8-bit messaging—set by default.
0x0004	4	FEAT_UDH	UDH (Binary)—set by default.
0x0008	8	FEAT_UCS2	UCS2 / Unicode—set by default.
0x0010	16	FEAT_ALPHA	Alpha source address (from parameter).
0x0020	32	FEAT_NUMER	Numeric source address (from parameter).
0x0200	512	FEAT_FLASH	Flash messaging.
0x2000	8192	FEAT_DELIVACK	Delivery acknowledgments.
0x4000	16384	FEAT_CONCAT	Concatenation—set by default.

The requested features parameter is set by bitmask, that is we need to add the decimal values together to get the necessary final value to use. Some values are set by default as described above. As can be seen from the table, the value 8192 sets the delivery acknowledgements value, requesting Clickatell to only send messages to gateways that have delivery acknowledgements.

The values in the table are only a subset of the full set of features available from Clickatell. For more details on the settings and parameters, you should read the Clickatell HTTP APIs specification from `http://www.clickatell.com/downloads/http/Clickatell_HTTP.pdf`.

Sending an email through ActionMailer

ActionMailer is the default framework in Rails used for sending and receiving emails. Before sending emails, we will need to configure ActionMailer first. Go to `config` and open up the appropriate environment configuration file (in development mode we will normally be using `development.rb`). Append the following to the end of the file and change the configuration appropriately:

```
config.action_mailer.delivery_method = :smtp
config.action_mailer.server_settings =
{
   :address => <your smtp server> ,
   :port => <smtp server port>,
   :domain => <your server domain name> ,
   :authentication => :login,
   :user_name => <your username> ,
   :password => <your password>
}
```

`address` and `port` are the address and port of the SMTP server that we're using to send the emails. `Domain` is the domain the mailer uses to identify itself to the server specified in `address`. You should normally use the top-level domain name of the machine that is sending the email. Use `authentication` if your SMTP server requires authentication to log into the system. If you use authentication you should also enter your SMTP user name and password in `user_name` and `password` respectively.

Now that ActionMailer is configured, generate the `Mailer` model through the generate script:

```
$./script/generate mailer Mailer
```

This creates a Mailer model in our `app/model` folder. The Mailer class in `mailer.rb` inherits from `ActionMailer::Base` and is the class we will use to send emails out.

```
class Mailer < ActionMailer::Base
  def mail(template, contact)
    @recipients = contact[:email]
    @subject = 'Big Business Marketing Message'
    @from = <sender email>
    @body['text'] = template.message_body(:email, contact)
  end
end
```

Each method in the mailer class sets up the environment for sending a particular email. In our case, we have only one email to send so we need only one method. The method sets up the environment by setting up instance variables containing data for the email's header and body. In our case, we set the recipient to the contact email and hard-code a marketing message as its subject. Next we set the sender email address and then the body of the email message from the message template. `Body` is a hash used to pass values to the email template. In this case, the message template's email body is passed to the email template as a variable named `@text`.

Let's create, then look at the email template named `mail.text.html.rhtml`. (`RAILS_ROOT/app/views/mailer/`). This file is in named in this format:

<method>.<content>.<type>.rhtml

The method is the name of the method in the `Mailer` class, in this case, mail. The content and type are the MIME type of the text to be sent. In this case we're sending an HTML message so the content type is `text/html`.

```
<div id='header'>Big Business Banner/div>
<%= @text%>
<div id='footer'>Copyright Big Business 2007</div>
```

Note that the email body from the message template has some HTML tags as well, and this goes well into this email template.

Customizing text messages according to the individual recipient

Finally, the messages in the message template can be customized according to the individual recipient. In this mashup we use the display name as well as additional text to be added for each recipient, if any. The text for the SMS message for example, goes like this:

Dear #{display_name}, New product just in! Check out our latest product offers at http://some.big_business.com! #{additional_message}

Notice that both display name and the additional text message customization look like the string replacement syntax in Ruby. This is because we evaluate this text as a Ruby string inside the Job class in RAIL_ROOT/app/model/MessageTemplate.rb:

```ruby
class MessageTemplate < ActiveRecord::Base
  has_many :jobs
  def message_body(type,contact)
    display_name = contact[:display_name]
    additional_message = contact[:additional_message]
    case type
      when :email : eval '"' + self.email_body + '"'
      when :sms : eval '"' + self.sms_body + '"'
      when :fax : eval '"' + self.fax_body + '"'
      else 'Incorrect type of message requested'
    end
  end
end
```

By evaluating the text as a Ruby string, we replace the values specified in the message body with the required values from the contact information. Whenever we need the message text, we just call it like this:

```ruby
res = Net::HTTP.post_form(URI.parse('http://api.clickatell.com/http/
sendmsg'),
    {'session_id' => $clickatell_session_id,
     'cliMsgId' => template.id,
     'to'=>contact[:mobile_no],
     'from' => 'Chapter 3',
     'text' => template.message_body(:sms, contact),
     'callback' => '3',
     'deliv_ack' => '1',
     'req_feat' => '8192' })
```

This little trick gives us great flexibility when doing text replacement on the messages for individual recipients.

This wraps up the mashup. Run this script to send the messages once you have set up the templates and the jobs.

Using the mashup

To recap the chapter, this is the sequence to follow in using the mashup:

1. Start up the server
2. Create one or more message templates
3. Create a job
4. Run the rake script to process the job

If you have set up things correctly you should receive the three marketing messages, through the email, SMS, and fax.

Summary

What we've learned in this chapter is to extract information from online spreadsheets through CSV and use that information to send messages through three different communications channels—email, SMS, and fax. We created a marketing message mashup using Google Spreadsheets and/or EditGrid, both online spreadsheets, Clickatell, a bulk SMS provider, as well as Interfax, an Internet fax provider.

4
Book sales tracking mashup plugin

What does it do?

This mashup plugin allows you to add a feature to your website to track the sales ranking and customer reviews of a particular product from Amazon.com. It also allows visitors to your website to buy the product directly by creating a shopping cart and adding the product to that shopping cart—to be eventually purchased through Amazon.com.

A book sales tracking and shopping cart feature

You have just published your first book and it has been hard. A whole 9 months of your life has been dedicated to writing that book and you want to make sure that you get the best out of it. What you want is to track its sales, know what your readers think about the book, and tie it in with your existing website. You also want to allow readers to directly buy the book off your website but you don't want to spend the next 9 months of your life writing an application to do this! What you're looking for is a mashup between your website and an online book seller like Amazon.com.

Requirements overview

These are the requirements for your book sales tracking and shopping cart mashup:

- Provide information on the book
- Track and chart the sales of the book through the online book seller

- Provide customer reviews on your site to show customer feedback that is posted on the online book seller

- Provide a shopping cart that is integrated into your website that enables visitors to your website to buy your book easily

- Allow visitors to your website to also buy related books through your website in order for your to earn some extra income from product recommendation

Design

This mashup will mostly use the Amazon E-Commerce Services (ECS) API, though we will use some part of Joe Gregorio's Sparklines web service to chart out the progress of the sales ranking from week to week. This is how we will implement the mashup:

Provide information

We will use the `ItemLookup` web service from Amazon ECS to get these particular details of your book:

- Title
- Author
- Publication date
- Price and currency of a new item
- A picture of the book cover

We will also use the `SimilarityLookup` web service from Amazon ECS API to find books that are related to your book.

Track sales ranking with a chart

We will create a rake script that is executed every 24 hours to get the latest sales ranking using the `ItemLookup` web service from Amazon ECS API. The sales ranking is then stored in the server. Whenever the info page of the book mashup is called, we will recall the historic sales ranking information and use the Sparklines web service to create a sparkline to show its progress.

Show customer reviews

We will use the `ItemLookup` web service from Amazon ECS API to get the customer reviews and display them. If there are too many reviews in a single page, we will paginate the reviews.

Provide a shopping cart

We will use the `CartCreate` web service from Amazon ECS API to create a shopping cart for the mashup. `CartCreate` will create a remote shopping cart on Amazon.com and place the book in it. Then we will provide a button that redirects the visitor to the Amazon.com checkout page for purchase.

Allow visitors to buy related books

We will use the `ItemLookup` web service from Amazon to get books that are related to or similar to your book. We will then allow your visitors to add them to the cart using the `CartAdd` web service.

With the design in place, let's look at the mashup APIs we're going to use, in detail.

Mashup APIs on the menu

For this mashup, to access the Amazon ECS APIs we will be using the Amazon ECS Ruby module developed by Herryanto Siatono and to show the sales ranking and number of customer reviews, we will be using Joe Gregorio's Sparklines web service.

Amazon E-Commerce Services API

The Amazon E-Commerce Services (ECS) API is a web service API accessible through SOAP and REST that provides access to Amazon.com's online retail platform. Using these web services, developers can:

- Find items that are available on sale on Amazon.com, either by Amazon.com itself or by other merchants
- Get detailed information on the items including pricing and availability
- Get customer reviews on the items, including customer ratings
- Find items that are similar
- Create and manage remote shopping carts at Amazon.com

To use the Amazon ECS API as a developer you need to register for an Amazon Web Service (AWS) access key ID. This access ID is used with every request that you send to the Amazon ECS.

Registering for an Amazon Web Service access key ID

To register for the AWS access key ID, go to `http://www.amazon.com/gp/aws/registration/registration-form.html`. If you're an existing Amazon.com customer, you can provide your email address and your account password. If you don't have an existing Amazon Web Services account, you will be asked to create one.

Once you create the Amazon Web Services account, you will be sent an email and also redirected to the success page. Select the Amazon E-Commerce Service link as the service you would like to explore. When you enter the Amazon E-Commerce web services link, you will see a small button to your right: **Your Web Services Account**. Click on it and it will show you a list of actions you can do with your web services account. Click on the **AWS Access Identifiers** link to see your access key ID.

Registering as an Amazon Associate

Associates is Amazon.com's affiliate marketing program and it allows you to earn money by recommending purchases on Amazon.com. When you register to be an associate, you will receive an associate ID. In the mashup shown in this chapter, we will include an associate ID in your shopping cart in order for you to earn extra money.

To join the Associates program, go to `http://affiliate-program.amazon.com/join` and click on the 'Apply now' button. Enter your email address and account password (you should have an account by now) for your account. You will need to fill up a form and provide information on your site, after which you will be shown an associate ID, which you can use in your mashup.

Amazon ECS Ruby library

The Amazon ECS library (`http://rubyforge.org/projects/amazon-ecs`) is a Ruby package that provides easy access to the Amazon ECS APIs. This library accesses the Amazon ECS REST APIs using Hpricot (`http://code.whytheluckystiff.net/hpricot`) and is flexible enough to allow use of all Amazon ECS APIs, even those not directly supported with convenience methods.

Sparklines web service

Sparkline is the name proposed by Edward Tufte for *small, high resolution graphics embedded in a context of words, numbers, images*. A normal chart usually tries to display as much information as possible and is placed separately from the text but sparklines are part of the text itself and displays a simple, to-the-point graphic. Tufte describes sparklines as *data-intense, design-simple, word-sized graphics*.

Sparklines have been implemented in many different languages, including Ruby. However for this mashup, instead of coding up sparklines, we will use a sparkline web service offered by Joe Gregorio (`http://bitworking.org/projects/sparklines`).

The service consists of a single CGI program (`http://bitworking.org/projects/sparklines/spark.cgi`) written in Python that takes query parameters that describe the sparkline. The web service produces three types of sparklines:

- Discrete — One vertical bar per data point
- Smooth — all the points plotted as a continuous line
- Impulse — Like discrete, but all the lines start at zero

For this mashup we will be using the 'smooth' sparkline that is most commonly used. To create a sparkline with this web service, the easiest way is to provide a set of comma-delimited data to the URL given and to display the URL as an image.

For example, this snippet shows how to display this sparkline:

in an HTML page:

```
<img src= "http://bitworking.org/projects/sparklines/spark.cgi?t
    ype=smooth&d=88,84,82,92,82,86,66,82,44,64,66,88,96,80,24,26,
        14,0,0,26,8,6,6,24,52,66,36,6,10,14,30&height=14&limits=0,100
        &min-m=true&max-m=true&last-m=true&min-color=red&max-
        color=blue&last-color=green&step=3"/>
```

What we will be doing

For this mashup we will be creating a new Rails application to demonstrate how you can integrate this feature into your website. The Rails application will have a left-hand sidebar that shows your book, its details, and a list of similar books. The sidebar also shows the most recent sales rank from Amazon and a list of historical sales ranking for the past 10 days, displayed in a sparkline. Your visitors can also view comments and ratings from other readers posted on Amazon.com.

This mashup also enables you to create a remote shopping cart at Amazon.com to let your visitors buy directly through you. At the same time, it allows you to earn some extra money by being an Amazon Associate and referring other similar books to your visitors and allowing your visitors to add them to the remote shopping cart. When your visitors are ready to buy, the mashup will redirect them to Amazon.com for checkout and payment.

This is the sequence of actions we will take to create this mashup:

- Create a Rails application
- Install the Amazon ECS Ruby library
- Create the books controller
- Create the Amazon Rails library and use it to get information on the book
- Create the sidebar view to display the book information and similar books
- Get customer reviews and create the customer comments and ratings view
- Create a rake script to get the sales ranking for each day and populate it into a YAML file
- Get the sales ranking history from the YAML file and use the information to create a sparkline representing the sales ranking history
- Create a remote shopping cart and add your book as the first item
- Add a link for each similar book to allow your visitors to add it to the shopping cart

Note that this mashup doesn't require database access at all. Even the sales ranking history is stored in a YAML file to be retrieved and displayed. This is ideal in the case where your existing website doesn't have a database and you're not keen to pay your hosting company additional money for one. However if you have an existing database you can easily add another table and add in some simple ActiveRecord models to represent the history.

Also note that there is very little that you are actually processing or even storing at your mashup—almost everything is residing at Amazon.com or the sparkline web service.

Creating a new Rails project

As before, creating the Rails project is the easiest part.

`$rails Chapter4`

This will create a new blank Rails project.

Installing the Amazon ECS Ruby library

To install the Amazon ECS Ruby library, run this command at the console (this can be anywhere):

```
$gem install amazon-ecs --include-dependencies
```

This will install the Amazon ECS Ruby gem from the remote gem repository and will also install Hpricot if you don't have Hpricot installed.

Creating the books controller

Next, we will need to create the one and only controller in this whole mashup. Create a file called `books_controller.rb` in the `RAILS_ROOT/app/controllers` folder. The books controller is a very simple controller. Its main job is to control or redirect the process flow of the mashup. The controller includes our Amazon Rails library, which we will create in the next section. Almost all the methods we call in the controller come from this Amazon Rails library.

```
class BooksController < ApplicationController
  include Amazon
  @@book_asin = '0974514055'
  def sidebar
    @book = get_book_details @@book_asin
    @similars = get_similar_products @@book_asin
  end
end
```

 One of the key pieces of information Amazon.com uses in its retail and web services platform is the ASIN or the Amazon Standard Item Number. The ASIN is an alphanumeric string that uniquely identifies items in Amazon.com. All items on Amazon.com have an ASIN, even if they are not on sale. For books, the ASIN and the ISBN number are the same.

We hard-coded the book ASIN as we're only interested in your book. Note that this file is not the end product; we will be filling up the rest of the methods as we go along.

Creating the Amazon Rails library

This is a Ruby module that we include in your book controller. It contains the main processing logic of the mashup. It is used mainly to communicate with the Amazon ECS API provided by Amazon.com, using the Amazon ECS Ruby library by Herryanto Siatono.

Create a Ruby file in the RAILS_ROOT/lib folder called amazon.rb. For those uninitiated in Ruby on Rails, all Ruby files placed here are directly accessible to the Rails application during run time. This is why we only need to add the line include Amazon in the controller.

```ruby
require 'amazon/ecs'
module Amazon
  @@key_id = <your Amazon.com access key ID>
  @@associate_id = <your associate ID>
  # get the details of the book given the ASIN
  def get_book_details(asin)
    book = Hash.new
    res = ecs.item_lookup(asin, :response_group => 'Large')
    book[:title] = res.first_item.get("title")
    book[:publication_date] = res.first_item.get("publicationdate")
    book[:salesrank] = res.first_item.get("salesrank")
    book[:image_url] = res.first_item.get("mediumimage/url")
    book[:author] = res.first_item.get("itemattributes/author")
    book[:isbn] = res.first_item.get("itemattributes/isbn")
    book[:price] = res.first_item.get("price/currencycode") +
                   res.first_item.get("price/formattedprice")
    book[:total_reviews] =
                   res.first_item.get("customerreviews/totalreviews")
    book[:average_rating] =
                   res.first_item.get("customerreviews/averagerating")
    book[:offer_listing_id] =
                   res.first_item.get("offerlisting/offerlistingid")
    return book
  end
# get similar products to a given ASIN
  def get_similar_products(asin)
    similars = Array.new
    res = ecs.send_request(:aWS_access_key_id => @@key_id, :
            operation => 'SimilarityLookup', :item_id => asin, :
            response_group => 'Small,Images' )
    res.items.each do |item|
      similar = Hash.new
      similar[:asin] = item.get('asin')
      similar[:title] = item.get('itemattributes/title')
      similar[:author] = item.get('itemattributes/author')
      similar[:small_image] = item.get_hash('smallimage')
      similars << similar
    end
    return similars
  end
  protected
  # configure and return an Ecs object
```

```
    def ecs
      Amazon::Ecs.configure do |options|
        options[:aWS_access_key_id] = @@key_id
        options[:associate_tag] = @@associate_id
      end
      return Amazon::Ecs
    end
  end
```

Note that as before, this is not how the file will finally look. We will be adding more functions in terms of methods, as we go along.

We will need to require the Amazon ECS Ruby library, and also define the AWS access key ID and associate ID that you have acquired from Amazon.com in a previous section. Define both of them in class variables, as they are not going to change.

First, we define a convenient method that returns the Amazon::Ecs object that is configured with the access key ID and the associate ID.

Next, define two instance methods. The first is to get the book's details and the second is to get books that are related or 'similar' to your book. Similarity is based on books that customers bought, that is, customers who bought X also bought Y. This assures us that the customer is really interested in those books. In both methods you need to provide an ASIN. In our case the ASIN is from the book controller, where we hard-coded your book's ASIN.

Let's look at the get_book_details method. We use the Amazon::Ecs.item_lookup method from the Amazon ECS Ruby library, passing in the ASIN and requesting a Large response group. This method wraps around the ItemLookup web service from the Amazon ECS API. This response group returns various pieces of information, which we subsequently extract into a Hash and display in the view.

Response groups control the kind of information returned by the Amazon ECS API request. For example, a Large response group returns most of the available information on the item, whereas the Medium and Small response groups return less. Besides these generic response groups, there are very specific ones. For example, if you want to have pricing information you can include the Offer response group as part of the response. You can request more than one response group in a single request. Just place the response groups you want in the response group parameter, separated by commas. For example in our mashup, in the get_similar_products method we requested both the Small and Image response groups.

The `get_similar_products` method on the other hand uses a web service directly from the Amazon ECS API called `SimilarityLookup`. `SimilarityLookup` does not have an equivalent wrapper method in the Amazon ECS Ruby library. However, the Amazon ECS Ruby library is flexible enough to allow other requests through the `Amazon::Ecs#send_request` method by placing the web service name through the `:operation` parameter. We also request two response groups to be returned, that is, `Small` and `Images`. As in `get_book_details`, we extract the information we need from the returned response and place it in a Hash, which in turn is placed in an array of similar items and returned to the view.

Creating the sidebar

The Amazon Rails library is the brain of our mashup but it's not visible or exciting. Let's create something visible next, the sidebar.

First, create the layout used for all templates in the book views. Create a file in the folder `RAILS_ROOT/app/views/layouts` named `books.rhtml`:

```
<!DOCTYPE html PUBLIC "-//W3C//DTD XHTML 1.0 Transitional//EN"
    "http://www.w3.org/TR/xhtml1/DTD/xhtml1-transitional.dtd">
<html xmlns="http://www.w3.org/1999/xhtml" xml:lang="en" lang="en">
 <head>
   <meta http-equiv="content-type" content="text/html;charset=UTF-8" />
   <title>Chapter 4</title>
   <%= javascript_include_tag :defaults %>
   <%= stylesheet_link_tag 'main' %>
 </head>
<body>
<%= yield %>
</body>
</html>
```

Note that Rails will, by default, use the `books.rhtml` as the layout for the other view templates, replacing the `yield` with the actual content of the view. We also link to a stylesheet called `main.css`, which is not listed here but included in the source package.

Next, create a folder called `RAILS_ROOT/app/views/books` and a view file called `sidebar.rhtml` in this folder.

```
<table class="main">
   <tr valign="top">
    <td class="sidebar">
   <div class="info" id="bookBox">
  <table class="box">
         <tbody><tr>
         <td class="topLeft"> </td>
```

```
            <td class="topCenter">
                <div class="center">
                    <h1><%= h @book[:title]%></h1>
                    <h2><%= h @book[:author]%></h2>
                    <%= image_tag @book[:image_url]%>
                    <p/>
                    <strong><%= h @book[:price]%></strong>
                    <p/>
                    <span>Published <%= h @book[:
                       publication_date]%></span>
                </div>
                <div>
                    <strong><%= h @book[:salesrank]%></
                                              strong>
                </div>
                <br/>
                <div>
                <strong>Other books you might be
                        interested in</strong>
                <br/>
                <table>
                <% @similars.each { |similar|%>
                    <tr><td align='center'>
                    <%= image_tag(similar[:small_image][:
                       url], :border => 0) %>
                    </td></tr>
                    <tr><td align='center'>
                    <%= h similar[:title]%>
                    </td></tr>
                    <tr><td align='center'>
                           
                    </td></tr>
                <% }%>
                </table>
                </div>
            </td>
            <td class="topRight"> </td>
        </tr>
        <tr>
            <td class="bottomLeft"> </td>
            <td class="bottomCenter"> </td>
            <td class="bottomRight"> </td>
        </tr>
    </tbody></table>
</div>
</td>
</table>
```

This view file will show the sidebar with the details of the book. Now let's quickly preview the fruits of your labor! Start the server with:

```
$./script/server
```

Then go to http://localhost:3000/books/sidebar.

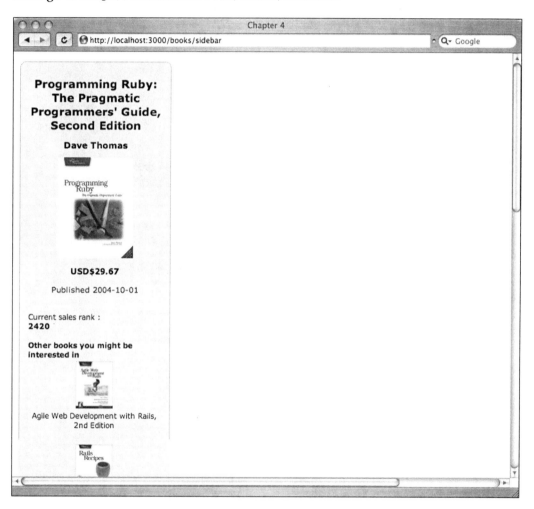

Note the blank space to the right of the page. This is deliberate. After all, the sidebar is a part of your website, not your entire site. For example, this blank space could be your existing blog. We will also be using it later on for the customer reviews as well as the shopping cart.

You may notice that the `sidebar.rhtml` view template uses CSS style classes from the `main.css` stylesheet. I did not show this stylesheet in a listing, so as not to distract from the flow of the project. This means that if you copied the code from this chapter directly you will not see what is shown in the figure above. However, if you download the code package from Packt Publishing's website you will find the `main.css` stylesheet; place it in `RAILS_ROOT/public/stylesheets`.

Getting customer reviews

Next, we want to get customer reviews that have been posted on Amazon.com and display them to the right of the sidebar. To do this, we will add a picture just below the sales ranking. The picture will display the average customer rating of the book, using the rating system in Amazon.com, which is 0 stars to 5 stars. Clicking on this picture will show the customer reviews in blank space to the right of the sidebar. The Amazon ECS API allows 5 customer reviews to be retrieved in each call, so we will also do some simple pagination for the customer reviews. Let's get to work!

First, add in the highlighted line into the `sidebar.rhtml` file at the location shown in the snippet below.

```
<div class="center">
    <h1><%= h @book[:title]%></h1>
    <h2><%= h @book[:author]%></h2>
    <%= image_tag @book[:image_url]%>
    <p/>
    <strong><%= h @book[:price]%></strong>
    <p/>
    <span>Published <%= h @book[:
        publication_date]%></span>
</div>
<div class="right-float"><%= link_to_
remote(image_tag("#{@book[:average_rating]}.
gif", :border => 0), :update => 'update_area',:
url => {:action => 'reviews' ,:page => 1})
%></div>
<div>
    Current sales rank : <br/>
    <strong><%= h @book[:salesrank]%></strong>
</div>
</td>
<td><div id="update_area"></div></td></tr>
</table>
```

Here, we are using a `link_to_remote` on a dynamically generated image name to call an action named `review`, which will update an HTML element with the ID `update_area`. Place the `div` element with the ID `update_area` at the bottom of the page. You will notice that the image links to #{@book[:average_rating]}.gif. This produces, depending on the average rating of the book (which changes from time to time) strings like 4.5.gif or 4.0.gif or 0.5.gif and so on depending on the average rating provided by the customers. You will need to create these appropriate images and place them in the RAILS_ROOT/public/images folder.

Next, add the following action in the `books_controller.rb` file:

```
def reviews
    @reviews = get_customer_reviews @@book_asin, params[:page].to_i
    @page = params[:page].to_i
end
```

The `get_customer_reviews` method in this action comes from our Amazon Rails library again, so add this method in the `amazon.rb` file:

```
# get customer reviews of the product given the ASIN
  def get_customer_reviews(asin,page=1)
    res = ecs.item_lookup(asin, :review_page => page, :response_group
=> 'Reviews')
    reviews = res.first_item/"customerreviews/review"
    reviews.collect { |review|
      Amazon::Element.get_hash(review)
    }
  end
```

The `get_customer_reviews` method, like the `get_book_details` method, uses `Amazon::Ecs.item_lookup` to retrieve the reviews. However, this time we are asking for the `Reviews` response group, which we will convert into a Hash and return it to the view.

Lastly we need to create the reviews view to display the reviews. Create a file named `reviews.rhtml` in RAILS_ROOT/app/views/books:

```
<h1>Customer reviews</h1>
<% @reviews.each { |review| %>
<table class='reviews'>
    <tr><th><%= h review[:summary]%></th></tr>
    <tr><td><div class="left-float"><%= h review[:date]%></div>
<div class="right-float">
<%= image_tag("#{review[:rating]}.0.gif")%>
</div></td></tr>
    <tr><td><%= CGI.unescapeHTML review[:content]%></td></tr>
```

```
</table>
<% } %>
<div class='left-float'><%= link_to_remote '<< previous', :update =>
'update_area', :url => {:action => 'reviews', :page => @page - 1}
unless @page == 1%></div>
<div class='right-float'><%= link_to_remote 'next >>', :update =>
'update_area', :url => {:action => 'reviews', :page => @page + 1} %></
div>
```

Notice that the image for the rating follows a similar format to that for the average
rating. However because Amazon.com doesn't allow customers to put fractions
of a star as a rating, the rating will always be a whole number. We also need to
unescape the HTML in `review[:content]` using `CGI.unescapeHTML` in order to
display the HTML formatting in the text properly. In case you are wondering, `CGI` is
already included in the Rails framework, which explains why you can use it without
requiring it earlier on.

We also provide a simple pagination mechanism that allows us to move to the next
page of reviews.

Here's how it turns out. Click on the rating graphic to bring up the customer reviews:

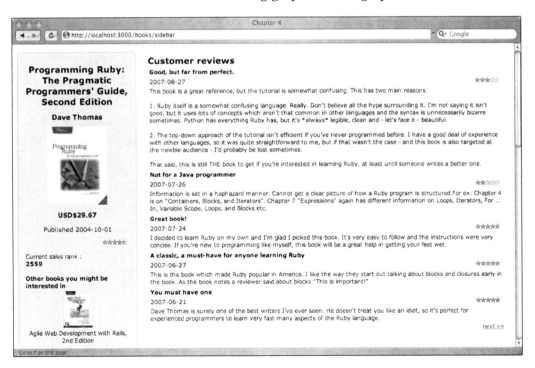

Getting the daily sales ranking

Now that we have the customer reviews, let's do something about the sales ranking. Amazon.com provides only the most current sales ranking, which we have already displayed in the sidebar. Unfortunately it doesn't display any historic sales ranking and therefore we don't know how the book sales have performed over a period of time. To do this, we need to keep a history of the sales ranking.

We will keep the historic sales ranking in a YAML file instead of ActiveRecord although this is also possible. However ActiveRecord is overkill if you do not already have a database. What we're going to do is to create a rake script that runs on a regular basis (depending on how often you want to check the sales ranking) and which stores the ranking in a sequence in a YAML file.

Create a rake script named `salesrank.rake` in the `RAILS_ROOT/lib/tasks` folder:

```
namespace :chapter4 do
  desc 'Get daily sales ranking'
  task :salesrank => :environment do
    begin
      salesrank = Amazon.salesrank('0974514055')
      SalesRank.add(salesrank)
    rescue
      puts $!
    end
  end
end
```

The rake script itself is quite simple. It just calls a class method in the Amazon Rails library to retrieve the current sales ranking, and then calls another class method in the SalesRank library to update the YAML file.

Let's look at the new method we are adding to the Amazon library:

```
# get the current sales rank for the product given the ASIN
def self.salesrank(asin)
  Amazon::Ecs.configure do |options|
    options[:aWS_access_key_id] = @@key_id
    options[:associate_tag] = @@associate_id
  end
  res = Amazon::Ecs.item_lookup(asin,
              :response_group => 'SalesRank')
  res.first_item.get('salesrank').to_i
end
```

The `Amazon.salesrank` method takes in the ASIN from the rake script and calls `Amazon::Ecs.item_lookup`, requests the `SalesRank` response group, then extracts it from the response and returns it as an integer.

For the sales rank-related features we will create a new SalesRank library. Create an empty file named `salesrank_history.yml` in the `RAILS_ROOT/config` folder and a file named `sales_rank.rb` in the `RAILS_ROOT/lib` folder:

```
module SalesRank
  def self.history
    history = YAML.load_file(RAILS_ROOT +
                       '/config/salesrank_history.yml')
    history ? history : []
  end
  def self.add(rank)
    current = history.last(10) << rank
    File.open( RAILS_ROOT + '/config/salesrank_history.yml',
                                         'w' ) do |out|
      YAML.dump( current , out )
    end
  end
end
```

The `salesrank_history.yml` file is a YAML file that contains the history of the sales ranking over a period of time.

Run the rake script. Once the rake script has retrieved the most recent sales ranking, we will add it to the sales ranking history using the `SalesRank.add` method. Firstly, the method takes the current history from the `salesrank_history.yml` file as an Array. However, we limit the history to the last 10 (this number is arbitrary; you can use any number) sales ranking values and append the latest rank to the end of the array. Then we re-open the `salesrank_history.yml` file and write the entire contents of the array to it, overwriting the previous content. This ensures that we will only have at most 11 last readings of the sales ranking at any point in time.

Now that we have the rake script, we can use a scheduler to run it periodically. A good period is to run it once every day in order to get the latest daily sales ranking of your book.

Displaying the sales ranking sparkline

We have the historic sales ranking now but we need to display it nicely using a sparkline. To do this we can opt for the simplest way of getting the image, which is to just place the values into the URL string itself.

Add this class method to `sales_rank.rb`:

```
def self.sparkline
    hist = history
    min = hist.sort.first - 100 > 0 ? hist.sort.first - 100 : 0
    max = hist.sort.last + 100
"http://bitworking.org/projects/sparklines/spark.
cgi?type=smooth&d=#{hist.join(',')}&height=15&limits=#{min},#{max}&m
in-m=true&max-m=true&last-m=true&min-color=red&max-color=blue&last-
color=green&step=10"
  end
```

Firstly we need to find out the minimum and the maximum sales ranking of the book within the period and put a buffer of 100 ranks below and above it respectively. Then, we plug in the data from the history, set the maximum and minimum limits into the web service URL, and return it.

Now that we have the sparkline image, let's put it in the sidebar, just next to the sales ranking numbers.

```
<div style="clear: both;"/>
<br/>
    Current sales rank : <br/>
<%= image_tag SalesRank.sparkline %>
    <strong><%= h @book[:salesrank]%></strong>
</div>
```

This is how it will look:

Creating a shopping cart

The last feature for this mashup is to allow your visitors to buy your book directly from your website. Visitors to your website can add your book and other similar books to a shopping cart. Payment still goes through Amazon.com and the shopping cart is located remotely at Amazon.com but you will be able to fully control and manipulate it.

Firstly, add in a `create_new_cart` method in the `books_controller.rb` file as below:

```
def create_new_cart
  @cart = session[:cart] = create_cart (params[:offer_listing_id])
    redirect_to :action => :cart
end
```

This method calls the `create_cart` method in the Amazon Rails library, passing in the Offer Listing ID of a copy your book, and returns a hash providing the cart's details. Note that we're using the Offer Listing ID instead of the product ASIN.

We store this hash into the session and redirect the flow to the cart view. Let's quickly turn to the Amazon Rails library. Add in a method named `create_cart` in the `amazon.rb` file:

```
# create a new cart with an item given the Offer Listing ID
  def create_cart(offerListingId)
    cart = Hash.new
    res = ecs.send_request(:aWS_access_key_id => @@key_id,
          : operation => 'CartCreate', 'Item.1.OfferListingId' =>
          offerListingId, 'Item.1.Quantity' => 1)
    cart[:cart_id] = res.doc.at("cartid").inner_html
    cart[:hmac] = res.doc.at("hmac").inner_html
    cart[:urlencoded_hmac] = res.doc.at("urlencodedhmac").inner_html
    cart[:purchase_url] =  res.doc.at("purchaseurl").inner_html
    return cart
  end
```

We use the `CartCreate` web service from Amazon ECS API, passing in the book's Offer Listing ID as well as the quantity we require. For simplicity's sake we will hard-code the quantity to 1. You can add up to 10 products in a single `CartCreate` web service call, each passing the Offer Listing ID like this: `Item.1.OfferListingId, Item.2.OfferListingId, Item.3.OfferListingId` and so on; but to keep things simple we'll only add your book to this shopping cart when we're creating it.

An offer listing ID is an alphanumeric token that uniquely identifies an item, as opposed to an ASIN, which identifies a product. While it is possible to add an item to a cart using an ASIN, the preferred means of adding an item is by specifying an Offer Listing ID. This is because an Offer Listing ID, not an ASIN, guarantees that an item can be purchased. Some items (for example variation abstractions or collections) may have an ASIN but not an Offer Listing ID. Items that do not have an Offer Listing ID cannot be purchased.

We will also need at least three values in the cart hash. The Cart ID uniquely identifies a remote shopping cart at Amazon.com, where our newly created shopping cart is located. The HMAC (Hash Message Authentication Code) is an encoded alphanumeric token, which is used to authenticate the cart. Both values must be present to use any of the shopping cart-related web services from Amazon. com ECS API. The purchase URL is the URL that is submitted to purchase the items in a remote shopping cart.

Now that we have the `create_new_cart` action, link a nice shopping cart image (which you'll need to put in `RAILS_ROOT/public/images`) to it in the `sidebar.rhtml` file as shown in the snippet below:

```
<div class="center">
    <h1><%= h @book[:title]%></h1>
    <h2><%= h @book[:author]%></h2>
    <%= image_tag @book[:image_url]%>
    <p/>
    <strong><%= h @book[:price]%></strong>
    <p/>
    <span>Published <%= h @book[:publication_date]%></span>
</div>
<div style="clear: both;"/>
<div class="left-float"><%=link_to_remote(image_tag('add_to_cart.gif',
    :border => 0), :update => 'update_area', :url => {:action =>
    'create_new_cart', :offer_listing_id =>  @book[:offer_listing_id]}
    )%></div>
<div class="right-float"><%= link_to_remote(image_tag("#{@book[:
    average_rating]}.gif", :border => 0), :update => 'update_area',:url
    => {:action => 'reviews' ,:page => 1}) %></div>
<div style="clear: both;"/>
```

As in the customer review, we will place the shopping cart in the `<div>` element with the ID `update_area`.

The `create_new_cart` action redirects to a cart view, which updates (through AJAX) the `<div>` element. Create a method in the `books_controller.rb` file:

```
def cart
    @cart = get_cart session[:cart]
end
```

In the `amazon.rb` file, add the `get_cart` method to retrieve the remote shopping cart from Amazon.com using the `CartGet` web service, passing in the cart hash we created when we created the shopping cart (and which we have placed in a session).

```
# get an existing cart
  def get_cart(cart)
    res = Amazon::Ecs.send_request(:operation => 'CartGet',
          :cart_id => cart[:cart_id], 'HMAC' => cart[:hmac])
    items = Array.new
    subtotal = nil
    purchase_url =  res.doc.at("purchaseurl").inner_html
    cartitems = res.doc.at("cartitems")
    cartitems.each_child { |child|
      if child.name == 'cartitem'
        item = Hash.new
        item[:title] = child.at("title").inner_html
        item[:quantity] = child.at("quantity").inner_html
        item[:asin] = child.at("asin").inner_html
        item[:price] = child.at("price/formattedprice").inner_html
        items << item
      elsif child.name == 'subtotal'
        subtotal = child.at("formattedprice").inner_html
      end
      }
    return {:items => items, :subtotal => subtotal,
                  :purchase_url => purchase_url}
  end
```

This method returns a hash containing the items in the shopping cart, the subtotal, and purchase URL. This hash is passed to the view and is used for displaying the shopping cart information. Create a `cart.rhtml` file in the RAILS_ROOT/apps/views/books folder:

```
<h1>Your shopping cart</h1>
You have the following books in your shopping cart:
<p/>
<table>
    <tr>
            <th class="item_column">Item</th>
            <th class="qty_column">Quantity</th>
```

```
                <th class="price_column">Price</th>
        </tr>
<%. @cart[:items].reverse.each { |item| %>
        <tr>
                <td><%= h item[:title]%> </td>
                <td><%= h item[:quantity]%> </td>
                <td><%= h item[:price]%> </td>
        </tr>
<% } %>
<tr>
        <td></td>
        <td></td>
        <th><%= h @cart[:subtotal]%> </th>
</tr>
</table>
<%= link_to (image_tag('buy.jpg', :border => 0), @cart[:purchase_url]
)%>
```

Note that we attach the purchase URL to the 'Buy Now!' image (which once again you'll need to put in the RAILS_ROOT/public/images folder) to redirect the visitor to Amazon.com for payment.

This is how the page looks like after clicking on the 'Add to Shopping Cart' image button.

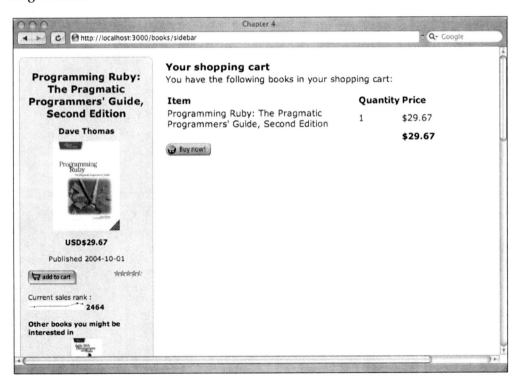

Adding similar books to the shopping cart

To increase your earnings, you want to be an Amazon Associate and sell some books that are related to yours, so you want to allow your visitors to add these similar books to the shopping cart. To do this, we need to modify some of the methods we have already created.

Change the `get_similar_products` method in the Amazon Rails library to include the Offer Listing ID in the returned response.

```
# get similar products to a given ASIN
  def get_similar_products(asin)
    similars = Array.new
    res =  ecs.send_request(:operation => 'SimilarityLookup', :item_id
       =>  asin, :response_group => 'Small,Images,Offers' )
    res.items.each do |item|
      similar = Hash.new
      similar[:asin] = item.get('asin')
      similar[:title] = item.get('itemattributes/title')
      similar[:author] = item.get('itemattributes/author')
      similar[:offer_listing_id] = item.get("offerlisting/
                                      offerlistingid")
      similar[:small_image] = item.get_hash('smallimage')
      similars << similar
    end
    return similars
  end
```

Note that the response group requested now includes the `Offers` response group, which gives us the Offer Listing ID. Now change the `sidebar.rhtml` file as shown in the snippet below:

```
<div>
    <strong>Other books you might be interested in</strong>
    <br/>
    <table>
    <% @similars.each { |similar|%>
        <tr><td align='center'>
      <%= link_to_remote(image_tag(similar[:small_image][:url], :border
        => 0), :update => 'update_area', :url => {:action => 'add_item', :
        offer_listing_id => similar[:offer_listing_id], :quantity => 1})%>
        </td></tr>
        <tr><td align='center'>
        <%= h similar[:title]%>
        </td></tr>
        <tr><td align='center'>
         
        </td></tr>
    <% }%>
    </table>
</div>
```

The change links the similar book image to an `add_item` action in the book controller, passing in the Offer Listing ID and the quantity. Next, we need to add a new method in the `books_controller.rb` file:

```
def add_item
    item = {:offer_listing_id => params[:offer_listing_id],
                        :quantity => params[:quantity]}
    @results = add_item_to_cart(session[:cart], item)
    redirect_to :action => :cart
end
```

This method calls the `add_item_to_cart` method in the Amazon library, passing on the remote shopping cart and item to be added to the shopping cart. Create this method in the `amazon.rb` file:

```
# add a new item to an existing cart
def add_item_to_cart(cart,item)
    res = ecs.send_request(:operation => 'CartAdd',
    :cart_id => cart[:cart_id], 'HMAC' => cart[:hmac],
    'Item.1.OfferListingId' => item[:offer_listing_id],
    'Item.1.Quantity' => item[:quantity])
end
```

This method looks very much like the `create_cart` method except that it calls the `CardAdd` web service instead of the `CartCreate` web service.

And we're done! This is how it looks with the additional lines added to the shopping cart.

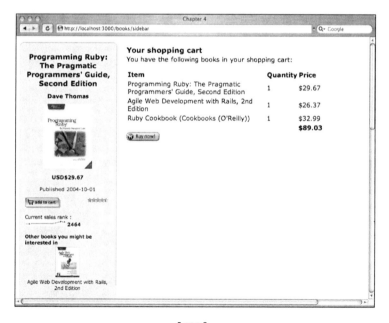

Summary

We've learned about Amazon's E-Commerce API web service and how we can use it to retrieve information on the products sold by Amazon.com and its merchants. We learned how to retrieve and store historic sales ranking information in a YAML file and create a sparkline chart using a web service based on the historic sales ranking. We also learned how to create a remote shopping cart in Amazon.com, then display and manipulate it.

5

Job board mashup application

What does it do?

The job board mashup application is a fully fledged web application (running in the Facebook interface) that allows a user to perform some functions and features of a job board. This chapter describes how some functions of a job board can be performed and enhanced by mashing up APIs from various sources.

Job board

A job board is a web application that 'converts' visits to a web site into actual candidates registering for consideration for a job. It can belong to a company that is recruiting its own employees or a third-party provider that helps companies to recruit.

The basic functions of job board are:

- Acquiring candidates
- Storing and providing access to candidate profiles
- Processing candidate profiles
- Acquiring job postings
- Storing and providing access to job postings
- Processing job postings
- Providing value-added functions to candidates and employers

In this mashup we will show how some of a job board's functions can be duplicated using various existing APIs on the Internet.

Requirements overview

We will define and map some of the functions of a job board and create mashups to support these functions. We're not going to cover all the functions of a job board (there are too many to cover) and we will be using numerous APIs from different providers to provide these functions.

The functions are:

- Create a Facebook application that extracts and displays the user's profile. Facebook is used here as a marketing tool to acquire candidates.

- Search for jobs through Indeed according to the user's Facebook profile. Most job boards will have their own database of job postings but here we emulate acquiring job postings by using a job search engine.

- Display the location of the jobs found using the user's profile in Google Maps. Displaying job locations in a map provides more visual impact to candidates.

- Search and display news on the recruiting companies through the Daylife platform. News on the recruiting company provides more information on the company and its products and services.

- Search and display blog postings in the blogosphere on the recruiting companies through Technorati. Blog postings on the recruiting company provide a different view of the company through the eyes of employees, ex-employees, customers, or partners.

Design

This mashup application takes input and provides output to many different mashup APIs. We will break down the process of creating this mashup into different steps. The final application is not a single piece of software but a mashup in every sense.

We are going to use Facebook as a marketing tool, tapping its social network for candidates. To do this we will create a Facebook application. This means while the software resides within our server, the interface is through Facebook.

Searching for jobs through Indeed is displayed through the Facebook application but displaying them on Google Maps is more conventionally displayed in our own interface. News and blog entries on the company offering the job are displayed when clicked on within Google Maps, in a separate panel to the side of the map.

Mashup APIs on the menu

We are going to use five different mashup APIs in our mashup application:

- Facebook
- Google Maps
- Indeed
- Daylife
- Technorati

We're also going to use a few technologies to access these APIs:

- RFacebook for accessing Facebook
- YM4R/GM for accessing Google Maps
- Net::HTTP for accessing Indeed, Daylife and Technorati
- XmlSimple for parsing input form Indeed, Daylife, and Technorati

Here's a quick rundown and introduction to the APIs and tools.

Facebook

Facebook (`http://www.facebook.com`) is a social networking tool that connects you to other people that you know on Facebook. It has the largest registered user base among college-focused sites in the United States with an estimated 34 million users as of September 2007.

In May 2007, Facebook opened up its network to application developers by launching a set of APIs for third-party developers, called the Facebook Platform. Since then there has been a flurry of third-party applications developed on Facebook and as of September 2007 there are more than 4,500 such applications deployed on its platform.

Facebook Platform

The Facebook Platform consists of several parts:

- Facebook REST APIs
- Facebook Query Language (FQL)
- Facebook Markup (FBML)

Facebook REST APIs allow you to write applications (either completely external or attached to the Facebook interface) that use Facebook data or write data to user's Facebook accounts.

FQL allows you to write SQL-like queries in your applications to request Facebook data. FQL is used instead of the REST APIs if you want to have finer control on what data you want from Facebook. For example if you only want a small subset of data from Facebook, or if you want to concatenate data from a few sources in Facebook, then you might not want to call two or more APIs to do the work where a single FQL query will do the job. However, FQL as its name implies is only available for reading data off Facebook.

FBML is a markup language that allows your application to integrate well into the Facebook application. It is set of HTML-like tags that can be used at various places in the Facebook application. FBML can be integrated in many different parts of a Facebook application, though the two main parts are the profile page and the canvas page.

We will be accessing Facebook through the RFacebook Ruby library and Rails plugin.

RFacebook

RFacebook (`http://rfacebook.rubyforge.org/index.html`) is a Ruby interface to the Facebook APIs. You can use the REST APIs, FQL, and FBML through RFacebook. There are two parts to RFacebook—the gem and the plugin. The plugin is a stub that calls RFacebook on the Rails library packaged in the gem. RFacebook on Rails library extends the default Rails controller, model, and view. RFacebook also provides a simple interface through an RFacebook session to call any Facebook API. RFacebook uses some meta-programming idioms in Ruby to call Facebook APIs.

Google Maps

Google Maps is a free web-based mapping service provided by Google. Google provides a free JavasSript API library that allows developers to integrate Google Maps into their own applications. In this mashup we will be using only the online mapping function and not the geocoding capabilities of Google Maps. We will be using the YM4R/GM plugin to access the online map. For more information on getting a Google Maps API key please refer to Chapter 2.

Indeed

Indeed is a job search engine that allows users to search for jobs based on keywords and location. It includes job listings from major job boards and newspapers and even company career pages.

Indeed provides a search API through its web services offering. To register for the web service API go to `http://www.indeed.com/jsp/createaccount.jsp` and register for an account. Once you have signed up you will receive a search API key. You are allowed to make up to 99,999 queries in a single day. The web service API provided by Indeed is only available through a GET request from a REST URL.

Technorati

Technorati (`http://www.technorati.com`) is an Internet search engine that specializes in searching blogs. As of August 2007, Technorati had indexed 94 million blogs on the Internet. Technorati provides a set of APIs for developers to help them integrate Technorati data into their applications and to create mashups.

To create a developer account in Technorati, go to `http://technorati.com/signup/` and sign up for an account. Once you have signed up you will be provided with an API key. The number of queries you make on Technorati each day is tracked and you are not allowed to make more than 500 queries in a single day, unless you have a commercial agreement with Technorati.

Technorati provides a number of APIs of which search is only one. You are also able to get information on its members and the blogs its members own as well as various blog statistics.

Daylife

Daylife (`http://www.daylife.com`) is a news aggregation site that gathers news items from sources around the world and presents them in a meaningful and connected way. One of the key features in Daylife is its ability to connect different stories and topics together. Daylife also offers a platform for third-party applications to use its data. Daylife provides a set of APIs around their News objects through a REST interface. APIs provided include those used for Articles, Images, Quotes, Topics, and Searches.

To use the Daylife platform you need to register at `http://developer.daylife.com/member/register`. After registering you will be given an API access key and a shared secret.

To send a request to the Daylife APIs, we need to compose a URL that specifies an API endpoint and a list of input parameters. Input parameters are provided as URL-encoded name value pairs.

This what an endpoint looks like:

```
http://freeapi.daylife.com/<resultformat>/publicapi/<version>/
<NewsObject name>_<method name>
```

Note that the current version is 4.2 and therefore the version number above is 42. Daylife provides resultsets in three formats; that is in XML (xmlrest), in serializable PHP objects (phprest) and in JSON (jsonrest). In this mashup we will use the XML format only.

Input parameters are appended to the API endpoint as an '&'-separated list of name-value pairs of arguments as a query string using the standard HTTP GET formatting.

For example, a call to search for news containing the text "ruby on rails" and a request for the resultset in an XML format looks like this:

```
http://freeapi.daylife.com/xmlrest/publicapi/4.2/search_getRelatedArt
icles?accesskey=<accesskey>&signature=<signature>&query=ruby+on+rails
```

where <accesskey> is your assigned API access key, and <signature> is replaced by an MD5 hashed signature. To create the signature, we concatenate the API access key, the shared secret, and a core input that varies according to the API called. We will be describing how to create the signature in detail when we do it later.

Net::HTTP

For a more detailed discussion on Net::HTTP please refer to Chapter 3. We will only be sending GET requests to the REST APIs in this mashup, so our code will be in this form:

```
response = Net::HTTP.get_response(URI.parse('http://www.packtpub.com'))
```

XmlSimple

XmlSimple (http://xml-simple.rubyforge.org/) is a Ruby API that allows XML formatted data to be easily read and written to. It is a Ruby translation of the Perl module XML::Simple and is written on top of REXML, an XML parser that is included in the Ruby distribution.

To install XmlSimple, run this at the command line:

```
$gem install xml-simple
```

The main use for XmlSimple in our mashup is to read the XML response that is sent by the API and convert the XML into a nested hash. For example, when we send a request query to Technorati using its search query, this is the returned XML response:

```
<?xml version="1.0" encoding="utf-8"?>
<!-- generator="Technorati API version 1.0 /search" -->
<!DOCTYPE tapi PUBLIC "-//Technorati, Inc.//DTD TAPI 0.02//EN"
"http://api.technorati.com/dtd/tapi-002.xml">
<tapi version="1.0">
<document>
<result>
    <query>Ruby on Rails</query>
    <querycount>42254</querycount>
    <rankingstart></rankingstart>
</result>
<item>
    <weblog>
        <name>Urubatan's Weblog</name>
        <url>http://www.urubatan.info</url>
        <rssurl>http://www.urubatan.info/feed/</rssurl>
        <atomurl></atomurl>
        <inboundblogs>8</inboundblogs>
        <inboundlinks>11</inboundlinks>
        <lastupdate>2007-10-16 14:17:27 GMT</lastupdate>
    </weblog>
    <title>Ruby out of the Rails - Nitro and Og</title>
    <excerpt> The Ruby language, started to grow inside the enterprises
and to be the topic in many blogs after the Rail framework showed up,
but Rails is not the only option for developing web applications with
Ruby, there are other frameworks, and one of the others is called
Nitro Framework, this one has almost the same age as Rails</excerpt>
    <created>2007-10-16 14:17:27 GMT</created>
    <permalink>http://www.urubatan.info/2007/10/ruby-out-of-the-rails-
                    nitro-and-og/</permalink>
</item>
</document>
</tapi>
```

Running this through XmlSimple with this code:

```
XmlSimple::xml_in(xml_input, 'force_array' => false)
```

results in a nested hash like this:

```
{"document"=>
 {"result"=>
  {"querycount"=>"42255", "rankingstart"=>{},
                  "query"=>"Ruby on Rails"},
   "item"=>
   {"permalink"=>
     "http://www.urubatan.info/2007/10/ruby-out-of-the-rails-nitro-
            and-og/",
    "title"=>"Ruby out of the Rails - Nitro and Og",
    "excerpt"=>
     " The Ruby language, started to grow inside the enterprises and
        to be the topic in many blogs after the Rails framework showed
        up, but Rails is not the only option for developing web
        applications with Ruby, there are other frameworks, and one of
        the others is called Nitro Framework, this one has almost the
        same age as Rails",
    "weblog"=>
    {"inboundlinks"=>"11",
     "rssurl"=>"http://www.urubatan.info/feed/",
     "name"=>"Urubatan's Weblog",
     "atomurl"=>{},
     "url"=>"http://www.urubatan.info",
     "inboundblogs"=>"8",
     "lastupdate"=>"2007-10-16 14:17:27 GMT"},
    "created"=>"2007-10-16 14:17:27 GMT"}},
 "version"=>"1.0"}
```

By setting the attribute force_array to false in this example, we allow elements in the nested hash not to be an array if there is only 1 element. From the nested hash we can extract the data that we need.

We will be using XmlSimple pretty extensively in many of the subsequent sections.

What we will be doing

The following section describes the steps we will be taking to create the mashup.

Acquire candidates through Facebook

The first and longest step is to acquire candidates through a Facebook application. These are the steps we will take to create this Facebook application:

1. Create a Rails application
2. Create a Facebook application
3. Install and configure the RFacebook plugin and gem

4. Extract the user's Facebook user profile using RFacebook

5. Display the user profile information we need and create a form to send the user profile to the search page

6. Deploy and configure the Facebook application

Search for jobs through Indeed

Next, we will enable searching for jobs through Indeed while displaying the jobs in the Facebook application. The Facebook application also allows you to display the location of the jobs found in a map and this redirects to our mashup. The steps to achieve this are:

1. Create the action and use Net::HTTP to send the search parameters to Indeed

2. Parse the results with XML:Simple and display the search results in the Facebook application

Display jobs in Google Maps

Displaying Google Maps is done in our own mashup interface:

1. Use the search results to display the location of the jobs in the map

2. Create a link on each job to show the news and stories on the company

Search and display job news from Daylife

Searching and displaying job news extracted from Daylife:

1. Use Net::HTTP to accesss Daylife APIs to extract Daylife news data and display it on the web page

Search and display job stories from Technorati

Searching and displaying job news extracted from Technorati:

1. Use Net::HTTP to access Technorati's REST APIs and extract blog information

Acquiring candidates through Facebook

We will be creating a Facebook application and displaying it through Facebook. This application, when added into the list of a user's applications, allows the user to search for jobs using information in his or her Facebook profile.

Facebook applications, though displayed within the Facebook interface, are actually hosted and processed somewhere else. To display it within Facebook, you need to host the application in a publicly available website, then register the application. We will go through these steps in creating the Job Board Facebook application.

Creating a Rails application

We begin this mashup by creating a Rails application.

```
$rails Chapter5
```

This will create a new Ruby on Rails application. Note that in this application we will not be using ActiveRecord or accessing any databases to retrieve or store data. All data will be retrieved and parsed from the various APIs we will be using.

Creating a Facebook application

Next, create a Facebook application. To do this, you will need to first add a special application in your Facebook account—the Developer application. Go to http://www.facebook.com/developers and you will be asked to allow Developer to be installed in your Facebook account.

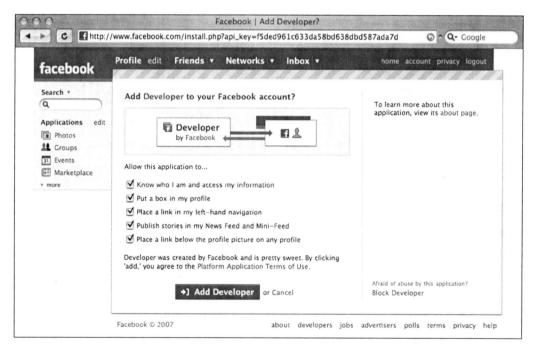

Add the Developer application and agree to everything in the permissions list.

You will not have any applications yest, so click on the **create one** link to create a new application. Next you will be asked for the name of the application you want to create. Enter a suitable name; in our case, enter 'Job Board' and you will be redirected to the Developer application main page, where you are shown your newly created application with its API key and secret.

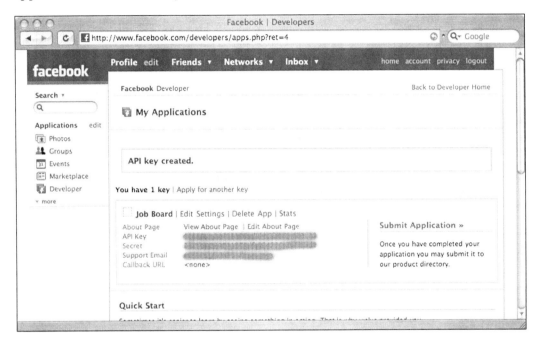

You will need the API key and secret in a while.

Installing and configuring RFacebook

RFacebook consists of two components—the gem and the plugin. The gem contains the libraries needed to communicate with Facebook while the plugin enables your Rails application to integrate with Facebook. As mentioned earlier, the plugin is basically a stub to the gem. The gem is installed like any other gem in Ruby:

```
$gem install rfacebook
```

To install the plugin go to your RAILS_ROOT folder and type in:

```
$./script/plugin install svn://rubyforge.org/var/svn/rfacebook/trunk/
rfacebook/plugins/rfacebook
```

Next, after the gem and plugin is installed, run a setup rake script to create the configuration file in the RAILS_ROOT folder:

```
$rake facebook:setup
```

This creates a facebook.yml configuration file in RAILS_ROOT/config folder. The facebook.yml file contains three environments that mirror the Rails startup environments. Open it up to configure the necessary environment with the API key and secret that you were given when you created the application in the section above.

```
development:
    key: YOUR_API_KEY_HERE
    secret: YOUR_API_SECRET_HERE
    canvas_path: /yourAppName/
    callback_path: /path/to/your/callback/
    tunnel:
      username: yourLoginName
      host: www.yourexternaldomain.com
      port: 1234
      local_port: 5678
```

For now, just fill in the API key and secret. In a later section when we configure the rest of the Facebook application, we will need to revisit this configuration.

Extracting the Facebook user profile

Next we want to extract the user's Facebook user profile and display it on the Facebook application. We do this to let the user confirm that this is the information he or she wants to send as search parameters.

To do this, create a controller named search_controller.rb in the RAILS_ROOT/app/controllers folder.

```
class SearchController < ApplicationController
  before_filter :require_facebook_install
  layout 'main'
  def index
  view
    render :action => :view
  end
  def view
    if fbsession.is_valid?
      response = fbsession.users_getInfo(:uids =>
                 [fbsession.session_user_id], :fields =>
                 ["current_location", "education_history",
```

```
                "work_history"])
    @work_history = response.work_history
    @education_history = response.education_history
    @current_location = response.current_location
  end
end
```

Note the `before_filter` we've added to this controller. This filter is a part of RFacebook and forces the user to install the application whenever this controller is used. Let's look at the `view` action.

`fbsession` is the current user's Facebook session represented in Rails. `fbsession` allows you to call any existing method in the set of Facebook REST APIs through a commonly used Ruby meta-programming idiom. There is a method in the Ruby `Kernel` module (which is included in the base `Object` class and therefore available to every Ruby object) called `method_missing`. This is called every time any Ruby object is sent a message it cannot handle (that is, it is called when there is a 'missing method'). Normally the Ruby interpreter will raise an error if this happens but this method (like any method in Ruby) can be overridden to process the message. This meta-programming idiom is widely used in many Ruby libraries and frameworks, including Ruby on Rails. For example, in ActiveRecord, the find_by_xxx methods are implemented in this way.

In the case of RFacebook, `method_missing` is overridden in `fbsession` (which is an instance of `RFacebook::FacebookSession`) to call the corresponding Facebook API. In the above code, the method `users_getInfo` is called in `fbsession`. This is translated into the Facebook API `facebook.users.getInfo`. The general rule is to drop 'facebook' and convert the dot (.) to an underscore (_). The parameters passed to the API are passed as a Hash. In this case, we are passing the current user's Facebook session UID and a list of fields we want from the API.

RFacebook stores the response in a format called Facepricot, which is an extended form of Hpricot, but with some specific and simplified methods for getting Facebook data from the returned response document. In our Job Board Facebook application, we're looking specifically for three pieces of information — the user's education history, work history, and current location.

Displaying the user profile and creating the search form

Now that we have the information let's go to the corresponding view and see how we can display it. Create a file called `view.rhtml` in the `RAILS_ROOT/app/views/search` folder:

```
<h1>
    Job Board
</h1>
<p>Select to include your education and work history.</p>
<% form_tag :action => "search" do %>
<label>Education history   <%= check_box_tag
        'education'%></label>
<ul>
<%
education = []
    @education_history.education_info_list.each { |education_info|
    education << education_info.concentrations.concentration_list
    %>
    <li><%= h education_info.name %>(<%= h education_info.year%>) -
    <%= h education_info.concentrations.concentration_list.join ", "
    %></li>
    <% } %>
</ul>
<%= hidden_field_tag 'education_info', education.join(", ") %>
<label>Work history   <%= check_box_tag 'work'%></label>
<ul>
<%
work = []
@work_history.work_info_list.each { |work_info|
    work << work_info.position
    %>
    <li><%= h work_info.company_name %> (<%= h work_info.start_date%>
     - <%= work_info.end_date%>) - <%= h work_info.position%>
    </li>
    <% } %>
</ul>
<%= hidden_field_tag 'work_info', work.join(", ") %>
<label>Other keywords</label>
<p>Enter additional keywords to search jobs on (separate keywords with
commas) </p>
<%= text_field_tag 'keywords'%>
<br/>
<label>Job location</label>
<p>Where should the jobs be located?</p>
<% locations = []
    locations << @current_location.city << @current_location.country
%>
```

```
<%= text_field_tag 'location', locations.compact.delete_if {|item|
item == '' }. join(', ')%>
<p/>
<%= submit_tag "search" %>
<% end %>
```

Let's take a look at how to display the education history. This is sample response format from the Facebook API documentation:

```
<education_history list="true">
  <education_info>
    <name>Harvard</name>
    <year>2003</year>
    <concentrations list="true">
      <concentration>Applied Mathematics</concentration>
      <concentration>Computer Science</concentration>
    </concentrations>
  </education_info>
</education_history>
```

Note that the education_history element has an attribute list=true, which indicates that there can be one or more education info elements. To get the list of education info elements, just attach _list to education_info to get education_info_list and use that as a method name. This will produce an Array of education_info elements, which we iterate to get and display the information.

```
<%
education = []
@education_history.education_info_list.each { |education_info|
    education << education_info.concentrations.concentration_list
  %>
    <li><%= h education_info.name %>(<%= h education_info.year%>) -
<%= h education_info.concentrations.concentration_list.join ", " %></
li>
  <% } %>
```

Repeat this with work history.

```
<%
work = []
@work_history.work_info_list.each { |work_info|
    work << work_info.position
  %>
    <li><%= h work_info.company_name %> (<%= h work_info.start_date%>
          - <%= work_info.end_date%>) - <%= h work_info.position%>
    </li>
  <% } %>
```

We wrap a form around the displayed information and place check boxes next to education and work history to let the user choose if they want to use the data in their education history, work history, both, or none at all, in the job search. The fields we are using are the work positions and the education history concentrations. We also place the current location of the user as indicated in the user profile in a text field. This allows the user to search jobs in their current location by default or change it according to the location that they want.

The search form will call a `search` action in the search controller, which we will describe in the next part. For now we need to deploy the Facebook application and then configure it.

Deploying and configuring the Facebook application

Facebook applications, as mentioned earlier, are displayed through Facebook but hosted elsewhere. When a user accesses our application through Facebook, Facebook will call our application and return the results to the user.

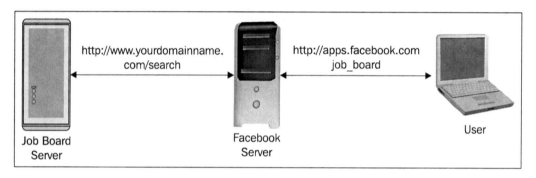

As a result, the Facebook application needs to be accessible by Facebook and this means it needs to be hosted in a publicly available Internet site. This also means that our Facebook application cannot be deployed locally on your desktop PC even for testing purposes.

If you don't happen to have access to a server on the Internet or have access to a publicly available hosting account, there is another way of deploying your Facebook application. Assuming that you're running your application on your PC at home and accessing it through an ISP, you can use a dynamic DNS service to point an Internet domain name to the IP address that the ISP assigned to your PC. You will usually need to install a small application on your PC that will automatically update the DNS entry whenever your ISP-assigned IP address changes. There are many freely available dynamic DNS services on the Internet. This is the same technique we used in Chapter 2 to enable us to geolocate the user of the application through Hostip.info. We will use this technique again in Chapter 6.

The caveat is that if you run your Facebook application on your home PC, you will need to keep it running all the time, unless it is acceptable that the application can be unavailable when it is not turned on. Also you should be aware that many ISPs do not allow their subscribers to run services on their home PCs and some even block off certain ports, in particular the HTTP port.

No matter where you plan to run the Facebook application, you can start the application as you start any Rails application.

```
$./script/server
```

After you have started up the Facebook application, you need to go back to the Facebook Developer application in your Facebook account to configure it. Click on the Edit Settings link for the application. There are a number of settings you need to configure here.

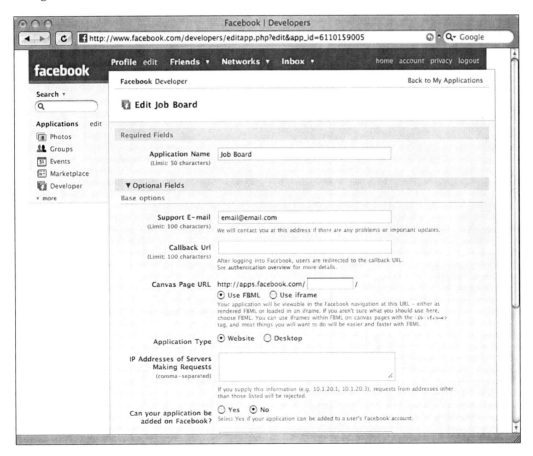

The callback URL is the public URL of your Facebook application. For our Job Board application, assuming that you are hosting on yourdomainname.com, you should use `http://www.yourdomainname.com:3000/search`.

Note that the default port number for the server script in the `RAILS_ROOT/script` folder is 3000. You can change it like this:

```
$./script/server -p 80
```

There are several ways of integrating your application in Facebook and the two most common ways are as a canvas page and as a profile box. The canvas page provides the most real estate for your application as it provides a boxed area that covers most of the page except for top and left navigation bars.

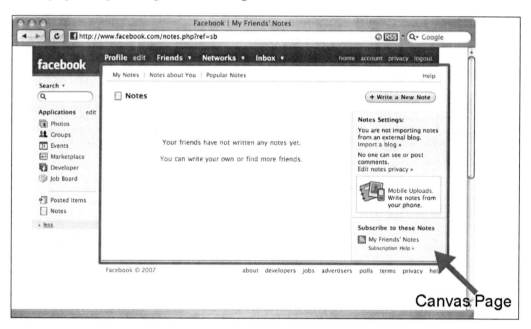

The canvas page URL is the URL you want to use to identify the canvas page of your application. In our application this is `http://apps.facebook.com/job_board/`.

Now let's go back quickly to the RFacebook configuration we left alone earlier on:

```
development:
    key: YOUR_API_KEY_HERE
    secret: YOUR_API_SECRET_HERE
    canvas_path: /job_board/
    callback_path: /search
    tunnel:
      username: yourLoginName
```

```
host: www.yourexternaldomain.com
port: 1234
local_port: 5678
```

Note the two highlighted settings. The `canvas_path` setting is the setting you have just placed in your Canvas Page URL while the `callback_path` is the relative path from your application. You can ignore the tunnel settings unless you wish to tunnel a remote domain name to your local machine.

Another configuration you need to set for the canvas page is whether to display the page as FBML (Facebook Markup Language) or to load your application as an iframe within Facebook. Generally speaking, using FBML will result in faster display and more consistent look-and-feel but the set of available markup is much more limited. In addition, there are many things not possible with FBML. In our application we will be using an iframe.

We also want our application to be added to a user's Facebook account, so select Yes for that setting. You will notice that once we click on the **Yes** radio button, a whole new set of configuration settings appears.

We want to re-direct the user to our canvas page once he or she has agreed to install the application, so enter `http://apps.facebook.com/job_board/` in the Post-Add URL setting. As we are not integrating with the user's profile in this application, the other profile-related settings can be ignored.

The next setting to configure is the left-side navigation link. We want to display a nice little logo and enable our user to access our application by clicking on a link in the left navigation bar, so enter `http://apps.facebook.com/job_board/` in the Side Nav URL setting.

Finally, before we complete the configuration, create a small (16 pixel by 16 pixel) image in JPG, GIF, or PNG format for your application and upload it in the icon setting.

To add the finishing touches, we want to make our Job Board application's look and feel very similar to the rest of Facebook even though it's using an iframe. The trick is to use Facebook's static stylesheets to style your views. Remember in the search controller we had this line:

```
class SearchController < ApplicationController
  before_filter :require_facebook_install
  layout 'main'
```

This changes the layout of views from this controller to using a layout file called `main.rhtml`. So to make the look and feel uniform, let's create this `main.rhtml` under `RAILS_ROOT/app/views/layouts`:

```
<!DOCTYPE html PUBLIC "-//W3C//DTD XHTML 1.0 Transitional//EN"
        "http://www.w3.org/TR/xhtml1/DTD/xhtml1-transitional.dtd">
<html xmlns="http://www.w3.org/1999/xhtml" xml:lang="en" lang="en">
<head>
  <meta http-equiv="content-type" content="text/html;charset=UTF-8"
    />
  <title>Job Board</title>
  <%= javascript_include_tag :defaults %>
  <%= stylesheet_link_tag
    'http://static.ak.facebook.com/css/base.css' %>
</head>
<body>
  <%= yield %>
</body>
</html>
```

The highlighted code shows that our main layout uses the base stylesheet used by Facebook as well.

Now let's take a quick view of your new application!

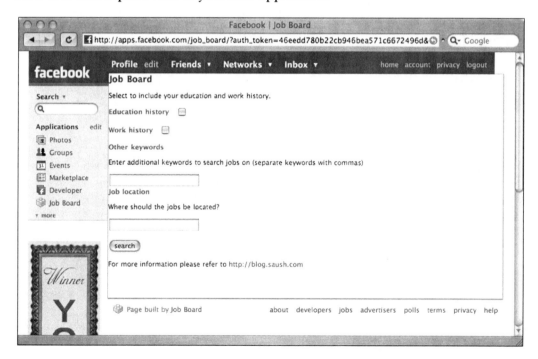

Searching for jobs through Indeed

Now that we have the Facebook application providing search parameters, we will use these parameters and send a search query to Indeed, then parse the results and display them in the Job Board canvas page.

Creating the search action

First, let's create the search action in the search controller. Modify `search_controller.rb` to add in a search method:

```ruby
class SearchController < ApplicationController
  before_filter :require_facebook_install
  layout 'main'
  def index
  view
    render :action => :view
  end
  def view
    if fbsession.is_valid?
        response = fbsession.users_getInfo(:uids => [fbsession.
                   session_user_id], :fields => ["current_location",
                   "education_history", "work_history"])
        @work_history = response.work_history
        @education_history = response.education_history
        @current_location = response.current_location
    end
  end
  def search
    query = []
    query << params[:work_info] if params[:work]
    query << params[:education_info] if params[:education]
    query << params[:keywords]
    url = 'http://api.indeed.com/search'
    hash = {'key' => 'YOUR_INDEED_API_KEY',
            'q'=> query.join(", "),
            'limit' => 20,
            'latlong' => 1}
    hash['l'] = params[:location]
    parameters = URI.escape(hash.to_a.collect {|pair| pair.join('=')}.
                 join('&'))
    res = Net::HTTP.get_response(URI.parse(url + '?' + parameters))
    case res
    when Net::HTTPSuccess, Net::HTTPRedirection
      results = XmlSimple::xml_in(res.body, 'force_array' => false)
      @jobs_found = results['results']['result']
    else
```

```
      puts res.error!
    end
  if @jobs_found.nil?
    @jobs_found = []
    flash[:notice] = "No jobs found"
    else
      session[:jobs] = @jobs_found
    end
  end
end
```

First, we get the parameters from the search form and push them into an array, query, if the user wanted to use that parameter. Next, we fashion the URL parameters out of various parameters required by Indeed, including the API key, the search parameters, the maximum number of jobs to retrieve, and whether to include the latitude and longitude information of the job. We also attach the location to search for the job, if the user has entered any location information.

After formatting the URL parameters properly, we attach them to Indeed's API search REST URL and use Net::HTTP to send a GET request to the URL. Note that we are using GET because Indeed does not support POST requests for the search.

As before we get a returned response object that has data embedded in its body. In this section we use XmlSimple to extract the XML in the response body and format it into a nested hash. Please refer to the earlier section on XmlSimple if you have not installed it. Note that we set the force_array configuration to false in order not to produce arrays to for single values.

Finally, we get the hash that we're interested in (that is, the jobs that are returned) and pass it on to the view. We also store the hash of jobs into a session to be processed later by the map and others.

Parsing and displaying the search results

Let's move on to the view. Create a file called search.rhtml in the RAILS_ROOT/app/views/search/ folder:

```
<h1>Job Board search results</h1>
<span class="message"><%= h flash[:notice] %></span>
<br/><%= link_to "Back to search", "http://apps.facebook.com/job_
board", :target => '_top'%>  
<%= link_to "Display jobs on a map", "http://www.yourdomainname.com/
map", :target => '_top'%><br/>
<ol>
<%@jobs_found.each { |job|  %>
<li class="title">
```

```
<a href="<%= job['url']%>" target="_new"><%= h job['jobtitle']%>, <%=
h job['company']%>
</a>
</li>
<div class="description">
<div class="underline">Location</div>
<%= h job['city'] %>, <%= h job['country'] %>
<div class="underline">Description</div>
<%= job['snippet'] %>
</div>
<% } %>
</ol>
<br/>
<span id=indeed_at><a href="http://www.indeed.com/">jobs</a>
by <a href="http://www.indeed.com/" title="Job Search">
<img src="http://www.indeed.com/p/jobsearch.gif" style="border: 0;
vertical-align: middle;" alt="job search">
</a></span>
```

The code here is quite self-explanatory. We take the jobs found from calling Indeed's API search and display them accordingly on the page. Remember that this is still a page in the Facebook application. For the next API we are mashing up with, we will be using our own site, so place a link on the page back to our mashup application. We also wrap up the page by including the obligatory link back to Indeed.

Display jobs in Google Maps

Displaying locations on Google Maps has been covered extensively in Chapter 2, so I will not go into the details of setting up the various plugins to do this but go straight into the code. However note that this mashup does not do any geocoding so we don't need to install GeoKit. We only need YM4R/GM.

Displaying the location of the jobs on the map

To display the location of the jobs, we need a new controller. Create a file called map_controller.rb in RAILS_ROOT/app/controllers:

```
require 'net/http'
require 'cgi'
class MapController < ApplicationController
  layout 'main'
  def index
          @jobs = session[:jobs]
          @map = GMap.new("map_div")
```

```
            @map.control_init(:large_map => true, :map_type => true)
            markers = {}
            count = 1
            @jobs.each { |job|
                info = <<END
<div style='width: 350px'>
<label>#{job['jobtitle']} (#{job['company']})</label> <br/>
#{job['snippet'].capitalize}</div>
END
                markers[count] =
                    GMarker.new([job['latitude'],
                                 job['longitude']],
                        :title => job['jobtitle'],
                        :info_window => info)
                count = count + 1
            }
            @map.overlay_global_init(GMarkerGroup.new(true,
                                     markers),"job_markers")
            # zoom to the source
            @map.center_zoom_init([@jobs.first['latitude'],
                            @jobs.first['longitude']], 12)
        end
    end
```

First, take the jobs out from the session where we stored them earlier on. We will need them in the view, so make them an instance variable. Next, create the map object and initialize it as described in Chapter 2. Then create a marker for each of the jobs and put them into a hash. Finally, overlay these markers on the map and zoom in to the map to display it.

Create a file named `index.rhtml` in `RAILS_ROOT/app/views/map`:

```
<table width="1024px">
    <tr>
            <td valign="top">
            <%= GMap.header %>
            <%= javascript_include_tag("markerGroup") %>
            <%= @map.to_html%>
            <%= @map.div(:width => 640, :height => 480)%>
    </td>
    <td>
            <div id="display" style="height:480px;overflow:
                                     auto;width:384px">
                <%= render :partial => 'jobs'%>
            </div>
```

```
      </td>
    </tr>
</table>
<p/>
<%= link_to 'Back to Facebook Job Board application',
    'http://apps.facebook.com/job_board'%>
```

As in Chapter 2, we add the GMap headers and include the marker group JavaScript files then convert the `map` object from the action into HTML and place the div element in the page. This will show us the map of jobs that have been found from Indeed.

We're also going to place a list of the jobs that we've found earlier on next to the map—so render a job partial next to it and set the style to overflow to the height of the map. This allows you to view the map all the time even as you scroll through the list of jobs found.

Create a file called `_jobs.rhtml` in the `RAILS_ROOT/app/views/map`:

```
<h2><%= @jobs.size %> jobs displayed.</h2>
<ol>
    <% count = 1
    @jobs.each { |job|   %>
        <li class="title">
            <a href="#" onclick="job_markers.showMarker(<%= count
                %>);return false;"><%= h job['jobtitle']%>, <%= h
                job['company']%>
            </a>
        </li>
        <div class="description">
            <div class="underline">Location</div>
            <%= h job['city'] %>, <%= h job['country'] %>
            <div class="underline">Description</div>
            <%= job['snippet'] %>
        </div>
        <%
        count += 1
        } %>
</ol>
<span id=indeed_at><a href="http://www.indeed.com/">jobs</a>
        by <a href="http://www.indeed.com/" title="Job Search">
            <img src="http://www.indeed.com/p/jobsearch.gif"
            style="border: 0; vertical-align: middle;"
            alt="job search">
        </a></span>
```

Note that this is very similar to the jobs listing in the Facebook application. The main difference is that while clicking on the job title in the Facebook application shows the job URL, clicking on the job title here will show the map showing the location of the job.

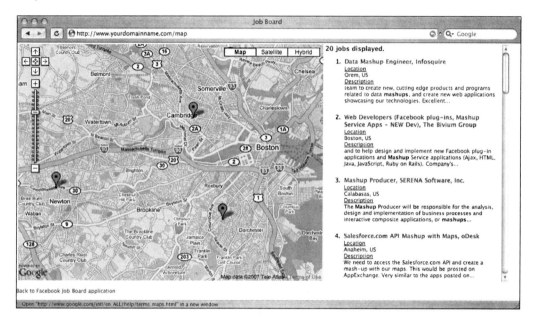

Creating a link on each job to show the news and blog articles

Next we want to find out more about the companies that posted the jobs. In each job, we want to place a link to search Internet news on the company and another to search for blog articles that mention the company.

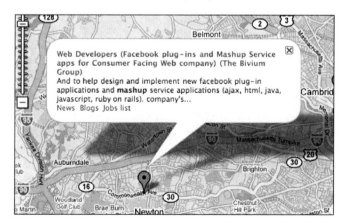

When we click on the link we want to display the list of news or blog articles to the right of the map, where the list of jobs is now. We are going to do this using AJAX to replace the HTML with the list of news or blog articles. However, we also want to be able to go back to the list of jobs that we had originally.

To do this, modify the index method of the map controller and add a few new lines into the information box that is popped up when we click on the marker:

```
@jobs.each { |job|
            info = <<END
<div style='width: 350px'>
<label>#{job['jobtitle']} (#{job['company']})</label> <br/>
#{job['snippet'].capitalize}</div>
<span><a href="#" onclick="new Ajax.Updater('display', '/map/news?comp
any=#{job['company']}', {asynchronous:true, evalScripts:true}); return
false;">News</a></span> 
<span><a href="#" onclick="new Ajax.Updater('display', '/map/blogs?
company=#{job['company']}', {asynchronous:true, evalScripts:true});
return false;">Blogs</a></span> 
<span><a href="#" onclick="new Ajax.Updater('display', '/map/list',
{asynchronous:true, evalScripts:true}); return false;">Jobs list</a></
span>
END
            markers[count] =
                GMarker.new([job['latitude'],
                            job['longitude']],
                    :title => job['jobtitle'],
                    :info_window => info)
            count = count + 1
        }
```

Remember that the AJAX links will not work unless you have added the default JavaScript libraries in your layout file `main.rhtml`:

```
<!DOCTYPE html PUBLIC "-//W3C//DTD XHTML 1.0 Transitional//EN"
        "http://www.w3.org/TR/xhtml1/DTD/xhtml1-transitional.dtd">
<html xmlns="http://www.w3.org/1999/xhtml" xml:lang="en" lang="en">
<head>
  <meta http-equiv="content-type" content="text/html;charset=UTF-8" />
  <title>Job Board</title>
  <%= javascript_include_tag :defaults %>
  <%= stylesheet_link_tag
                        'http://static.ak.facebook.com/css/base.css' %>
</head>
<body>
<%= yield %>
</body>
</html>
```

I will describe what the news and blog links will do in the next few sections but let's look at what happens when you click on the job list link. Add a new method in the map controller:

```
def list
  @jobs = session[:jobs]
end
```

Then create a file called `list.rhtml` in `RAILS_ROOT/app/views/map`:

```
<%= render :partial => 'jobs'%>
```

This view simply renders the same partial that we created earlier on.

The next two mashup APIs we are using are search based, like Indeed. The main idea behind using these two APIs is to search for information on the company that is posting the job then display them in the same right panel as the job list.

Searching and displaying news from Daylife

In this mashup we will use only one API endpoint from the Search API, which is `getRelatedArticles`. We will be searching for news the same way as we did searches on Indeed, that is, constructing the REST URL and sending a GET request to Daylife using `Net::HTTP`.

Searching for news on the company

To search for news on the company that posted the job, add a new method in the map controller:

```
def news
    server = 'freeapi.daylife.com'
    protocol = 'xmlrest'
    version = '4.2'
    service_name = 'search'
    method_name = 'getRelatedArticles'
    access_key = 'YOUR API ACCESS KEY'
    shared_secret = 'YOUR SHARED SECRET'
    query = params[:company]
    core_input = query
    url = "http://#{server}/#{protocol}/publicapi/#{version}/
          #{service_name}_#{method_name}"
    hash = {}
    hash[:signature] = Digest::MD5.hexdigest(access_key +
                        shared_secret + core_input)
    hash[:accesskey] = access_key
    hash[:query] = query
```

```
parameters = URI.escape(hash.to_a.collect {|pair| pair.join('=')}.
              join('&'))
res = Net::HTTP.get_response(URI.parse(url + '?' + parameters))
case res
when Net::HTTPSuccess, Net::HTTPRedirection
  results = XmlSimple::xml_in(res.body, 'force_array' => false)
  @results = results['payload']['article']
  if @results.nil?
    flash[:notice] = "No news found for this company."
    @results = {}
  end
else
  flash[:notice] = res.error!
end
end
```

As with searching through Indeed, we send a GET request to Daylife using `Net::HTTP` and parsing the resulting XML into nested hashes. However we need to specify the return format and an API version. We also need to create a signature that is sent along with the API access key with each call.

```
hash[:signature] = Digest::MD5.hexdigest(access_key + shared_secret +
core_input)
```

To create the signature, we concatenate the API access key, the shared secret, and a core input that varies according to the API called. For the API we are calling, this core input is the query we want send to Daylife. This concatenated string is then hashed with the MD5 hash function to return the signature.

We also need a view corresponding to the action method. Create a file called `news.rhtml` in the `RAILS_ROOT/app/views/map` folder:

```
<h1>News (by <%= link_to "Daylife", "http://www.daylife.com"%>)</h1>
<span class="notice"><%= h flash[:notice] %></span>
<br/>
<ol>
<% @results.each { |article| %>
   <li class="title">
         <a href="<%= article['url']['content']%>" target="job"><%= h
                 article['headline']['content'] %></a>
         <div class="description">
               <%= article['excerpt']['content'] %>
         </div>
   </li>
<% } %>
</ol>
```

This will be displayed to the right of the online map.

Searching and displaying blog articles from Technorati

Technorati provides a set of REST APIs for developers to extract and integrate their data in other applications. The APIs can be called using GET or POST requests. We will be using the Technorati API search to search for blog articles that discuss the recruiting company.

Searching for blog entries on the company

As with the Indeed and Daylife searches, we will be using Net::HTTP to send a GET request to Technorati and then parsing the XML that is returned using XmlSimple. The steps are straightforward and don't need much explanation at this stage.

First, add a new method in the map controller:

```
def blogs
    url = 'http://api.technorati.com/search'
    hash = {'key' => 'YOUR TECHNORATI API KEY',
            'query'=> params['company'],
            'authority' => 'n'}
    parameters = URI.escape(hash.to_a.collect {|pair|
                 pair.join('=')}.join('&'))
    res = Net::HTTP.get_response(URI.parse(url + '?' + parameters))
    case res
    when Net::HTTPSuccess, Net::HTTPRedirection
      results = XmlSimple::xml_in(res.body, 'force_array' => false)
      @stories = results['document']['item']
      flash[:notice] = "No blog entries found for this company."
                       if @stories.nil?
    else
      flash[:notice] = res.error!
    end
  end
```

Then create a view corresponding to the blogs action. Create a file called blogs. rhtml in the RAILS_ROOT/app/views/map folder:

```
<h1>Blogs entries (by <%= link_to "Technorati", "http://www.
technorati.com"%>)</h1>
<span class="notice"><%= h flash[:notice] %></span>
<br/>
<ol>
<% unless @stories.nil?
@stories.each { |story| %>
```

```
<li class="title">
        <a href="<%= h story['permalink']%>" target="job"><%= h
            story['title']%></a>
        <div class="description">
            <%= story['excerpt']%>
        </div>
    </li>
<% }
end
%>
</ol>
```

And we're done with the mashup!

Summary

Mashup applications are complete applications that use APIs in a synergistic way to provide value that does not exist before. In this mashup application, we showed how a job board could benefit from mashing up APIs from various providers including Facebook, Google Maps, Indeed, Daylife, and Technorati. The combination of the services and the uniqueness of the emergent services show how new applications can add extra value to their existing functions by mashing up external services and integrating them as part of their own.

6
Trip organizer mashup application

What does it do?

The trip organizer is a web mashup application that has features and functions that allow users to view information on a location for the purpose of organizing a trip. This mashup uses different APIs to provide these generic functions:

- Mapping
- Information
- Translation

The purpose of this application is to provide a complete set of information for a traveler before the trip. This application also provides a showcase of mashup APIs, as a large number of mashup APIs are used to construct it.

Requirements overview

The trip organizer is an application that wraps various types of information around a location that the user enters. As a result, the concept of a 'location' is central in the design of this mashup. A location is a city or a large town in a country, for example, Athens, Greece or New York, United States. The types of information on a location shown in this mashup are:

- Map view of the location
- Summary information on the location
- Places of interest around the location

- Hotels around the remote location filtered by availability according to a set of dates and sorted by the number of stars for the hotel, with the location of each hotel shown on the map
- Weather forecast of the location for today and the next six days
- Pictures of the location or associated locations
- Currency exchange rate of the remote location in comparison with the user's home country
- Time zone and current time in the remote location, and a comparison with the user's home time zone

Design

The fundamental design of the system is simple. We will create an object called Location, which will encapsulate all the information that is required for the mashup. Then, using a web application we will extract the information from the Location object and display it on a single web page.

The Location object will hide away all the implementation of extracting information from the various API providers, so most of the action will reside in this object. For the currency conversion, we will also create a Currency object, which the Location object calls, to abstract the currency conversion implementation.

Little to almost no processing is done in this mashup application as the API providers will be doing most of the processing. The mashup's main work is in taking input from the user, getting information from the various providers and displaying it appropriately back to the user. Where needed, data from one provider is passed on to a second provider.

Mashup APIs on the menu

This application will need to get services from various providers to display information on a remote location. In this mashup we will be using the largest number of APIs compared to the applications in the other chapters in this book. APIs accessed in this mashup are:

- Google Maps (mapping)
- FUTEF Wikipedia (location information)
- WebserviceX Currency Convertor (currency conversion)
- Yahoo Geocoding Services (location geocoding)
- WeatherBug (weather)

- Kayak (hotel search)
- GeoNames (location information)
- Flickr (location images)
- Hostip.info (IP geocoding)

For most of the APIs, with the exception of YM4R/GM and WebserviceX we will be using their REST APIs (even though some of them provides multiple types of interfaces) and accessing them using Open URI.

Google Maps

Google Maps is a free web-based mapping service provided by Google. Google provides a free JavaScript API library that allows developers to integrate Google Maps into their own applications. In this mashup we will be using only the online mapping function and not the geocoding capabilities of Google Maps. We will be using the YM4R/GM plugin to access the online map.

To access Google Maps you need an API key. For more information on getting a Google Maps API key please refer to Chapter 2.

FUTEF

Wikipedia is a multilingual web-based encyclopedia that has more than 2 million English-language articles as of November 2007. FUTEF (`http://futef.com`) is a service that provides search access through APIs to Wikipedia. FUTEF provides a free search API for non-commercial, low volume access. You are required to present an application ID to access FUTEF services. To request an application ID, go to the FUTEF API documentation page at `http://api.futef.com/apidocs.html`. FUTEF APIs are REST-based and return only JSON formatted data.

WebserviceX Currency Converter

WebserviceX (`http://www.webservicex.net`) is a web service provider that offers various types of free web services, and the currency converter is one of them. The currency converter converts a unit of a currency to another. WebserviceX APIs are SOAP based.

Yahoo Maps Geocoding API

The Yahoo Maps geocoding API (`http://developer.yahoo.com/maps/rest/V1/geocode.html`) allows you to find information on a location, including longitude and latitude data. Although Yahoo's website indicates only US addresses, the Yahoo Maps geocoding API allows you get information on any location, including those outside of the United States.

The geocoding APIs provide precision of data at several levels:

- Address
- Street
- Zip
- Zip+4
- City
- State
- Country

The information returned by the geocoding API includes:

Latitude	The latitude of the location.
Longitude	The longitude of the location.
Address	Street address of the result, if a specific location could be determined.
City	City in which the result is located.
State	State in which the result is located.
Zip	Zip code, if known.
Country	Country in which the result is located. The result is an ISO 3166-1 country code.

As the Yahoo Maps geocoding API returns only the country code, in this chapter we will use the GeoNames API to extract the country name. Yahoo Map geocoding services are free for non-commercial use.

WeatherBug

WeatherBug (`http://weatherbug.com`) is a website that provides weather information. WeatherBug has live data from over 8,000 WeatherBug Tracking Stations across the US and from more than 50,000 other weather stations around the globe. In this chapter we will be using WeatherBug's international weather information API through its REST-based API.

To register for the WeatherBug API, go to `http://apireg.weatherbug.com` and follow the instructions given. You will need to agree to the terms and conditions and provide some additional information. WeatherBug APIs are free for non-commercial use.

WeatherBug provides a list of APIs that can be used. We will be using the Forecast API, which returns a 7-day forecast based on our input. WeatherBug APIs return responses in XML, RSS, and pipe-delimited formats. The returned response for the Forecast API is only in RSS.

Kayak

Kayak (`http://www.kayak.com`) is a travel search engine that searches through travel sites around the world to bring various travel products into a single location. Kayak's search engine looks for travel products from flights and hotels to rental cars and cruises. Kayak provides various tools and utilities through its lab, but the one that we will be using in this chapter is its hotel RSS feed (`http://www.kayak.com/labs/rss`).

GeoNames

GeoNames (`http://www.geonames.org`) is an extensive geographical database and is available for download or access through web services, free of charge, under a creative commons attribution license. GeoNames provide a set of REST-based web services around the geographical database that returns either XML or JSON responses. In this chapter we will be using three web service APIs from GeoNames:

- Country information
- Time zone information
- Places information (from Wikipedia)

Flickr

Flickr (`http://www.flickr.com`) is a web-based photo sharing application that provides an extensive set of APIs for developers. Usage for non-commercial purposes is free. Access to the APIs requires you to register for a Yahoo ID and also apply for an application key. To apply for any application key, go to `http://www.flickr.com/services/api/keys/apply` and fill in a simple form requesting your name and a description of your usage of Flickr APIs. You will be given both an application key and a shared secret. Afterwards you can edit the details of the application key to provide additional information like the name of the application and a public application description, though this is optional.

The application key is necessary for every Flickr API request but the shared secret is only necessary for API requests that require authentication. You can request Flickr APIs through three different formats:

- REST
- XML-RPC
- SOAP

Flickr will respond to you in any one of five formats (which you can specify):

- REST
- XML-RPC
- SOAP
- JSON
- PHP

In our mashup application, we will be using the REST request format. A REST request defaults to a REST response, which is basically a simple XML block in this format:

```
<?xml version="1.0" encoding="utf-8" ?>
<rsp stat="ok">
    [xml-payload-here]
</rsp>
```

If an error occurs, the following is returned instead:

```
<?xml version="1.0" encoding="utf-8" ?>
<rsp stat="fail">
    <err code="[error-code]" msg="[error-message]" />
</rsp>
```

Flickr also provides secured API calls by requiring users to log in for certain method calls. We will not be using any secured APIs in this chapter.

Hostip.info

Hostip.info (http://www.hostip.info) is a website that provides free geocoding of IP addresses. Hostip.info offers an HTTP-based API as well as its entire database for free for integration. We used Hostip.info in Chapter 2 through GeoKit but in this chapter we will be using it directly through its REST interface.

Open URI

Open URI is an easy-to-use wrapper library included in Ruby 1.8 onwards. It wraps around Net::HTTP, Net::HTTPS, and Net::FTP and allows URLs to be opened and used like files. For convenience, open URI aliases and replaces `Kernel::open` to allow opening of files, pipes, URIs from a single method. This means that you can use `open` directly like this:

```
open('http://ws.mashup-api.com')
{
    |data| results = data.read
}
```

Open URI is the simpler, alternative library used to access URLs. It is simpler to use than Net::HTTP but has limitations as you cannot specify the HTTP method to use. This effectively prevents us from using Open URI for REST-like interfaces that require usage of HTTP methods. However, Open URI is probably the better library to use for getting data from a URL.

In this chapter we will be using only Open URI.

What we will be doing

The following section describes the steps we will be taking to create the mashup. The basic steps are:

1. Create the Rails application
2. Create the basic Location object
3. Create a location search form
4. Create an online map to show the location found
5. Create the tabs for the information
6. Get general information from Wikipedia using FUTEF
7. Get places information from Wikipedia through GeoNames
8. Get hotel information from Kayak
9. Get weather information from WeatherBug
10. Display pictures of the location using Flickr
11. Show currency exchange rate from WebserviceX
12. Show remote location time compared with local time

Creating a Rails application

We begin this mashup as before by creating the usual Rails application.

```
$rails Chapter6
```

This will create a new Ruby on Rails application.

Creating the basic Location object

Our design revolves around a main Location object that provides all the information that we need for a user-specified location. This can be used for the remote location and the user's home location, which is detected from the requesting IP address. Therefore our first but most important task is to build a basic Location class that will store the information we need as well as to derive basic information on the location.

Create a file called `location.rb` in the `RAILS_ROOT/lib` folder:

```ruby
require 'open-uri'
require 'cgi'
require'pp'
YAHOO_GEOCODE_URL = 'http://local.yahooapis.com/MapsService/V1/
geocode'
YAHOO_APP_ID = '<your Yahoo APP ID>'
GEONAMES_SEARCH_URL = 'http://ws.geonames.org/search'
GEONAMES_COUNTRY_URL = 'http://ws.geonames.org/countryInfo?country='
class Location
attr_accessor :location, :lat, :long, :city, :state, :country, :
country_code, :currency, :timezone
def initialize(location='Singapore')
    hash = {:appid => YAHOO_APP_ID, :location => location }
    parameters = URI.escape(hash.to_a.collect {|pair| pair.join('=')}.
                join('&'))
    results = ''
    open(YAHOO_GEOCODE_URL + '?' + parameters) { |s| results =
        XmlSimple::xml_in(s.read, 'force_array' => false)['Result'] }
    if results.class == Array then
      cities = '<ol>'
      results.each {|res|
        if res['Country'] == 'US' or res['Country'] == 'CA'
          cities += "<li><a href='/trip/map?location=#{res['City']},
                #{res['State']}, #{res['Country']}'>#{res['City']},
                #{res['State']}, #{res['Country']}</a></li>"
        else
          cities += "<li><a href='/trip/map?location=#{res['City']},
                #{res['Country']}'>#{res['City']},
```

```
                    #{res['Country']}</a></li>"
        end
    }
    cities += '</ol>'
    raise "More than one city with the same name found! Please
        choose one from below:" + cities
  end
  @country_code = results['Country']
  @state_code = results['State']
  @lat = results['Latitude'].to_f
  @long = results['Longitude'].to_f
  hash = {:q => location, :maxRows => 1, :style => 'FULL' }
  parameters = URI.escape(hash.to_a.collect {|pair| pair.join('=')}.
        join('&'))
  open(GEONAMES_SEARCH_URL + '?' + parameters) { |s| results =
      XmlSimple::xml_in(s.read, 'force_array' => false)['geoname'] }
  raise "Cannot find this city, please try again with a different
      state or country." if results == nil
  @city = results['name']
  @country = results['countryName']
  @timezone = results['timezone']['content']
  if @country_code == 'US' or @country_code == 'CA'
  @location = "#{@city}, #{@state_code}, #{@country}"
  else
  @location = "#{@city}, #{@country}"
  end
  end
end
  end
```

First, we needed to define a number of attribute accessors to store the information we need. We store the following information:

- A location string describing the city, for example, Paris, France
- The longitude and latitude of the location
- The name of the city, state, and country of the location
- The currency code of the currency used in that location
- The time zone of that location

Next, we created a constructor to define how Location objects are created. We want to allow the user to create a new Location object by passing in a location name parameter and we set a default location in case no parameters are passed in.

The first few lines in the constructor will be used repeatedly in the subsequent code:

```
hash = {:appid => YAHOO_APP_ID, :location => location }
parameters = URI.escape(hash.to_a.collect {|pair| pair.join('=')}.
join('&'))
results = ''
open(YAHOO_GEOCODE_URL + '?' + parameters) { |s| results = XmlSimple::
xml_in(s.read, 'force_array' => false)['Result'] }
```

The basic concept behind these few lines is to create a URL string and use it for a REST API call with Open URI. The first line creates a hash with the key names as the parameter names and the values as the parameter values. In this instance, we need to provide a Yahoo application ID and a location that we want to geocode. The next line converts this hash into a string of key-value pairs. We will then append this string to the geocoding URL and use Open URI to get a response from the Yahoo geocoding REST API.

`s.read` is the response retrieved from the API. Yahoo returns an XML response as shown below, which we then use XmlSimple to parse and convert into an array of hashes.

```
<ResultSet xsi:schemaLocation="urn:yahoo:maps http://api.local.yahoo.
com/MapsService/V1/GeocodeResponse.xsd">
    <Result precision="zip">
      <Latitude>48.856925</Latitude>
      <Longitude>2.341210</Longitude>
      <Address/>
      <City>Paris (Paris)</City>
      <State>France</State>
      <Zip/>
      <Country>FR</Country>
    </Result>
</ResultSet>
```

From this results hash, we extract the country code, state code, and longitude and latitude information. Note that unfortunately, the name of the city returned by Yahoo is not consistently usable. For example in the response above, the name of the city is *Paris (Paris)*, which is not usable for later mashup usage. We will deal with this in a while.

Sometimes more than one city is returned because there could be more than one city with the same name. For example, a search on *Birmingham* returns five Birminghams in the United States alone. This mashup can only display one location so we need to ask the user to choose exactly which one to show.

```
if results.class == Array then
    cities = '<ol>'
    results.each {|res|
        if res['Country'] == 'US' or res['Country'] == 'CA'
            cities += "<li><a href='/trip/map?location=#{res['City']},
                    #{res['State']}, #{res['Country']}'>#{res['City']},
                    #{res['State']}, #{res['Country']}</a></li>"
        else
            cities += "<li><a href='/trip/map?location=#{res['City']},
                    #{res['Country']}'>#{res['City']},
                    #{res['Country']}</a></li>"
        end
    }
    cities += '</ol>'
    raise "More than one city with the same name found! Please
            choose one from below:" + cities
end
```

A string with an HTML snippet of a list of locations found is created and an exception is raised. This will be caught later and the HTML snippet displayed to the user.

Coming back to the city name, we will use another mashup API, this time GeoNames, to get the proper city name, as well as the country name and the time zone.

```
hash = {:q => location, :maxRows => 1, :style => 'FULL' }
    parameters = URI.escape(hash.to_a.collect {|pair| pair.join('=')}.
                join('&'))
    open(GEONAMES_SEARCH_URL + '?' + parameters) { |s| results =
        XmlSimple::xml_in(s.read, 'force_array' => false)['geoname'] }
    raise "Cannot find this city, please try again with a different
        state or country." if results == nil
    @city = results['name']
    @country = results['countryName']
    @timezone = results['timezone']['content']
```

This returns the response (truncated for formatting purposes):

```
<?xml version="1.0" encoding="UTF-8" standalone="no"?>
<geonames style="FULL">
    <totalResultsCount>1398</totalResultsCount>
    <geoname>
            <name>Paris</name>
```

```
            <lat>48.8666667</lat>
            <lng>2.3333333</lng>
            <geonameId>2988507</geonameId>
            <countryCode>FR</countryCode>
            <countryName>France</countryName>
            <fcl>P</fcl>
            <fcode>PPLC</fcode>
            <fclName>city, village,...</fclName>
            <fcodeName>capital of a political entity</fcodeName>
            <population>2138551</population>
            <alternateNames>...</alternateNames>
            <elevation/>
            <adminCode1>A8</adminCode1>
            <adminName1>Île-de-France</adminName1>
            <adminCode2>75</adminCode2>
            <adminName2>Paris</adminName2>
            <adminCode3>751</adminCode3>
            <adminName3>Arrondissement de Paris</adminName3>
            <adminCode4>75056</adminCode4>
            <adminName4>Paris</adminName4>
            <timezone dstOffset="2.0" gmtOffset="1.0">Europe/Paris</
timezone>
    </geoname>
</geonames>
```

We get the city name, country name, and time zone from the response.

If you're observant you might notice that in fact, the information found from Yahoo's geocoding API can also be found in GeoNames and we might save on a mashup API call if we just used GeoNames only! So why did we use two mashup APIs instead of one?

Admittedly showing off how to use Yahoo's geocoding APIs is one of the minor reasons; the main reason is that the GeoNames returns too many records when the information is too ambiguous. This is true even when we filter off certain records by their feature code or feature class. For example, when searching for Paris, instead of returning names of cities or towns named Paris, it will return all populated places with names containing Paris. Yahoo's search on the other hand returns what we required—a list of cities or large towns.

This shows that we need to be careful when using mashup APIs and only careful study and research in using the API will give us the necessary data that we need to build our mashup.

To properly search through Yahoo Geocoding APIs, we should put in the state codes for the United States as well as Canada and we re-format the location string that is the original input:

```
if @country_code == 'US' or @country_code == 'CA'
    @location = "#{@city}, #{@state_code}, #{@country}"
else
    @location = "#{@city}, #{@country}"
end
```

This returns the Location object to the calling class.

Creating a search form

Now that we have the basic Location class, let's turn to the controllers and views to create a search form for our user. Create a controller named `trip_controller.rb` in the `RAILS_ROOT/app/controllers` folder:

```
class TripController < ApplicationController
  layout 'main'
  def index
  end
end
```

Create the corresponding `index.rhtml` template in a new `RAILS_ROOT/app/views/trip` folder:

```
<h1>Trip Organizer</h1>
<%= render :partial => 'search'%>
```

Also create the `_search.rhtml` partial in the same folder:

```
<div id='search_form'>
<% form_tag(:action => 'map') do -%>
<%= text_field_tag 'location', @location, :size => 30 %> <%= submit_
tag 'Find' %><br/>
<% end -%>
</div>
```

Creating the online map

Next, we will create the map action that will display a map on the screen. Add a map method in the `trip_controller.rb` file.

```
def map
session[:location] = Location.new(params[:location])
    @map = GMap.new("map_div")
    @map.control_init(:large_map => true, :map_type => true)
    @map.icon_global_init( GIcon.new(:image => "http://www.google.com/
                                        mapfiles/ms/icons/blue-pushpin.png",
    :shadow => "http://www.google.com/mapfiles/shadow50.png",
    :icon_size => GSize.new(32,32),
    :shadow_size => GSize.new(37,32),
    :icon_anchor => GPoint.new(9,32),
    :info_window_anchor => GPoint.new(9,2),
    :info_shadow_anchor => GPoint.new(18,25)),
    "icon_source")
    icon_source = Variable.new("icon_source")
    source = GMarker.new([session[:location].lat,
                        session[:location].long],
    :title => 'Source',
    :info_window => "Start here!",
    :icon => icon_source)
    @map.overlay_init(source)
    @map.center_zoom_init([session[:location].lat,
                    session[:location].long], 12)
    @location = session[:location].location
end
```

First, we create a new Location object based on the location entered by the user. We store this object in the session for later use. The next few lines use YM4R/GM to create a Google Map marker and set it on the map then zoom in on that location, similar to what we've done in Chapter 2 and Chapter 5 before this. Ensure that you download the plugin and amend the `gmaps_api_key.yml` file.

Next, we create the map template `map.rhtml` in the `RAILS_ROOT/apps/views/trip` folder:

```
<h1>My Trip Organizer</h1>
<table>
<tr>
<td id="info_panel">
    <a href='/trip'><span style='font-size: 4em;'>City360</span></a>
    <%= render :partial => 'search'%>
    <%= render :partial => 'tabs'%>
```

```
</td>
<td id="map_panel">
    <%= GMap.header %>
    <%= javascript_include_tag("markerGroup") %>
    <%= @map.to_html%>
    <%= @map.div(:width => 600, :height => 640)%>
</td>
</tr>
</table>
```

Note the second partial below the search form. We'll be discussing it in the following section.

Creating the tabs for the information

We will be using tabs to display the information on the location. For tabbing we will be using AJAX to load the data into the tab pages when needed. At the same time, whenever the data has been loaded already we don't want to load it again. For this we turn to the excellent AJAX Tabs code from Flinn Mueller at http://actsasflinn.com/Ajax_Tabs/index.html.

First, create a JavaScript file named tabs.js in the RAILS_ROOT/public/javascripts folder:

```
function tabselect(tab) {
  var tablist = $('tabcontrol1').getElementsByTagName('li');
  var nodes = $A(tablist);
  var lClassType = tab.className.substring(0,
              tab.className.indexOf('-') );
  nodes.each(function(node){
    if (node.id == tab.id) {
      tab.className=lClassType+'-selected';
    } else {
      node.className=lClassType+'-unselected';
    };
  });
}
function paneselect(pane) {
  var panelist = $('panecontrol1').getElementsByTagName('li');
  var nodes = $A(panelist);
  nodes.each(function(node){
    if (node.id == pane.id) {
      pane.className='pane-selected';
    } else {
      node.className='pane-unselected';
```

```
      };
    });
  }
  function loadPane(pane, src) {
    if (pane.innerHTML=='' || pane.innerHTML=='Loading...') {
      reloadPane(pane, src);
    }
  }
  function reloadPane(pane, src) {
    new Ajax.Updater(pane, src, {asynchronous:1, evalScripts:true,
    onLoading:function(request){pane.innerHTML='Loading...'}})
  }
```

Now, we need to create a layout file called `main.rhtml`, which we will place in `RAILS_ROOT/app/views/layouts`.

```
<!DOCTYPE html PUBLIC "-//W3C//DTD XHTML 1.0 Transitional//EN"
        "http://www.w3.org/TR/xhtml1/DTD/xhtml1-transitional.dtd">
<html xmlns="http://www.w3.org/1999/xhtml" xml:lang="en" lang="en">
<head>
  <meta http-equiv="content-type" content="text/html;charset=UTF-8" />
  <title>City360</title>
  <%= javascript_include_tag :defaults %>
  <%= javascript_include_tag 'tabs' %>
  <%= javascript_include_tag 'PopBox' %>
  <%= stylesheet_link_tag 'main' %>
</head>
<body>
  <%= yield %>
</body>
</html>
```

This JavaScript file requires the use of Prototype. In particular it uses the Ajax Updater from the Prototype JavaScript library to load the necessary page when `loadPane` or `reloadPane` is called. Notice in the `loadPane` function, if there is already information in the tab, it will not call `reloadPane`, which will always load the page.

Next, add in the following styles in your stylesheet. For this project, we use `main.css` in the `RAILS_ROOT/public/stylesheets` folder:

```
.tabselector, .tab-selector {
  width: auto;
  border-bottom: 1px solid #c0c0c0;
  padding: 10px 0 0 20px;
}
.tab-unselected {
```

```
    display: inline;
    padding: 2px 7px 0 7px;
    background-color: #f0f0f0;
    border: 1px solid #c0c0c0;
    border-bottom: 0;
    color: #c0c0c0;
}
.tab-selected {
    display: inline;
    padding: 3px 7px 1px 7px;
    background: #fff;
    border: 1px solid #c0c0c0;
    border-bottom: 0;
}
.tab-unselected a {
    padding: 6px;
    color: #a0a0a0;
}
.tab-selected a {
    font-weight: bold;
    color: #0066CC;
    padding: 6px;
}
.panes, .pane-selector {
    width: 97%;
    padding-left: 0px;
    margin: 2%;
    min-height: 300px;
    overflow: auto;
}
.pane-selected {
    list-style-type: none;
    display: block;
    padding: 10px;
}
.pane-unselected {
    list-style-type: none;
    display: none;
}
```

Finally, create the `_tabs.rhtml` partial in the RAILS_ROOT/app/views/trip folder:

```
<ul class="tabselector" id="tabcontrol1">
  <li class="tab-selected" id="info_tab">
    <%= link_to_function('Info', "tabselect($('info_tab'));
       paneselect($('info_pane'))") %></li>
  <li class="tab-unselected" id="places_tab">
    <%= link_to_function('Places', "loadPane($('places_pane'), '" +
       url_for(:action => 'places', :location => params[:location]) +
       "'), tabselect($('places_tab')); paneselect($('places_
       pane'))") %></li>
  <li class="tab-unselected" id="hotels_tab">
    <%= link_to_function('Hotels', "loadPane($('hotels_pane'), '" +
       url_for(:action => 'hotels', :location => params[:location]) +
       "'), tabselect($('hotels_tab')); paneselect($('hotels_
       pane'))") %></li>
  <li class="tab-unselected" id="weather_tab">
    <%= link_to_function('Weather', "loadPane($('weather_pane'), '" +
       url_for(:action => 'weather', :location => params[:location])
       + "'), tabselect($('weather_tab')); paneselect($('weather_
       pane'))") %></li>
  <li class="tab-unselected" id="pictures_tab">
    <%= link_to_function('Pictures', "loadPane($('pictures_pane'), '"
       + url_for(:action => 'pictures', :location =>
       params[:location]) + "'), tabselect($('pictures_tab'));
       paneselect($('pictures_pane'))") %></li>
<p>
  <li class="tab-unselected" id="currency_tab">
    <%= link_to_function('Currency', "loadPane($('currency_pane'), '"
       + url_for(:action => 'currency', :location =>
       params[:location]) + "'), tabselect($('currency_tab'));
       paneselect($('currency_pane'))") %></li>
  <li class="tab-unselected" id="time_tab">
    <%= link_to_function('Time', "reloadPane($('time_pane'), '" +
       url_for(:action => 'time', :location => params[:location]) +
       "'), tabselect($('time_tab')); paneselect($('time_pane'))")
       %></li>
</ul>
<ul class="panes" id="panecontrol1">
  <li id="info_pane" class="pane-selected">
    <%= render :partial => 'info' %>
  </li>
  <li id="places_pane" class="pane-unselected"></li>
  <li id="hotels_pane" class="pane-unselected"></li>
  <li id="weather_pane" class="pane-unselected"></li>
  <li id="pictures_pane" class="pane-unselected"></li>
  <li id="currency_pane" class="pane-unselected"></li>
  <li id="time_pane" class="pane-unselected"></li>
<ul>
```

Note that the first pane is a partial and is loaded when the page is displayed.

Getting information from Wikipedia

Now that we have the basic skeleton of the page ready, it is time to flesh it out with information. First up is information about the location from everyone's favorite online encyclopedia — Wikipedia.

First, we need to go back to the Location class and make some changes. Add these constants at the top of the class:

```
FUTEF_URL = 'http://api.futef.com/api/v1'
FUTEF_API_ID = '<YOUR FUTEF API ID>'
```

FUTEF returns JSON responses so make sure you have installed the Ruby JSON library:

```
require 'json'
```

Then add in this method:

```
def info
  hash = {:appid => FUTEF_API_ID, :query => @city}
  parameters = URI.escape(hash.to_a.collect {|pair| pair.join('=')}.
              join('&'))
  results = ''
  open(FUTEF_URL + '?' + parameters) { |s| results =JSON.parse(s.
        read) }
  results['records']
end
```

As before, we create a hash from the parameters and form a URL parameter string from it. Then, attaching it to the FUTEF URL, we use Open URI to request information from Wikipedia through FUTEF. Note that we're making a query on the city only, and not the full location string. The returned result is in JSON format, which we parse through the JSON library to get an array of hashes similar to what we did with XmlSimple.

The information retrieved will be placed in the info tab. As mentioned, the info tab is a partial that is shown when the main page is loaded. As such we will not be adding any actions in `trip_controller.rb`. Create a partial template called `_info.rhtml` in the `RAILS_ROOT/app/views/trip` folder:

```
<div>
<% session[:location].info.each { |info|%>
    <%= info['text']%><p>
    <%= link_to (info['url']), info['url']%><p>
<% } %>
</div>
```

The code is pretty simple. Using the Location object already instantiated previously and stored in the session, we call the info method, then iterate through the information retrieved.

We're ready for a first look at our application. Go to the text box after opening: `http://localhost:3000/trip` and type in a city and country of your choice. In order not to confuse Yahoo Maps geocoding service, you should enter both city and country, though sometimes for unique cases (especially in the United States, where the data is more accurate) you can get away with just entering the city.

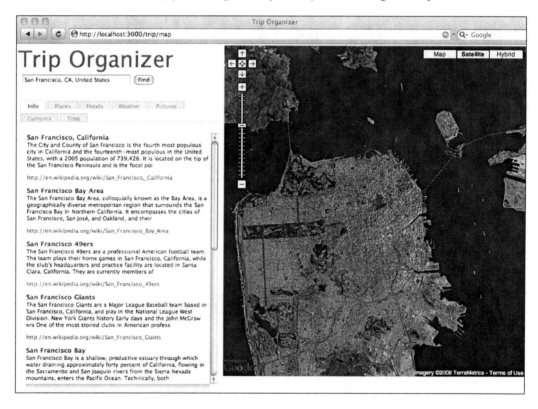

Getting places information

Next, we want to get information on places of interest within that city or its surroundings. To do this we will turn to Wikipedia again though this time we will access it through GeoNames instead.

First, we need to add in the URL for the GeoNames Wikipedia search web service that we're using. Add this constant at the top of the `location.rb` file:

```
GEONAMES_WP_URL = 'http://ws.geonames.org/findNearbyWikipedia'
```

Then create a method named `places_of_interest` in the `location.rb` file:

```
def places_of_interest
  hash = {:radius => 20, :maxRows => 20, :lat => @lat, :lng => @long
        }
  parameters = URI.escape(hash.to_a.collect {|pair| pair.join('=')}.
        join('&'))
  pp GEONAMES_WP_URL + "?" + parameters
  results = ''
  open(GEONAMES_WP_URL + "?" + parameters) { |s| results =
        XmlSimple::xml_in(s.read, 'force_array' => false) }
  pp results
  results['entry']
end
```

The `radius` here indicates the radius of the search for a place, around the given `longitude` and `latitude`. The `maxRows` parameter tells GeoNames how many records we want to retrieve. What is returned is a list of interesting places centered around the given coordinates.

Having retrieved our data we need to create the action and view to display it. The action is quite simple; add the following method in `trip_controller.rb`:

```
def places
    @places = session[:location].places_of_interest
end
```

Then create a file called `places.rhtml` in the `RAILS_ROOT/app/views/trip` folder:

```
<div class="data">
<% unless @places.nil?%>
<% @places.each { |info|%>
<p>
    <h2><%= link_to_remote info['title'], :url => {:action => 'show_
        place', :long => info['lng'], :lat => info['lat'],
        :summary => "<div style='width:350px;'><h1>#{info['title']}
        </h1><table><tr valign='top'><td>#{info['summary']}</
        td><td> #{image_tag info['thumbnailImg'] unless
        info['thumbnailImg'].empty?}</td></tr></table></div>" }%></h2>
    <div>
    <table>
    <tr valign='top'>
    <td>
    <%= info['summary']%>
    </td><td>
    <%= image_tag info['thumbnailImg'] unless info['thumbnailImg'].
        empty?%><br/>
    </td>
```

```
        </tr>
        </table>
        <%= link_to 'more', info['wikipediaUrl']%>
        </div>
    </p>
    <% }
    else %>
    The places of interest tab is not available at the moment. You can try
    again later by doing the same search.
    <% end %>
    </div>
```

In this page we display the title, summary, and a thumbnail image provided in the article. We also link to the map using the given longitude and latitude, passing the summary in. When the user clicks on the link, the location of the place of interest is shown on the map to the right. To do this, we do an AJAX call to the action `show_place`, so we add this method in `trip_controller.rb`:

```
def show_place
    @map = Variable.new("map")
    icon_place = Variable.new("icon_place")
    @marker = GMarker.new([params[:lat],params[:long]],
                :title => "Place of interest",
                :info_window => params[:summary],
                :icon => icon_place)
end
```

This action gets the previously created map variable and proceeds to add a new marker to indicate the place of interest, passing the summary as the information window to pop up when the icon is clicked. Notice that we used a new icon called `icon_place`, and we need to create this when we first create the map. Add the highlighted portion into the `map` method in the `trip_controller.rb` file:

```
def map
    session[:location] = Location.new(params[:location])
    @map = GMap.new("map_div")
    @map.control_init(:large_map => true, :map_type => true)
    @map.icon_global_init( GIcon.new(:image =>
            "http://www.google.com/mapfiles/ms/icons/blue-pushpin.png",
    :shadow => "http://www.google.com/mapfiles/shadow50.png",
    :icon_size => GSize.new(32,32),
    :shadow_size => GSize.new(37,32),
```

```
        :icon_anchor => GPoint.new(9,32),
        :info_window_anchor => GPoint.new(9,2),
        :info_shadow_anchor => GPoint.new(18,25)),
        "icon_source")
    @map.icon_global_init( GIcon.new(:image => "http://maps.google.
                            com/mapfiles/ms/micons/yellow-dot.png",
        :shadow => "http://maps.google.com/mapfiles/ms/micons/
                msmarker.shadow.png",
        :icon_size => GSize.new(32,32),
        :shadow_size => GSize.new(59,32),
        :icon_anchor => GPoint.new(9,32),
        :info_window_anchor => GPoint.new(9,2),
        :info_shadow_anchor => GPoint.new(18,25)),
        "icon_place")
    icon_source = Variable.new("icon_source")
    source = GMarker.new([session[:location].lat,
            session[:location].long],
        :title => 'Source',
        :info_window => "Start here!",
        :icon => icon_source)
    @map.overlay_init(source)
    @map.center_zoom_init([session[:location].lat,
            session[:location].long], 12)
    @location = session[:location].location
  end
```

To display the marker on the map, we need to do some JavaScript magic, using an RJS template. The RJS template will dynamically add in the JavaScript code that places the marker on the right location on the map. Create a show_place.rjs file in the RAILS_ROOT/app/views/trip folder:

```
page << @map.clear_overlays
page << @map.add_overlay(@marker)
```

The first line in the RJS template clears the map of existing markers. The second line adds the marker to the map.

This is how the application looks with the new tab:

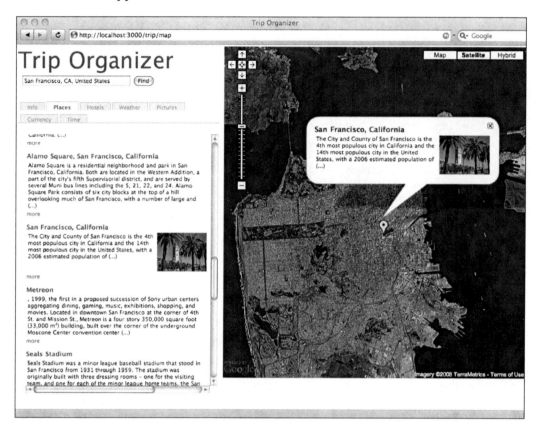

Getting hotel information

The next tab is the hotels tab. In this tab we process information from Kayak and display hotels that are available around the location. Kayak is one of the biggest travel search websites around since its merger with SideStep and its information on hotels is quite comprehensive.

We start off with adding a new method in the Location class. At the top of the location.rb file, add the following to enable usage of XmlSimple:

```
require 'xmlsimple'
```

Then add the necessary constant used in Kayak:

```
KAYAK_HOTEL_URL = 'http://www.kayak.com/h/rss/hotelrss'
```

Next, add in a `hotels` method:

```
def hotels
    hotels = []
    results = ''
    if @country_code == 'US' or @country_code == 'CA' then
      hotel_search = KAYAK_HOTEL_URL + "/#{CGI::escape(@country_
      code)}/#{CGI::escape(@state_code)}/#{CGI::escape(@city)}"
    else
      hotel_search = KAYAK_HOTEL_URL + "/#{CGI::escape(@country_
      code)}/#{CGI::escape(@city)}"
    end
    open(hotel_search) { |s| results = XmlSimple::xml_in(s.read,
    'force_array' => false)['channel']['item'] }
    unless results.nil?
      results.each {|hotel|
        hotels << Hotel.new(hotel)
      }
    end
    hotels
  end
```

Kayak searches for locations in the United States and Canada differently. For these two countries, you need to provide a state code, while the rest of the world doesn't require a state code. This is a sample of the returned feed (truncated for formatting purposes):

```
<?xml version="1.0"?>
<rss version="2.0"  xmlns:kyk="http://www.kayak.com/h/rss/
hotelextension">
    <channel>
          <title>Kayak.com Hotels in San Francisco, CA</title>
          <link>http://www.kayak.com</link>
          <description>Recent prices for hotels in San Francisco,
                  CA</description>
          <language>en-us</language>
          <pubDate>Sat, 29 Mar 2008 04:05:22 EDT</pubDate>
          <lastBuildDate>Sat, 29 Mar 2008 04:05:22 EDT</lastBuildDate>
          <docs>http://www.kayak.com/h/labs/rss</docs>
          <managingEditor>webmaster@kayak.com</managingEditor>
          <webMaster>webmaster@kayak.com</webMaster>
          <item>
                  <title>The Opal @ $20 ***</title>
    <link>http://www.kayak.com/k/redirect/in?ai=&amp;p=&amp;url=%2Fh%2
          Fhotel%2Fid%2F38126</link>
```

```
                      <description>A classic five story hotel, The Opal
                         San Francisco was constructed in 1908 in the heart
                         of the city...</description>
                      <pubDate>Sat, 29 Mar 2008 04:05:22 EDT</pubDate>
                      <guid>http://www.kayak.com/h/hotel/id/38126</guid>
                      <kyk:stars>3</kyk:stars>
                      <kyk:price>19.90</kyk:price>
                      <kyk:currency>USD</kyk:currency>
                      <kyk:hotelname>The Opal</kyk:hotelname>
                      <kyk:city>San Francisco</kyk:city>
                      <kyk:state>CA</kyk:state>
                      <kyk:country>US</kyk:country>
                      <kyk:thumbnail>http://www.kayak.com/himg/29/9d/da/
                         leonardo-t11124-t11124_ext_01_a-thumb.jpg</kyk:
                         thumbnail>
               </item>
   . . .
   </channel>
   </rss>
```

As before, we use XmlSimple to extract the information from the returned response. However, this time we extract the information into Hotel objects and return an array of Hotel objects. Create a Hotel class in the `location.rb` file:

```
class Hotel
  attr_accessor :name, :link, :thumbnail, :stars, :price, :
description, :currency
  def initialize(hotel)
    @name = hotel['hotelname']
    @link = hotel['guid']
    @thumbnail = hotel['thumbnail']
    @stars = hotel['stars']
    @price = hotel['price']
    @description = hotel['description']
    @currency = hotel['currency']
  end
end
```

You might realize that the returned response is an RSS feed and you might wonder why we don't parse it as such. This is because the Kayak hotel feed has Kayak-specific extensions defined in Kayak's proprietary namespace tags, and Ruby's default RSS parser cannot handle namespaces by default. Extracting it using XmlSimple turns out to be a simpler way to consume the RSS compared to extending the RSS parser to parse Kayak's tags.

Finally, create a simple view to display the hotels that we have retrieved. Add the following code to your `trip_controller.rb` file.

```
def hotels
    @hotels = session[:location].hotels
end
```

Then, create a file named `hotels.rhtml` in the `RAILS_ROOT/app/views/trip` folder:

```
<div class="data">
    <% @hotels.each { |hotel| %>
            <h2><%= link_to hotel.name,  hotel.link %> <%= image_tag
                  "#{hotel.stars}.gif" if hotel.stars %></h2>
            <p><%= hotel.price %> <%= hotel.currency %></p>
            <%= image_tag hotel.thumbnail %><%= hotel.description%>
            <p>
    <% }%>
    <% if @hotels.nil? then %>
    No hotels found for this city.
    <% end%>
</div>
```

Make sure you have some hotel star images in the `RAILS_ROOT/public/images` folder This is how it looks:

Getting weather information

The weather tab uses WeatherBug to provide information on the weather today as well as the following six days. As before, the first thing to create is a method in the Location class to call the WeatherBug API.

First, at the top of the `location.rb` file, add the following to enable the Ruby RSS library:

```
require 'rss/1.0'
require 'rss/2.0'
```

Then, add the necessary constants used in the Location class:

```
WEATHERBUG_APP_KEY = '<YOUR WEATHERBUG APP KEY>'
FORECAST_URL = "http://#{WEATHERBUG_APP_KEY}.api.wxbug.net/
getForecastRSS.aspx?ACode=#{WEATHERBUG_APP_KEY}"
```

Next, create a Weather class and a Forecast class to contain the forecast information, in the `location.rb` file:

```
class Weather
  attr_accessor :forecasts, :today
end
class Forecast
  attr_accessor :title, :description
  def initialize(initial = {})
    @title = initial[:title]
    @description = initial[:description]
  end
end
```

Note that a Weather object will contain one or more Forecast objects. Then, create a method called `weather` in the Location class:

```
def weather
    parameters = "lat=#{@lat}&long=#{@long}&unitType=1"
    rss = ''
    open(FORECAST_URL + '&' + parameters) { |s| rss = RSS::Parser.
        parse(s.read, false) }

    weather = Weather.new
    weather.today = Forecast.new(:title =>  rss.items.first.title, :
        description => rss.items.first.description)
    weather.forecasts = []
    rss.items[1,rss.items.size - 1].each {|item| weather.forecasts <<
        Forecast.new({:title => item.title, :description => item.
        description}) }
    weather
  end
```

As before, we use Open URI to call WeatherBug's REST API to retrieve forecast
information in an RSS 2.0 formatted feed. This is a sample of the returned response,
truncated for better formatting:

```
<rss version="2.0">
    <channel>
            <title>Forecast for Paris 2e, France</title>
            <link>http://weather.weatherbug.com/France/Paris 2e-weather/
                local-forecast/7-day-forecast.html?ZCode=Z5546&amp;
                Units=0</link>
            <description>Weatherbug, the owner of the world's largest
                weather network is now providing an API to it's weather
                data in the form of RSS. This will enable it's
                enthusiastic users to build their own applications.</
                description>
            <language>en-us</language>
            <lastBuildDate>Fri, 28 Mar 2008 23:00:00 GMT</lastBuildDate>
            <ttl>60</ttl>
            <aws:weather xmlns:aws="http://www.aws.com/aws"><aws:api
             version="2.0" />
            <aws:WebURL>http://weather.weatherbug.com/France/Paris 2e-
             weather/local-forecast/7-day-forecast.html?ZCode=Z5546&amp;
             Units=0</aws:WebURL>
            <aws:forecasts type="Detailed" date="Fri, 28 Mar 2008
            23:00:00 GMT">
                    <aws:location>
                            <aws:city>Paris 2e</aws:city>
                            <aws:citycode>62840</aws:citycode>
                            <aws:country>France</aws:country>
                    </aws:location>
                    <aws:forecast>
                            <aws:title alttitle="SAT">Today</aws:title>
                            <aws:short-prediction>Mostly Sunny</aws:short-
                            prediction>
                            <aws:image isNight="0" icon="cond026.
                            gif">http://deskwx.weatherbug.com/images/
                            Forecast/icons/cond026.gif</aws:image>
                            <aws:description>Today</aws:description>
                            <aws:prediction> Scattered clouds.  Mild,
                            Breezy. Temperature of 57&amp;deg;F.  Winds
                            18mph SW. Humidity will be 80% with a dewpoint
                            of 36&amp;deg; and comfort level of
                            54&amp;deg;F. There is a 30% chance of
                            precipitation.</aws:prediction>
                            <aws:high units="°F">57</aws:high>
                            <aws:low units="°F">37</aws:low>
                    </aws:forecast>
            . . .
            </aws:forecasts>
    </aws:weather>
```

```
<image>
        <title>Forecast from WeatherBug</title>
        <width>142</width>
        <height>18</height>
        <link>http://weather.weatherbug.com/France/Paris 2e-weather/
                local-forecast/7-day-forecast.html?ZCode=Z5546&amp;
                Units=0</link>
        <url>http://www.weatherbug.com/aws/imagesHmPg0604/
                img_wxbug_logo_whiteBG.gif</url>
</image>
<item>
        <title>Today's forecast for Paris 2e, France</title>
        <description>
                <![CDATA[
                <img src="http://deskwx.weatherbug.com/images/
                Forecast/icons/cond026.gif" border="0" alt="Current
                Conditions"/>  
                <b> Scattered clouds.  Mild, Breezy. Temperature
                of 57&deg;F.  Winds 18mph SW. Humidity will be 80%
                with a dewpoint of 36&deg; and comfort level of
                54&deg;F. There is a 30% chance of precipitation.</b>
                <br />
                <b>High:</b> 57 °F<br />
                <b>Low:</b> 37 °F
                ]]>
        </description>
        <pubDate>Fri, 28 Mar 2008 23:00:00 GMT</pubDate>
        <guid isPermaLink="false">WorldForecastTxt-Fri, 28 Mar 2008
         23:00:00 GMT-Today</guid>
        <link>http://weather.weatherbug.com/France/Paris 2e-weather/
         local-forecast/7-day-forecast.html?ZCode=Z5546&amp;Units=0&
         amp;rnd=1</link>
</item>
        . . .
</channel>
</rss>
```

However, this time we use Ruby's built-in RSS library to extract the information. Finally the weather method will return a Weather object.

WeatherBug's RSS feed like Kayak's is in RSS 2.0 format and also uses proprietary tags. Why do we use the default RSS library to parse the feed this time round instead of XmlSimple? This is because although WeatherBug has proprietary namespace tags, the information is actually repeated in the non-proprietary tags. It is even conveniently formatted in HTML for easy reuse! For simplicity, this time around we use the RSS information directly.

We now turn to the controller and view again. The `weather` action in the Trip controller is trivial. Create a `weather` method in `trip_controller.rb`:

```
def weather
    @weather = session[:location].weather
end
```

Next, create a file called `weather.rhtml` in the `RAILS_ROOT/app/views/trip` folder:

```
<h2><%= @weather.today.title%></h2>
<p><%= @weather.today.description %></p>
<% @weather.forecasts.each { |f| %>
<h2><%= f.title %></h2>
<p><%= f.description %></p>
<% } %>
```

This gives us today's weather forecast in that location as well as the forecast for the next 6 days.

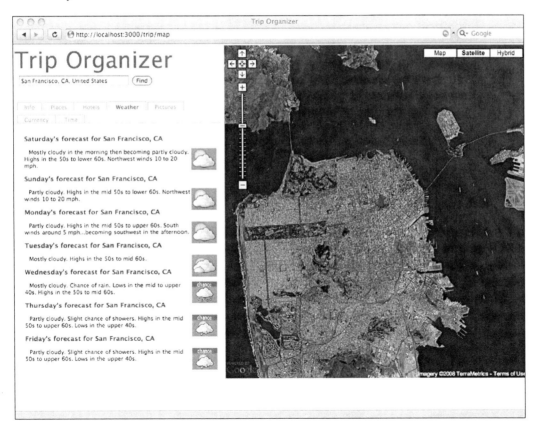

Displaying pictures of the location

Next in line is to display pictures of the remote location by searching through Flickr and showing thumbnails of pictures we find that are labeled or tagged with the name of the location. As always, we start off by adding a new capability to the Location class.

First, define the constants we need to connect to Flickr in the Location class:

```
FLICKR_API_KEY = '<YOUR FLICKR API KEY>'
FLICKR_SEARCH_URL = "http://api.flickr.com/services/rest/?api_
key=#{FLICKR_API_KEY}&method=flickr.photos.search"
```

Then, create a `pictures` method in the Location class:

```
def pictures
    hash = {:text => @location, :sort => 'relevance', :per_page => 32}
    parameters = URI.escape(hash.to_a.collect {|pair| pair.join('=')}.
                  join('&'))
    results = ''
    pics = []
    open(FLICKR_SEARCH_URL + '&' + parameters) { |s| results =
        XmlSimple::xml_in(s.read, 'force_array' => false) }
    results['photos']['photo'].each { |p|
      pics << ["http://farm#{p['farm']}.static.flickr.com/
        #{p['server']}/#{p['id']}_#{p['secret']}_s.jpg",
        "http://farm#{p['farm']}.static.flickr.com/#{p['server']}/
        #{p['id']}_#{p['secret']}.jpg", p['title']]
    }
    pics
  end
```

We use the public, unauthenticated API method called `flickr.photos.search`, which returns a list of public photos based on given search criteria. This method also allows us to sort the pictures according to various criteria. In this chapter we sort the pictures by relevance to the location name. The default number of pictures returned by Flickr is 100 and the maximum is 200 but we arbitrarily set it to 32 to speed up the response. You can visit `http://www.flickr.com/services/api/flickr.photos.search.html` to find out more on the other criteria.

The response from Flickr is in XML format as below (truncated to show only three pictures):

```
<?xml version="1.0" encoding="utf-8" ?>
<rsp stat="ok">
<photos page="1" pages="62639" perpage="32" total="2004419">
<photo id="2042120799" owner="73362533@N00" secret="69d5799a36"
```

```
               server="2135" farm="3" title="San Francisco Fog IR"
               ispublic="1" isfriend="0" isfamily="0" />
    <photo id="1013470973" owner="21063397@N00" secret="d3231b3e2d"
               server="1382" farm="2" title="Approaching San Francisco"
               ispublic="1" isfriend="0" isfamily="0" />
    <photo id="103386109" owner="22191840@N00" secret="14c259d3f1"
               server="41" farm="1" title="San Francisco" ispublic="1"
               isfriend="0" isfamily="0" />
    </photos>
    </rsp>
```

What we need to do next is to re-create a URL that will show the Flickr-hosted image. From Flickr's API documentation at `http://www.flickr.com/services/api/misc.urls.html`, we know that one of the three possible formats for defining a Flickr image URL is:

```
http://farm{farm-id}.static.flickr.com/{server-id}/{id}_{secret}_
[mstb].jpg
```

The information on the farm ID, server ID, photo ID, and secret are from the information on the photo. The last options (mstb) are size suffixes where:

s	small square 75x75
t	thumbnail, 100 on longest side
m	small, 240 on longest side
-	medium, 500 on longest side
b	large, 1024 on longest side (only exists for very large original images)

Therefore, for each returned photo, we create an array of URL strings with the necessary data from the photo for both a thumbnail and medium size as well as the title of the picture as entered by the photo owner. The `pictures` method returns this array.

Now that we have an array of URLs it is pretty easy to display the pictures in the tab. Create a simple method in `trip_controller.rb` for the array of pictures retrieved from the Location object we stored in the session:

```
def pictures
    @pictures = session[:location].pictures
end
```

Create a file called `pictures.rhtml` in the `RAILS_ROOT/app/views/trip` folder:

```
<div>
<% @pictures.each { |pic|%>
    <%= image_tag pic[0] %>
<% } %>
</div>
```

This produces a neat matrix of thumbnail pictures of the location. To add a nice touch to this pictures tab, we want to let the user click on a picture and pop up the larger image in the middle of the screen. To do this, we're going to use John Reid's PopBox JavaScript code from `http://www.c6software.com/Products/PopBox/Default.aspx`.

Download the code from the site, and unzip the package. Copy the `PopBox.js` JavaScript file into the `RAILS_ROOT/public/javascript` folder, and the `magminus.gif` file into the `RAILS_ROOT/public/images` folder. Then change the `pictures.rhtml` file to the one below.

```
<div>
<% @pictures.each { |pic|%>
    <%= image_tag pic[0], :pbSrc => pic[1], :pbCaption => pic[2], :
        onclick => "Pop(this,50,'PopBoxImageLarge');"%>
<% } %>
</div>
```

The `:pbSrc` option sets the medium sized image; the `:pbCaption` option provides a caption for the large image. We also pop out the medium sized image when the thumbnail image is clicked on. Clicking on the image pops up the medium sized image while clicking on the popped out image brings it back to the thumbnail.

Showing currency exchange rate

The next tab shows the currency exchange rate between the user's home country and the remote location. For this, we will be using WebserviceX to convert from one currency to another. WebserviceX uses SOAP so the approach in getting the conversion is different from what we've used so far.

For the currency conversion, we will use a different approach than with the others. The Location class is a library under the `RAILS_ROOT/lib` folder and used as a library class for the entire Rails application. For currency conversion, we will create a model called Currency, which maps to a list of currencies around the world. This will provide us with the currency description to be used in our application.

First, we need to get the currency code data. ISO 4217 is an international standard describing three letter codes that define names of currencies. The first two letters of the three letters are normally the country codes as defined in ISO 3166-1 alpha 2, while the last letter is usually the initial of the currency itself. For example, the US dollar is USD and the Japanese yen is JPY. We need to import the ISO 4217 currency codes into our database.

Go to the ISO website at `http://www.iso.org/iso/support/faqs/faqs_widely_used_standards/widely_used_standards_other/currency_codes/currency_codes_list-1.htm` and copy the list of currencies into a spreadsheet, then save it as a comma delimited file (CSV) named `currency_codes.csv` in the `RAILS_ROOT/db/migrate` folder. The file should contain entries like this:

```
"AFGHANISTAN","Afghani","AFN"
"ALBANIA","Lek","ALL"
"ALGERIA","Algerian Dinar","DZD"
"AMERICAN SAMOA","US Dollar","USD"
"ANDORRA","Euro","EUR"
```

The first item is the country name, the second is the currency name, and the last is the ISO 4217 currency code. Now generate a migration file with:

`$./script/generate migration create_currencies`

This will create a migration file in the `RAILS_ROOT/db/migrate` folder named `001_create_currencies.rb`. Amend it as follows:

```
class CreateCurrencies < ActiveRecord::Migration
  def self.up
    create_table :currencies do |t|
      t.column :country, :string
      t.column :name, :string
      t.column :code, :string
    end
```

```
      end
    def self.down
      drop_table :currencies
    end
  end
```

Run the database migration with:

$rake db:migrate

This will create the database table we need. Next, we need to create the Currency class. Create a file called `currency.rb` in the RAILS_ROOT/app/models folder:

```
class Currency < ActiveRecord::Base
end
```

Then create another migration file, this time to populate the data into the database. Run the following:

$./script/generate migration currencies_data

This will create a file named `002_currencies_data.rb` in the RAILS_ROOT/db/migrate folder. Add the following code into this file:

```
require 'csv'
class CurrenciesData < ActiveRecord::Migration
  def self.up
    down
    CSV.open("#{File.dirname(__FILE__)}/currency_codes.csv",
             'r') do |row|
      currency = Currency.new({:country => row[0],
                               :name => row[1],
                               :code => row[2]})
      currency.save
    end
  end
  def self.down
    Currency.delete_all
  end
end
```

This migration file will open up the `currency_codes.csv` file you created earlier and write each line into the database. Now run the database migration again.

Now that we have the data in the database, let's flesh out the rest of the Currency class, in `currency.rb`. We will use the Currency class to do the conversion through WebserviceX.

```
require 'soap/wsdlDriver'
class Currency < ActiveRecord::Base
  WSDL_URL = "http://www.webservicex.net/CurrencyConvertor.asmx?WSDL"
  attr_accessor :amount
  def Currency.get(code)
    Currency.find(:first,
                  :conditions => ['code = ?', code])
  end
  def to(to_currency)
    driver = SOAP::WSDLDriverFactory.new(WSDL_URL).create_rpc_driver
    params = {'FromCurrency' => self.code,
              'ToCurrency' => to_currency.code}
    amount.to_f *  driver.ConversionRate(params).
                      conversionRateResult.to_f
  end
end
```

We will use SOAP to access the currency conversion web service provided by WebserviceX. As with Chapter 3, we need to require the necessary SOAP library and also have access to the WSDL provided by WebserviceX.

The `to` method takes in a Currency object and uses SOAP to send a request to the web service. The first line creates a local proxy object that is the stub to the remote service. Using this local proxy, we call the `ConversionRate` web service, passing in the `FromCurrency` and `ToCurrency` parameters. The returned result is extracted using the `conversionRateResult` method and converted to the correct converted amount accordingly.

Now that we are able to convert from one currency to another, we need to find out where our user is coming from and get the currency code of his or her country of origin. To do this, we will use Hostip.info to geocode our user's IP address. Note that for this part of the chapter, you will need to deploy your application on a publicly available IP address for testing because Hostip.info will not be able to geocode your local IP address. For testing purposes you can use the dynamic DNS mechanism to simulate a publicly available website, as described in Chapter 2 and Chapter 5.

Add the Hostip.info URL constant in the `currency.rb` file:

```
IP_GEOCODE_URL = "http://api.hostip.info/get_xml.
php?position=true&ip="
```

Then add a new class method:

```
def Currency.get_from_ip(ipaddr)
    results = ''
    open(IP_GEOCODE_URL + ipaddr) { |s| results = XmlSimple::xml_in(s.
```

```
read, 'force_array' => false) }
    country = results['featureMember']['Hostip']['countryName']
    Currency.find(:first, :conditions => ['country = ?',
        country.upcase])
end
```

This method sends a given IP address (retrieved from the user) and retrieves XML from Hostip.info indicating the estimated location of the machine with that IP address. This is a sample of the retrieved XML:

```xml
<?xml version="1.0" encoding="ISO-8859-1" ?>
<HostipLookupResultSet version="1.0.0" xmlns="http://www.hostip.info/
api" xmlns:gml="http://www.opengis.net/gml" xmlns:xsi="http://www.
w3.org/2001/XMLSchema-instance" xsi:schemaLocation="http://www.hostip.
info/api/hostip-1.0.0.xsd">
 <gml:description>This is the Hostip Lookup Service</gml:description>
 <gml:name>hostip</gml:name>
 <gml:boundedBy>
  <gml:Null>inapplicable</gml:Null>
 </gml:boundedBy>
 <gml:featureMember>
  <Hostip>
   <gml:name>Sugar Grove, IL</gml:name>
   <countryName>UNITED STATES</countryName>
   <countryAbbrev>US</countryAbbrev>
   <!-- Co-ordinates are available as lng,lat -->
   <ipLocation>
    <gml:PointProperty>
     <gml:Point srsName="http://www.opengis.net/gml/srs/epsg.xml#4326">
      <gml:coordinates>-88.4588,41.7696</gml:coordinates>
     </gml:Point>
    </gml:PointProperty>
   </ipLocation>
  </Hostip>
 </gml:featureMember>
</HostipLookupResultSet>
```

There's lots of interesting information here but what we're interested in looking at is the country name. Using this name we search our database and find the corresponding currency, then load it up and return the Currency object. This gives us the currency of the place from which the user is accessing our mashup.

Next, we need to get the currency used for the location. To do this, we will revisit our old friend the Location class. Add the following lines to the end of the constructor in the `location.rb` file:

```
def initialize(location='Singapore')
    hash = {:appid => YAHOO_APP_ID, :location => location }
    parameters = URI.escape(hash.to_a.collect {|pair| pair.join('=')}.
            join('&'))
    results = ''
    open(YAHOO_GEOCODE_URL + '?' + parameters) { |s| results =
        XmlSimple::xml_in(s.read, 'force_array' => false)['Result'] }
    if results.class == Array then
      cities = '<ol>'
      results.each {|res|
        if res['Country'] == 'US' or res['Country'] == 'CA'
          cities += "<li><a href='/trip/map?location=#{res['City']},
                #{res['State']}, #{res['Country']}'>#{res['City']},
                #{res['State']}, #{res['Country']}</a></li>"
        else
          cities += "<li><a href='/trip/map?location=#{res['City']},
                #{res['Country']}'>#{res['City']},
                #{res['Country']}</a></li>"
        end
      }
      cities += '</ol>'
      raise "More than one city with the same name found! Please
            choose one from below:" + cities
    end
    @country_code = results['Country']
    @state_code = results['State']
    @lat = results['Latitude'].to_f
    @long = results['Longitude'].to_f
    hash = {:q => location, :maxRows => 1, :style => 'FULL' }
    parameters = URI.escape(hash.to_a.collect {|pair| pair.join('=')}.
            join('&'))
    open(GEONAMES_SEARCH_URL + '?' + parameters) { |s| results =
        XmlSimple::xml_in(s.read, 'force_array' => false)['geoname'] }
    raise "Cannot find this city, please try again with a different
        state or country." if results == nil
    @city = results['name']
    @country = results['countryName']
```

```
        @timezone = results['timezone']['content']
        if @country_code == 'US' or @country_code == 'CA'
          @location = "#{@city}, #{@state_code}, #{@country}"
        else
          @location = "#{@city}, #{@country}"
        end
    @currency = Currency.find_by_country(@country.upcase)
      end
```

This will populate the currency attribute in the Location object with the corresponding Currency object.

Now that we are able to convert currencies as well as get both the local and remote currencies, we go to the controller and view to display it in the currency tab. As before, the action in the Trip controller is trivial. Add in a currency method in trip_controller.rb:

```
def currency
    @loc_currency = session[:location].currency
    begin
      @my_currency = Currency.get_from_ip(request.remote_ip)
    rescue
      @my_currency = nil
    end
  end
```

The first line gets the remote currency from the Location object in the session. The second line gets the local currency through the remote_ip method of the request object. Now create a currency.rhtml file in the RAILS_ROOT/views/trip folder:

```
<% if @my_currency.nil? then %>
<h2>Local currency</h2>
<p>
Currency conversion is not available because we cannot geocode your
current location.
</p>
<p>
The local currency is <%= @loc_currency.name%> (<%= @loc_currency.
code%>)
</p>
<% else %>
<h2>Current exchange rate</h2>
<p>
<% @my_currency.amount = 100%>
<%= number_to_currency(@my_currency.amount, :unit => '') %> <%= @
```

```
  my_currency.name%> = <%= number_to_currency(@my_currency.to(@loc_
  currency), :unit => '')%> <%= @loc_currency.name%>
</p>
<h2>Conversion</h2>
<p>Enter an amount and click on 'convert'.</p>
<p>
<% form_remote_tag (:url => {:action => 'convert'}, :update =>
  'converted_to') do %>
  <%= hidden_field_tag 'from_currency', @my_currency.code %>
  <%= hidden_field_tag 'to_currency', @loc_currency.code %>
  <%= text_field_tag 'amount', '100', :size => 5%> <%= @my_currency.
   name%> = <span id='converted_to'>? </span><%= @loc_currency.name%>
<%= submit_tag 'convert'%>
<% end %>
</p>
<p>
<% form_remote_tag (:url => {:action => 'convert'}, :update =>
  'converted_from') do %>
  <%= hidden_field_tag 'to_currency', @my_currency.code %>
  <%= hidden_field_tag 'from_currency', @loc_currency.code %>
  <%= text_field_tag 'amount', '100', :size => 5%> <%= @loc_
    currency.name%> = <span id='converted_from'>? </span><%= @my_
    currency.name%>  <%= submit_tag 'convert'%>
<% end %>
</p>
<% end%>
```

There are two parts to this template. In the first part, we calculate an equivalent amount of currency for the remote location for 100 units of the local currency and use Rails' number_to_currency helper method to format it into a currency format.

```
<h2>Current exchange rate</h2>
<p>
<% @local_currency.amount = 100%>
<%= number_to_currency(@local_currency.amount, :unit => '') %> <%= @
   local_currency.name%> = <%= number_to_currency(@local_currency.to(@
   remote_currency), :unit => '')%> <%= @remote_currency.name%>
</p>
```

In the second part, we provide a simple facility to convert any amount from and to the remote currency:

```
<h2>Conversion</h2>
<p>Enter an amount and click on 'convert'.</p>
<p>
<% form_remote_tag (:url => {:action => 'convert'}, :update =>
  'converted_to') do %>
```

```
<%= hidden_field_tag 'from_currency', @my_currency.code %>
<%= hidden_field_tag 'to_currency', @loc_currency.code %>
<%= text_field_tag 'amount', '100', :size => 5%> <%= @my_currency.
name%> = <span id='converted_to'>? </span><%= @loc_currency.name%>
<%= submit_tag 'convert'%>
<% end %>
</p>
<p>
<% form_remote_tag (:url => {:action => 'convert'}, :update =>
'converted_from') do %>
<%= hidden_field_tag 'to_currency', @my_currency.code %>
<%= hidden_field_tag 'from_currency', @loc_currency.code %>
<%= text_field_tag 'amount', '100', :size => 5%> <%= @loc_
currency.name%> = <span id='converted_from'>? </span><%= @my_
currency.name%>  <%= submit_tag 'convert'%>
<% end %>
</p>
```

In the code above, both remote forms link to the same action but they update
different HTML elements. Create the corresponding convert action in the
trip_controller.rb file:

```
def convert
    to_currency = Currency.get(params[:to_currency])
    from_currency = Currency.get(params[:from_currency])
    from_currency.amount = params[:amount]
    @converted_amount = from_currency.to(to_currency)
end
```

The code is quite similar to that of the default 100 units conversion except that both
currencies are already known. The converted amount is updated into the respective
HTML tags. Finally, create the convert.rhtml template in the RAILS_ROOT/app/
views/trip folder:

```
<%= number_to_currency(@converted_amount, :unit => '') %>
```

This template consists of one line that converts the number to a currency format.

Showing remote location time compared with local time

The last tab shows the current local time for your user as well as the current local time for the remote location. To do this, we need to find out the time zone from which your user is accessing this service as well as the time zone of the remote location. As with the currency conversion, we will use Hostip.info to geocode the IP address of your user. As before, this tab cannot be viewed properly if it is not accessed through a publicly available website.

Firstly, we need to install the TZInfo package:

```
$gem install tzinfo
```

We need to do this as the default Rails library for timezones does not take account of daylight savings time as of writing (see `http://dev.rubyonrails.org/ticket/4551` for more information). Remember from the constructor of the Location class we already have the time zone information.

At the top of the `location.rb` file, add the following:

```
require 'tzinfo'
```

Next, we need to make a change to allow us to create Location objects from IP addresses. We already have the necessary URL constant for Hostip.info, in the `location.rb` file:

```
IP_GEOCODE_URL = "http://api.hostip.info/get_xml.
php?position=true&ip="
```

Now, add a new class method in the Location class (which does the same thing as in the Currency class):

```
def Location.get_from_ip(ipaddr)
    results = ''
    open(IP_GEOCODE_URL + ipaddr) { |s| results = XmlSimple::xml_in(s.
        read, 'force_array' => false) }
    country = results['featureMember']['Hostip']['countryName']
    Location.new(country)
  end
```

As with the others in this chapter, we use Open URI to send a request to Hostip.info to get the name of the country, and XmlSimple to parse the XML formatted response. Once we have the name of the country, we create and return a Location object for that country.

Now that we have the information set up, let's show the actual time on the time tab. Add a new `time` method in the Trip controller in the `trip_controller.rb` file:

```
def time
    tz = TZInfo::Timezone.get(session[:location].timezone)
    @time = tz.now
    @own_loc = Location.get_from_ip(request.remote_ip)
    @own_time = TZInfo::Timezone.get(@own_loc.timezone).now
  end
```

The first line gets a `TZInfo::Timezone` object for the remote location through the Location object in the session and the second line returns the actual current time from the `Timezone` object. The third line gets the user's current location as a Location object, through his or her IP address. Using the user's current location, we get the user's time zone and return the user's current local time.

This information is passed on to a view template to be displayed in the time tab.
Create a file called `time.rhtml` in the `RAILS_ROOT/app/views/trip` folder:

```
<h2><%= @own_loc.location%></h2>
Timezone: <%= @own_loc.timezone %>
<div class="time"><%= @own_time.strftime "%I:%M %p " %></div>
<h2><%= session[:location].location%></h2>
Timezone : <%= session[:location].timezone%><br/>
<div class="time"><%= @time.strftime "%I:%M %p" %></div>
```

This template formats and displays the time for both the user's current location and
the remote location he entered.

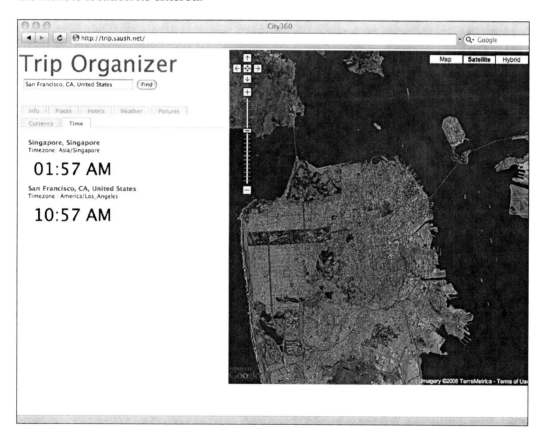

Showing nice exception pages

We've just completed a round of six information and utility tabs, and accessed a total of nine mashup APIs to retrieve various kinds of information for a remote location. Almost all the processing is done outside of your own application and the main activities in your application consist of calling the APIs and formatting the returned data. This means that the mashup application we just wrote is highly dependent on the Internet, your external access speed, and the availability of the remote APIs, all of which we normally cannot control.

This also means that exceptions and errors might occur, so controlling and managing exceptions and errors is very important. While it will take too long to start a section on Rails exception handling, a quick solution to this is to catch all exceptions gracefully from Rails and display a friendly message to your user.

Fortunately Rails has a very easy solution to this. `ActionController::Rescue`, which takes care of exception handling in the controller, has a method named `rescue_action_in_public`, which allows you to specify the handling of exceptions when the application is called from a non-local request (local meaning localhost or 127.0.0.1 and non-local meaning everything else). Just override this method in your `application.rb` file or in our case, `trip_controller.rb`:

```
def rescue_action_in_public(exception)
    render :template => 'error'
end
```

This will instruct your controller to render an error template in case of any exceptions that are raised. The `error.rhtml` file, in the `RAILS_ROOT/app/views` folder, can be as simple as:

```
<h1>Service not available at the moment</h1>
<p>
Something's not happening right, probably not getting data from the
remote service. Try again!
</p>
```

Also add in this method in `trip_controller.rb` to make all requests non-local:

```
def local_request?
    false
end
```

We will also need to change this parameter in your environment file (`development.rb` or `test.rb`) if you wish to see the nice error page in those environments:

```
config.action_controller.consider_all_requests_local = false
```

Summary

We have gone round accessing nine mashup APIs and have shown a set of information around a remote location. We displayed an online map of the remote location using Google Maps and a list of Wikipedia articles on the location using FUTEF. We retrieved and showed a list of places of interest around the location from Wikipedia through GeoNames. We've also used Kayak to retrieve a list of available hotels around the location. We retrieved the current weather forecast and those for the next six days from WeatherBug and displayed pictures of the location through Flickr. Finally we converted the user's local currency against the remote location's currency as well as showed the current local time in the user's location and the remote location by geocoding the user's IP address with Hostip.info.

7

Ticketing mashup application

What does it do?

This mashup allows an online event ticketing application to receive payment through PayPal, send SMS receipts, and add event records in the customer's Google Calendar account.

Online event ticketing

One of the most popular types of application on the Internet is the ticketing application. Online ticketing applications generally allow users to choose and buy tickets over the Internet. There are two types of ticketing applications:

1. Admission ticketing applications provide tickets for transportation and admission to facilities like amusement parks, museums, zoos, and others.

2. Event ticketing applications provide tickets for movies, theater shows, sports events, concerts, and similar events.

Event ticketing applications on the Internet include Fandango.com, MovieTickets.com, and Ticketmaster.com. Online event ticketing applications typically provide the following basic functions to their users:

- Show a catalogue of events and details of the events
- Show a catalogue of venues for the events
- Allow customers to select events, date, time, venue, seat, and number of tickets to attend the events
- Allow customers to pay for the tickets
- Create and send the tickets to the customers
- Allow customers to check the authenticity and validity of the tickets at the point of entry to the event

In addition other value-added functions can include:

- Sending reminders to the customers who have bought tickets to the event
- Adding the event to the customer's personal calendar
- Sending tickets or receipts in various forms including email and SMS
- Sending marketing emails to customers for promotional purposes

Requirements overview

This mashup shows how an online event ticketing application can use mashup APIs to perform some of these functions, simplifying the development and maintenance of the online event ticketing application. The functions we will replace in the online ticketing application are:

- Allowing customers to pay for tickets
- Adding the event to the customer's personal calendar
- Sending the tickets to the customer as an SMS

Design

In this mashup we will integrate with an existing online ticketing application and show how the three functions are replaced by mashup APIs from remote sites. The payment integration will be with PayPal for credit card payment only, while the calendar integration will be with Google Calendar. We will also revisit Clickatell and show how an electronic ticket can be sent via SMS.

The ticketing application we will use in this chapter is a movie ticketing application. Many of the functions are faked and hard-coded because we will not be writing a full-fledged movie ticketing application. The flow for the ticketing is as follows:

1. Customer selects movie and date of screening
2. Customer selects movie theater and screening time
3. Customer selects the number of tickets and types of tickets to buy
4. Customer enters payment details and Google Calendar credentials
5. Customer confirms the details
6. Application sends payment details to PayPal to request approval

7. Application creates event in customer's Google Calendar using the given Google credentials

8. Application sends SMS ticket to customer

9. Application forwards to a confirmation page

Bullet points 1 to 5 are fixed in this chapter. Our mashup will only come into the picture from point 6 onwards as we use PayPal. In this chapter we will not store any information in a database even though you will likely want to store the user details in a real application. Our design passes the information in one page form to the next page for processing.

Mashup APIs on the menu
The following are the APIs that are used in this chapter.

PayPal
PayPal is an Internet-based financial services company that provides payment and money transfer services through the Internet. PayPal also offers products for online merchants to accept payment over the Internet.

Website Payment Pro
Website Payment Pro is a payment solution offered by PayPal that provides the capabilities of a merchant account and gateway. Website Payment Pro includes:

- PayPal Direct Payment API, which enables a merchant to accept credit card payments directly on an e-commerce website
- PayPal Express Checkout, which allows customers to pay using their PayPal account

Website Payment Pro is accessible through different means including the PayPal Name-Value Pair (NVP) APIs, the PayPal SOAP APIs and its various SDKs. In this chapter we will be using Website Payment Pro through its NVP APIs with the Ruby-PayPal library.

PayPal Sandbox

The PayPal Sandbox is a self-contained environment in which developers can prototype and test PayPal applications. The Sandbox simulates almost every function available in the actual PayPal environment. Registering for a PayPal developer account provides a merchant account and 2 personal accounts for a developer to run test applications with those accounts. This includes email addresses, bank account numbers, and credit card account numbers as shown below.

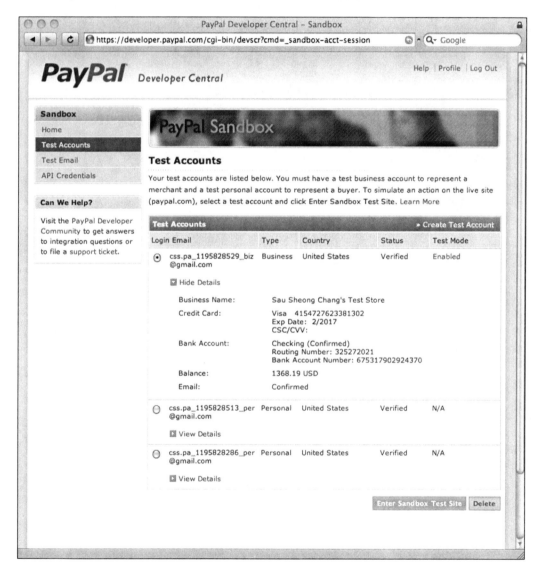

To register for a PayPal developer account, go to PayPal Developer Central at `https://developer.paypal.com`, click on 'Sign Up Now' and follow the online instructions. After you have a developer account, go to `https://www.sandbox.paypal.com` or click on the Sandbox tab in Developer Central, select a test user, and click on 'Launch Sandbox'.

In this chapter, all our testing will be with the SandBox only. To access the NVP APIs we will need API credentials. PayPal recommends using the API signature for credentials most of the time. You can find the API signature, API username, and API password in PayPal Developer Central.

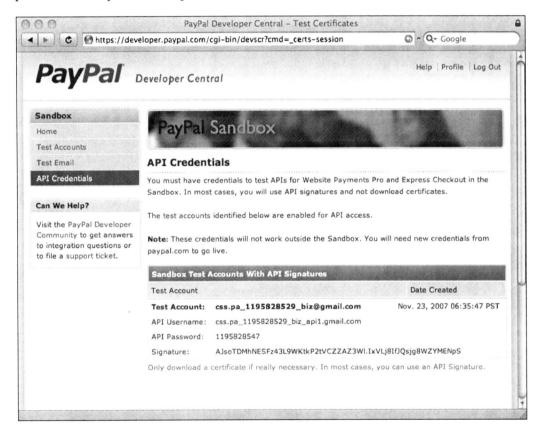

There are two types of methods of taking payment from a credit card (using Direct Payment) in PayPal:

- Final sale, where the merchant is asking for payment immediately
- Authorization, where the merchant is only asking for an authorization of the payment request and the merchant will capture the payment (or ask for money) at later time

In this chapter we will only deal with final sale payment requests.

Ruby-PayPal library

The Ruby-PayPal library (`http://rubyforge.org/projects/ruby-paypal`) is a lightweight wrapper library around the PayPal NVP APIs. It provides basic validation support for input into PayPal NVP APIs to reduce processing time if the input is erroneous. It also provides interpretation of the response from PayPal and an easy interface for Ruby developers.

To install it, type the following at a command prompt:

```
$gem install ruby-paypal
```

Google Calendar

Google Calendar is a web-based time and event management tool that is presented in the form of a web calendar. Google Calendar provides a set of APIs that allows client applications to view and update calendar events in the form of Google Data (GData) API feeds. To add or remove events from Google Calendar you need to be authenticated by Google. GData services support two types of authentication:

- ClientLogin, which is normally used for single-user desktop applications but gives your application full control of the authentication process. However your application needs to store your user's Google credentials.
- AuthSub, which is normally used for multi-user web applications and requires your application to redirect to Google's login. This method does not need to store your user's Google credentials.

Both authentication methods will return an authentication token to your application, which you will need to use in every request to a Google Calendar API. The GoogleCalendar library uses ClientLogin for its standalone API and this is the API we will also use in this chapter.

The Google Calendar API allows you to retrieve three types of calendars:

- A primary calendar that is created for the user when he or she signs up for a Google Calendar account
- A number of secondary calendars subsequently created by the user
- Imported calendars that are created by someone else but subscribed to by the user

Google calendars contain two main types of events:

- Single occurrence events that happen only once
- Recurrent events that occur at regular intervals

In this chapter we will be creating a single occurrence event in the user's primary calendar to indicate the movie-screening event.

GoogleCalendar library

Benjamin Francisoud's GoogleCalendar (`http://benjamin.francisoud.googlepages.com/googlecalendar`) provides a Ruby on Rails plugin to display Google Calendar events in Rails as well as a simple library that accesses Google Calendar services. In this chapter we will be using his library to create Google Calendar events.

To install the library type the following at the command prompt:

```
$gem install googlecalendar
```

Clickatell

Clickatell (`http://www.clickatell.com`) is a bulk SMS provider that provides SMS messaging services and gateways for over 600 networks in almost 200 countries for outbound messages, and 100 countries for inbound (two-way) messaging. We discussed Clickatell and SMS gateways in detail in Chapter 3 so I will not repeat the discussion here.

What we will be doing

The following section describes the steps we will be taking to create the mashup. The basic steps are:

1. Create the Rails application
2. Create the flow for the ticketing application
3. Create the PayPal NVP integration Ruby API
4. Integrate with PayPal for payment
5. Integrate with Google Calendar for event calendar
6. Integrate with Clickatell for sending SMS tickets

Creating a Rails application

We begin this mashup as before by creating the usual Rails application.

```
$rails Chapter 7
```

This will create a new Ruby on Rails application.

Creating the flow for the ticketing application

Before we can start the integration we need to build the flow for the ticketing application. The hard-coded flow for the ticketing is as follows:

1. Customer selects movie and date of screening

2. Customer selects movie theater and screening time

3. Customer selects the number of tickets and types of tickets to buy

4. Customer enters payment details and Google Calendar credentials

5. Customer confirms the details

This flow guides the customer to choose the movie, the date and the time of the screening, as well as the screening theater, then allows the customer to choose the types and number of tickets to buy. Finally the customer enters his or her payment details and Google Calendar credentials. You'll notice this design requires us to persist data between pages. In this chapter we will use one of the simplest methods to persist data between pages — storing it in the session.

To store data in the session, we create two simple data structures to abstract the two different types of data we need. The first type revolves around information about the movie, so we call it Movie. Create a file called movie.rb in the RAILS_ROOT/lib folder:

```
class Movie
  attr_accessor :name, :date, :time, :duration, :theater, :code
end
```

This is a very simple class, whose main purpose is to contain the data we need for processing later on. The name field is the name of the movie, while the code field is a simple string to represent the movie within the application. The time field is the start time of the movie screening and we use it to store a hash consisting of an hour and a min key. The duration field represents the number of minutes the movie will run while the theater field stores the name of the theater that will screen the movie.

The other data structure we will use is the `Payment` data structure, which we will use to store all information regarding the payment as well as additional information on the Google Calendar account and the mobile phone number to send the ticket to. Create a file called `payment.rb` in the `RAILS_ROOT/lib` folder:

```
class Payment
  attr_accessor :last_name, :first_name, :card_type,
                :card_no, :exp_date, :billing_zip,
                :google_acct, :google_pwd, :amount,
                :mobile_no
end
```

This class stores all the necessary payment information needed by PayPal, Google Calendar, and Clickatell later on. We will create and store objects of both classes in the session later on during the flow of the application.

Now that we have the data structures, let's turn to the main application. We will only need one main controller for this chapter: that is the `TicketingController`. Create a file called `ticketing_controller.rb` in the `RAILS_ROOT/app/controllers` folder.

We will first create a simple movies display and data selection page. Go to the `ticketing_controller.rb` file and add in the `movies` method:

```
class TicketingController < ApplicationController
  layout 'main'
  def movies
  end
end
```

Now add a `main.rhtml` file in the `RAILS_ROOT/app/views/layout` folder:

```
<!DOCTYPE html PUBLIC "-//W3C//DTD XHTML 1.0 Transitional//EN"
  "http://www.w3.org/TR/xhtml1/DTD/xhtml1-transitional.dtd">
<html xmlns="http://www.w3.org/1999/xhtml" xml:lang="en" lang="en">
<head>
  <meta http-equiv="content-type" content="text/html;charset=UTF-8"
    />
  <title>Chapter 7</title>
  <%= javascript_include_tag :defaults %>
  <%= stylesheet_link_tag 'main' %>
  <%= stylesheet_link_tag 'colors' %>
  <%= stylesheet_link_tag 'main2' %>
</head>
<body>
  <%= yield %>
</body>
</html>
```

Then add a `movies.rhtml` file in the `RAILS_ROOT/app/views/ticketing` folder:

```
<h2>Select Movie</h2>
<table>
<tr valign='top'>
  <td>
    <%= render :partial => '/ticketing/movies/bee_movie' %>
  </td>
  <td>
    <%= render :partial => '/ticketing/movies/enchanted' %>
  </td>
  <td>
    <%= render :partial => '/ticketing/movies/no_country_for_old_men'
      %>
  </td>
  <td>
    <%= render :partial => '/ticketing/movies/the_heartbreak_kid' %>
  </td>
</tr>
</table>
```

For simplicity, this view is hard-coded with four movies only. This is the `_bee_movie.rhtml` partial in the `RAILS_ROOT/app/views/ticketing/movies` folder, with the hard-coded details on the movie:

```
<%= render :partial => '/ticketing/movies/bee_movie_pic'%>
<p>
  <%= render :partial => '/ticketing/date_select', :locals =>
  {:movie_code => 'bee_movie', :movie_name => 'Bee Movie'}%>
</p>
<ul>
  <li><p>RELEASE DATE</p>11/02/2007 - Nationwide</li>
  <li><p>RUN TIME:</p>1 hr. 30 min.</li>
  <li><p>MPAA RATING:</p>(PG), for mild suggestive humor</li>
  <li><p>GENRE:</p>Animation</li>
  <li><p>STARRING:</p>Jerry Seinfeld, Renee Zellweger, Matthew
     Broderick, John Goodman, Chris Rock</li>
  <li><p>DIRECTOR(S):</p>Simon J. Smith, Steve Hickner</li>
  <li><p>PRODUCER(S):</p>Jerry Seinfeld, Christina Steinberg</li>
  <li><p>WRITER(S):</p>Spike Feresten, Barry Marder, Andy Robin, Jerry
     Seinfeld</li>
  <li><p>STUDIO:</p>Paramount Pictures</li>
</ul>
```

You will find the code for the other three movies in the source code. Copy them into the `RAILS_ROOT/app/views/ticketing/movies` folder. You may also wish to add the stylesheets, found in the source code, to make the page look more attractive.

This is the `_date_select.rhtml` partial in the `RAILS_ROOT/app/views/ticketing` folder:

```
<% form_tag(:action => 'movie_time') do -%>
<%= hidden_field_tag 'movie_code', movie_code%>
<%= hidden_field_tag 'movie_name', movie_name%>
<%= select_date(Date.today, :order => [:day, :month, :year],
    :use_short_month => true) %> <%= submit_tag 'buy' %>
<% end -%>
```

This is what the movies selection page looks like:

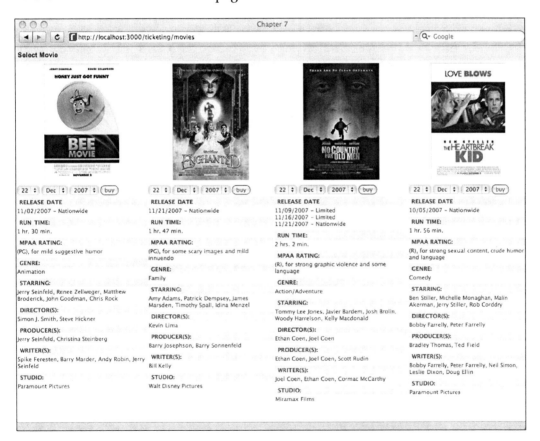

This page allows the customer to select the date of the movie screening. Once he or she has selected the date, he or she will be redirected to another page that allows him or her to select the theater and the starting time of the screening.

Create a method called `movie_time` in the `ticketing_controller.rb` file:

```
def movie_time
  movie = Movie.new
  movie.date = params[:date]
  movie.name = params[:movie_name]
  movie.code = params[:movie_code]
  movie.time = {}
  session[:movie] = movie
end
```

When we move to this page, we will store the date and the movie selected in the previous page into a new `Movie` object and place it in the session. Create the view to display the time and theater selection page by creating the `movie_time.rhtml` file in the `RAILS_ROOT/app/views/ticketing` folder:

```
<%
  values = (0..10).to_a
  options = options_from_collection_for_select(values,
           'to_i', 'to_s', 0)
%>
<h2>Select Movie Screening Time</h2>
<% form_tag(:action => 'payment_details') do -%>
<table >
  <tr valign='top'>
    <td width='150px'>
      <%= render :partial =>
          "/ticketing/movies/#{session[:movie].code}_pic"%>
    </td>
    <td>
      <%= render :partial =>
          "/ticketing/movies/#{session[:movie].code}_sypnosis"%>
      <p>Movie times</p>
      <div>
    AMC Van Ness 14 - San Francisco
      [<%= link_to '11:15 am', :action => :ticketing, :hour => '11',
        :min => '15', :duration => '90', :theater => 'AMC Van Ness 14
        - San Francisco'%>]
```

```
    [<%= link_to '1:15 pm', :action => :ticketing, :hour => '13',
        :min => '15', :duration => '90', :theater => 'AMC Van Ness 14
        - San Francisco'%>]
    [<%= link_to '5:30 pm', :action => :ticketing, :hour => '17',
        :min => '30', :duration => '90', :theater => 'AMC Van Ness 14
        - San Francisco'%>]
    [<%= link_to '9:15 pm', :action => :ticketing, :hour => '21',
        :min => '20', :duration => '90', :theater => 'AMC Van Ness 14
        - San Francisco'%>]
  </div>
  <div>
    Opera Plaza Cinemas - San Francisco
      [<%= link_to '11:15 am', :action => :ticketing, :hour =>
          '11', :min => '15', :duration => '90', :theater =>
          'AMC Van Ness 14 - San Francisco'%>]
      [<%= link_to '1:15 pm', :action => :ticketing, :hour => '13',
          :min => '15', :duration => '90', :theater =>
          'AMC Van Ness 14 - San Francisco'%>]
      [<%= link_to '5:30 pm', :action => :ticketing, :hour => '17',
          :min => '30', :duration => '90', :theater =>
          'AMC Van Ness 14 - San Francisco'%>]
      [<%= link_to '9:15 pm', :action => :ticketing, :hour => '21',
          :min => '20', :duration => '90', :theater =>
          'AMC Van Ness 14 - San Francisco'%>]
  </div>
  <div>
      <span> <%= link_to_unless request.env['HTTP_REFERER'].nil?,
                  'back', request.env['HTTP_REFERER'] %> </span>
  </div>
    </td>
  </tr>
</table>
<% end -%>
```

The movie times and theater are also hard-coded in this page. We will continue with the Bee Movie pages only from here.

This is how it looks:

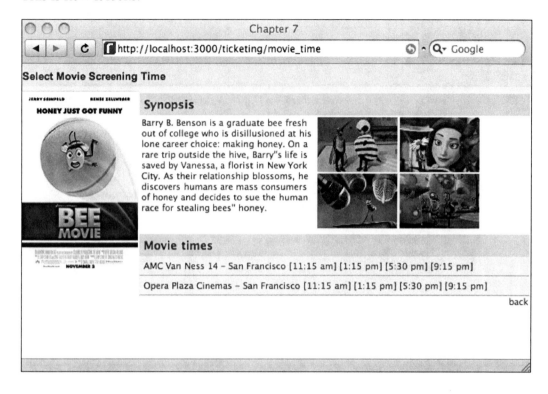

Selecting a movie theater and a screen time will re-direct the customer to choose the number and type of tickets that he or she wants to purchase. Create a `ticketing` method in the `ticketing_controller.rb` file:

```
def ticketing
  session[:movie].theater = params[:theater]
  session[:movie].time[:hour] = params[:hour]
  session[:movie].time[:min] = params[:min]
  session[:movie].duration = params[:duration]
end
```

Note how the `Movie` object in the session is updated with new information. Create the corresponding view template in the file `ticketing.rhtml` under the `RAILS_ROOT/app/views/ticketing` folder:

```
<%
  values = (0..10).to_a
  options = options_from_collection_for_select(values, 'to_i',
          'to_s', 0)
%>
```

```
<h2>Select Tickets</h2>
<% form_tag(:action => 'payment_details') do -%>
<table width="100%">
  <tr valign='top'>
    <td width='150px'>
      <%= render :partial =>
          "/ticketing/movies/#{session[:movie].code}_pic"%>
    </td>
    <td>
      <div>
       <div>Ticket<br>Type</div>
       <div>Ticket<br>Quantity</div>
       <div>Service*<br>Charge</div>
       <div>Ticket*<br>Price</div>
       <div> <br>Total*</div>
       <div></div>
      </div>
     <div>
      <div>
        <label>ADULT</label>
      <div>
        <%= select_tag 'adult_tix', options%>
       </div>
        <div>$0.00</div>
        <div>$0.00</div>
        <div>$0.00</div>
        <div></div>
       </div>
      <div>
        <label>CHILD</label>
      <div>
        <%= select_tag 'child_tix', options%>
       </div>
        <div>$0.00</div>
        <div>$0.00</div>
        <div>$0.00</div>
        <div></div>
       </div>
      <div>
        <label>SENIOR</label>
      <div>
        <%= select_tag 'senior_tix', options%>
      </div>
        <div>$0.00</div>
```

```
      <div>$0.00</div>
      <div>$0.00</div>
      <div></div>
    </div>
    <div>
      <div>Total</div> <span><%= link_to 'back', :action =>
          :movies %> <%= submit_tag 'continue'%></span>
      <div>$0.00</div>
      <div>$0.00</div>
      <div>$0.00</div>
      <div>$0.00</div>
      <div></div>
    </div>
  </div>
</td>
    </tr>
  </table>
<% end -%>
```

This is how the ticketing page looks (note, it is a dummy page and not a shopping cart—the real action takes place later in the chapter):

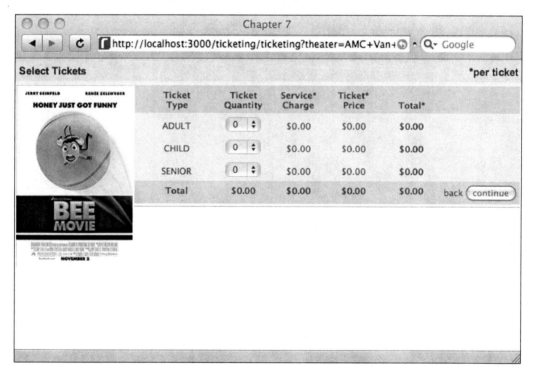

Now that we have all the information on the movie the customer wants to buy tickets for, we need to get the payment and other details from him or her. We will ask for these in a single payment details page. Create a method named `payment_details` in the `ticketing_controller.rb` file:

```
def payment_details
    session[:payment] = nil
end
```

This is a very simple method that will just show the `payment_details` view template. We will also remove any previous payment details information in the session. Now create the view template by adding a `payment_details.rhtml` file in the `RAILS_ROOT/app/views/ticketing` folder:

```
<%
  cards = %w(Visa Mastercard Amex Discover)
  card_options = options_from_collection_for_select(cards, 'to_s',
              'to_s', 'Visa')
%>
<h2 >Enter your Billing Information</h2>
<% form_tag(:action => 'confirm_payment') do -%>
<table width="100%">
  <tr valign='top'>
    <td width="150px">
      <%= render :partial =>
          "/ticketing/movies/#{session[:movie].code}_pic"%>
    </td>
    <td>
<div>
  <ul>
      <li>
        <label>First name:</label>
        <div><%= text_field_tag 'first_name'%></div>
        <label>Last name:</label>
        <div><%= text_field_tag 'last_name'%></div>
      </li>
      <li >
        <label>Credit Card Type:</label>
        <div>
          <%= select_tag 'card_type', card_options%>
        </div>
      </li>
      <li >
        <label>Card number:</label>
        <div>
```

```
      <%= text_field_tag 'card_no', '', :maxlength => 16%>
      <span>(no dashes or spaces)</span></div>
</li>
<li>
  <labelExp. Date:</label>
  <div>
  <%= select_month Date.today, :field_name => 'expdate_month'
      %>/<%= select_year Date.today, :start_year => 2007,
      :end_year => 2020, :field_name => 'expdate_year'%>
  </div>
  li>
    <li >
      <label>Billing Zip Code:</label>
        <div>
          <%= text_field_tag 'billing_zip', '', :maxlength =>
             8%>
        </div>
    </li>
  <li>
    <span><input  name="add_event" type="checkbox"></span>
    <label>Yes, I would like to add this as an event in my
          Google Calendar.</label>
  </li>
<li >
  <label>Google account:</label>
  <div><%= text_field_tag 'google_acct'%></div>
</li>
<li >
  <label>Google password:</label>
  <div><%= password_field_tag 'google_pwd'%></div>
</li>
<li >
  <label>Mobile no (to receive ticket confirmation):</label>
  <div><%= text_field_tag 'mobile_no'%></div>
</li>
<li >
  <label>Total:</label>
  <div>$10.00
  <%= hidden_field_tag 'amount', '10'%>
  </div>
</li>
<li >
  <span><%= link_to_unless request.env['HTTP_REFERER'].nil?,
          'back', request.env['HTTP_REFERER'] %> <%=
          submit_tag 'continue'%></span>
```

```
          </li>
    </ul>
          </div>
      </td>
    </tr>
  </table>
  <% end -%>
```

This is how the page looks:

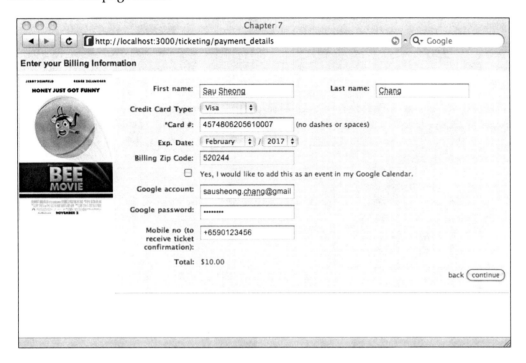

Note that the sample code in this chapter requires the customer to fill in all the information. In a real application, you would have required the user to register and log in first, perhaps even asked him or her to save details of a frequently used credit card in the database. You would also have stored his mobile phone number and details on his or her Google account, enough to add the event to his or her Calendar if he or she gave you prior permission.

Finally, we need to provide a page for the customer to review the information he or she has entered. Add a method `confirm_payment` in the `ticketing_controller.rb` file:

```
def confirm_payment
  if session[:payment].nil?
    payment = Payment.new
```

```
      payment.first_name = params[:first_name]
      payment.last_name = params[:last_name]
      payment.card_type = params[:card_type]
      payment.card_no = params[:card_no]
      payment.exp_date = {:month => params[:date][:expdate_month],
                           :year => params[:date][:expdate_year]}
      payment.billing_zip = params[:billing_zip]
      payment.google_acct = params[:google_acct]
      payment.google_pwd = params[:google_pwd]
      payment.mobile_no = params[:mobile_no]
      payment.amount = params[:amount]
      session[:payment] = payment
  end
end
```

As before, we create a Payment object to store the information entered by the customer then place it into the session. Create a file `confirm_payment.rhtml` in the `RAILS_ROOT/app/views/ticketing` folder to display all the fields in the session that we have just stored:

```
<h2>Confirm details</h2>
<% form_tag(:action => 'process_payment') do -%>
<table width="100%">
  <tr valign='top'>
    <td width="150px">
<%= render :partial =>
    "/ticketing/movies/#{session[:movie].code}_pic"%>
    </td>
    <td>
<div>
    <ul>
        <li>
          <label>Movie:</label>
          <div><%= session[:movie].name %></div>
        </li>
        <li>
          <label>Screening date:</label>
          <div><%= session[:movie].date[:day] %>/<%=
                   session[:movie].date[:month] %>/<%=
                   session[:movie].date[:year] %></div>
        </li>
        <li>
          <label>Screening time:</label>
          <div><%= session[:movie].time[:hour] %>:<%=
                   session[:movie].time[:min] %></div>
```

```
      </li>
      <li>
        <label>Theater:</label>
        <div><%= session[:movie].theater%></div>
      </li>
      <li>
        <label>Tickets:</label>
        <div>2 adults, 2 children, 1 senior</div>
      </li>
    </ul>
  <hr/>
  <ul>
      <li>
        <label>Name:</label>
        <div><%= session[:payment].first_name%> <%=
                session[:payment].last_name%></div>
      </li>
      <li>
        <label>Credit Card Type:</label>
        <div>
          <%= session[:payment].card_type%>
        </div>
      </li>
      <li>
        <label>Credit Card Number:</label>
        <div><%= session[:payment].card_no%></div>
      </li>
      <li>
        <label>Exp. Date:</label>
        <div>
          <%= session[:payment].exp_date[:month]%>/<%=
              session[:payment].exp_date[:year]%>
        </div>
      </li>
          <li>
            <label>Billing Zip Code:</label>
            <div><%= session[:payment].billing_zip%></div>
          </li>
      <li>
        label>Google account:</label>
        <div><%= session[:payment].google_acct%></div>
      </li>
      <li>
        <label>Mobile no:</label>
```

```
        <div><%= session[:payment].mobile_no%></div>
      </li>
      <li>
        <label>Total:</label>
        <div>$<%= session[:payment].amount%></div>
      </li>
      <li>
        <span><%= link_to_unless request.env['HTTP_REFERER'].nil?,
                'back', request.env['HTTP_REFERER'] %> <%= submit_tag
                'submit payment'%></span>
      </li>
   </ul>
</div>
    </td>
  </tr>
</table>
<% end -%>
```

This is what the confirmation page looks like:

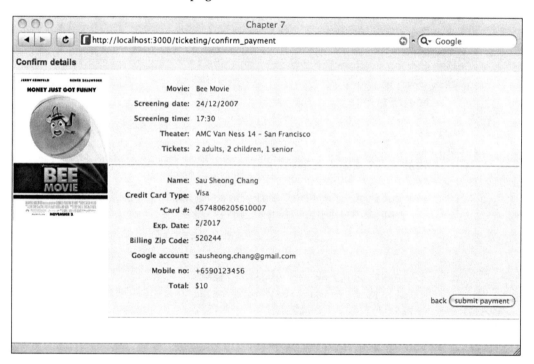

This concludes the basic flow to acquire enough information from the customer to begin the main processing. Finally, before we proceed to the integration with the mashup APIs, we need to create a method that will tie in all the integrations. Create a method called `process_payment` in the `ticketing_controller.rb` file:

```
def process_payment
  if do_payment.ack == 'Success' then
    send_sms
    add_to_calendar
  end
end
```

Note that there are three private methods called here. The first performs the payment transaction and we read its response to see if it is successful before continuing to send the SMS ticket and also adding to the Google Calendar. Finally, create a simple view template to show the success (or failure) of the payment processing. Create a file called `process_payment.rhtml` in the `RAILS_ROOT/app/views/ticketing` folder, and add a message of your choosing.

Next, we'll look into each integration in turn.

Integrating with PayPal for payment

The first integration with the mashup API is with PayPal. For this, we will use my Ruby-PayPal library, found in `http://rubyforge.org/projects/ruby-paypal`. To install it, type the following at a command prompt:

```
$gem install ruby-paypal
```

This library provides a simple wrapper around the PayPal NVP APIs and will provide us with the method calls to access the PayPal payment gateway. For this chapter we will be using Direct Payment only, which allows merchants with a PayPal business account to accept credit card payments through PayPal.

In this chapter we will be using the Sandbox test server and payment accounts provided by PayPal once you register with PayPal as a developer. Registration provides you with a merchant account as well as two test customer accounts with simulated credit card and PayPal accounts.

To process the credit card payment from the customer, we need to have the following information from the customer:

- Card type
- Card number
- CVV2

- Expiry date
- IP address of the customer making the request
- Payment amount
- Customer's first name
- Customer's last name

The CVV (Card Verification Value) is a security feature in credit and debit cards for preventing credit card fraud. CVV1 is encoded in the magstripe of the card and used during transactions in person. CVV2 is used when the card is not present with the merchant for example over the Internet, by mail or fax or phone. The CVV2 is not encoded in the magstripe and is usually printed on the back signature panel of the card.

Although the CVV2 value is not mandatory in the NVP API documentation, we will need it in a real production environment as PayPal will need it to do a CVV2 check. However you are not allowed to store CVV2. In this chapter, since we're using the Sandbox and the Sandbox ignores CVV2 (unless it is set to '000' in which case an error is returned), we will not use CVV2.

The card type must be of one of the few values supported by PayPal, which are Visa, Mastercard, American Express, Discover, Switch, and Solo. Switch and Solo are UK debit cards and require the currency to be in British pounds and the payment action to be authorization only (not final sale). In this sample application we will be using perhaps the most commonly used credit card at the moment, Visa.

The card number is the credit or debit card number. Although PayPal verifies the authenticity of the number that is sent, the Ruby-PayPal library also uses the Luhn algorithm and checks for the validity of the credit card number before sending it to PayPal's NVP API. The Luhn algorithm is a simple public domain checksum algorithm that is used for verifying ISO 7812 numbers. For more information on the Luhn algorithm please visit http://en.wikipedia.org/wiki/Luhn_algorithm.

Credit card numbers are a special type of ISO 7812 numbers and share a common numbering scheme. The first 6 digits of a credit card number is known as the Bank Identification Number (BIN) and they share a similar pattern. For example, all Visa card numbers start with the number 4 and all Mastercard card numbers start with number 51, 52, 53, 54, or 55. A simple check on such rules will provide a quick turnaround telling you if the card entered is valid or not. The Ruby-PayPal library also provides this simple check. For more information on credit card numbers you can visit http://en.wikipedia.org/wiki/Credit_card_number.

The expiry date is an important part of the credit card information as it tells us not only if the credit card has expired but can also be used to identify validity of the card. The format for the expiry date is MMYYYY where MM is a 2-digit string representing the month (with a leading 0 if necessary) and YYYY is a 4-digit string representing the year.

The IP address is the IP address of where the customer logs in. PayPal uses this as a means to detect fraud but you can use any valid IP address as an input.

The payment amount is the final amount to be paid by the customer, including any applicable taxes, shipping costs, and so on. This amount cannot exceed US $ 10,000 in any currency and the input format uses a dot ('.') as a decimal separator and a comma (',') as the optional thousands separator. If you read the NVP APIs you will notice a number of 'amount' fields like tax amount, item amount, shipping amount, handling amount, and so on. These amounts all add up to the final amount field and are optional.

The first and last name fields are 25-character long strings that represent the customer's first and last name respectively but there is no check on these fields.

The PayPal APIs for accepting credit card transactions are called the Direct Payment APIs and there are two ways of accepting payment in Direct Payment:

- The first is to do a final sale where the merchant is requesting full and final payment. To request a final sale, use the `do_direct_payment_sale` method.
- The second is to do an authorization of the payment request where the initial call is for the authorization of payment. Subsequently, the payment can be captured in separate request or requests.

In this chapter, we will do the simpler single transaction for final sale.

With the explanation above, let's create the method to process PayPal transactions. Add in the `require` statement at the beginning of the `ticketing_controller.rb` file to use the PayPal library:

```
require 'ruby-paypal'
```

Then create a new private method in the `ticketing_controller.rb` file:

```
def do_payment
    paypal = Paypal.new('<merchant_username>', '<merchant_password>',
            '<merchant_API_signature>')
    ipaddr = request.remote_ip
    amount = session[:payment].amount
    card_type = session[:payment].card_type
    card_no = session[:payment].card_no
```

```
month = session[:payment].exp_date[:month].to_i < 10 ? "0" +
    session[:payment].exp_date[:month] : session[:payment].
    exp_date[:month]
exp_date = "#{month}#{session[:payment].exp_date[:year]}"
first_name = session[:payment].first_name
last_name = session[:payment].last_name
#call direct payment for final sale and return a paypal response
    object return paypal.do_direct_payment_sale(ipaddr, amount,
    card_type, card_no, exp_date, first_name, last_name)
end
```

The first line creates the Paypal object that allows us to interact with the PayPal NVP APIs. The Ruby-PayPal library only supports the API signature method of establishing API credentials. By default the Ruby PayPal library connects to the Sandbox. In production mode, you can change the URL for the PayPal server by providing the URL as the fourth parameter to the Paypal object constructor method.

The last line calls the `do_direct_payment_sale` method, which in turn sends a request to PayPal to do a final sale direct payment with the various pieces of information we have gathered along the way.

The API responds with a `PayPalResponse` object that contains a standard set of information including:

- Acknowledgement status (ACK)
- Timestamp
- Version
- Build number
- Correlation ID (a debugging token)

If the ACK field is 'Error' additional fields describing the error are also provided. For Direct Payment we will also get the following additional information in the response:

- Amount (the same amount that has been sent in the method call)
- Address Verification System (AVS) system code
- Result of the CVV2 check by PayPal
- A unique Transaction ID of the payment transaction

The Address Verification System (AVS) is a system used to verify a credit card by checking the billing address of the credit card provided by the user with the address on file at the credit card company. AVS for Visa and Mastercard is used in very few countries (mostly in the US, Canada, and UK) though American Express uses AVS in more countries. AVS is only important if you have entered a billing address for the credit card.

PayPal also does a CVV2 check on our behalf if we submit the CVV2. However, if the transaction returns a 'Success' in the ACK field, there is normally no need to inspect CVV2 or AVS return codes. We would only inspect these codes if the returned ACK field is 'SuccessWithWarning' or 'Error'.

Note that for this chapter we have conveniently used PayPal for processing credit card payment from customers. In a real application, you are not allowed to only use Direct Payment without Express Checkout. This is because the following business rules of using PayPal Website Payment Pro need to be applied:

- Merchants need to present Express Checkout and associate messaging before asking for billing and shipping information.

- Merchants need to display PayPal as a payment option alongside other payment options if offered.

- Merchants need to show the PayPal graphic along with other payment graphics where applicable (for example, if we have shown the Visa graphic we need to show the PayPal graphic).

Integrating with Google Calendar

Next in line is the mashup with Google Calendar. The integration is relatively simple using the GoogleCalendar library and consists of two steps:

- Logging into GData services

- Adding a new Google Calendar event

First, add the `require` line at the top of the `ticketing_controller.rb` file:

```
require 'googlecalendar'
```

Then create a private method called `add_to_calendar` in `ticketing_controller.rb`:

```
def add_to_calendar
    gcal = GData.new
    #authenticate
    account = session[:payment].google_acct
    password = session[:payment].google_pwd
    gcal.login(account, password)
    #add new event
    time_start = Time.mktime(session[:movie].date[:year],
                             session[:movie].date[:month],
                             session[:movie].date[:day],
                             session[:movie].time[:hour],
                             session[:movie].time[:min])
    time_end = time_start +
```

```
                       (session[:movie].duration.to_i * 60)
      event =
        { :title=> "Watch movie #{session[:movie].name}",
          :content=> "Watch movie #{session[:movie].name}",
          :author=> "#{session[:payment].first_name}
                    #{ session[:payment].last_name }",
          :email=> session[:payment].google_acct,
          :where=> session[:movie].theater,
          :startTime =>
              time_start.utc.strftime('%Y-%m-%dT%H:%M:%SZ'),
          :endTime =>
              time_end.utc.strftime('%Y-%m-%dT%H:%M:%SZ') }
      gcal.new_event(event)
    end
```

We first log into GData services using the `login` method and this gives us an authenticated GData object. Next, we use this GData object and add a new event into the primary calendar using `new_event` and passing a hash of parameters into it.

This is what the customer's primary Google calendar looks like after you have added in a new event:

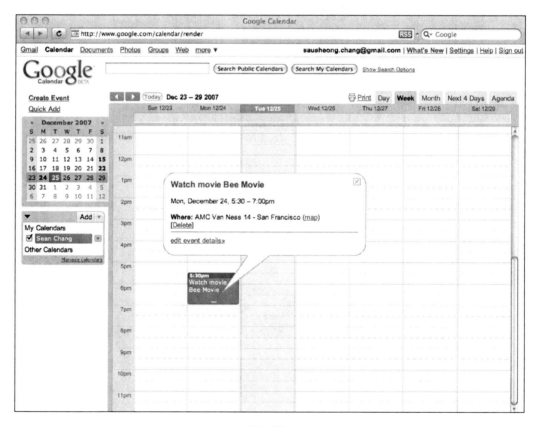

Integrating with Clickatell

Finally, we integrate sending an SMS ticket using Clickatell. As with Chapter 3, we will use Clickatell as the SMS gateway to send the SMS ticket. In Chapter 3 we used Clickatell directly from HTTP but in this chapter we will extract a simple Clickatell library into the RAILS_ROOT/lib folder and use it from the Ticketing controller.

Create a file called sms.rb in the RAILS_ROOT/lib folder:

```
class SMS
  def initialize(login,password,api_id)
    res = Net::HTTP.post_form(
        URI.parse('http://api.clickatell.com/http/auth'),
                 {'api_id' => api_id,
                  'user'=> login,
                  'password' => password})
    case res
    when Net::HTTPSuccess, Net::HTTPRedirection
      @clickatell_session_id = res.body.split(': ')[1]
    else
      puts res.error!
    end
  end
  def send(message, mobile_no)
    begin
      res = Net::HTTP.post_form(
        URI.parse('http://api.clickatell.com/http/sendmsg'),
                 {'session_id' => @clickatell_session_id,
                  'cliMsgId' => 'Chapter7',
                  'to'=> mobile_no,
                  'from' => '<a valid sender ID>',
                  'text' =>  message,
                  'callback' => '3',
                  'deliv_ack' => '1',
                  'req_feat' => '8192' })
      case res
      when Net::HTTPSuccess, Net::HTTPRedirection
        return true
      else
        return false
      end
    rescue
      puts "## Cannot send sms : #{$!}"
    end
  end
end
```

This is very similar to the code we have used in Chapter 3 except that we require that the user logs in before sending the SMS every time. Obviously this is not efficient and in a production environment this code should be re-factored to store the Clickatell session for a period of time before expiring and requiring re-authentication.

In the `ticketing_controller.rb` file, add the following `send_sms` method to send the ticket:

```
def send_sms
    sms = SMS.new('<Clickatell user name>', '<Clickatell password>',
        '<Clickatell API ID>')
    message = "You have bought 3 tickets for #{session[:movie].
            name} at #{session[:movie].theater} on #{session[:
            movie].date[:day]}/#{session[:movie].date[:
            month]}/#{session[:movie].date[:year]} #{session[:
            movie].time[:hour]}:#{session[:movie].time[:min]}. Your
            seat numbers are S10 to S13. Enjoy your movie!"
    sms.send(message, session[:payment].mobile_no)
    end
```

As mentioned, we will need to log in every time before sending the SMS ticket. Note that this method hard-coded the seat numbers, which in a realistic scenario the ticketing system will generate. We have also hard-coded the number of tickets bought for simplicity.

Summary

We have created a simple online event ticketing process flow and replaced a few components of the flow with mashup APIs to show the viability of re-using such functions with mashup APIs. First, we integrated with PayPal to provide payment processing for the ticket that was bought. Next we used Google Calendar and added a new event into the customer's primary calendar. Finally we sent the ticket as an SMS to the customer.

8
Expenses claims mashup plugin

What does it do?

This mashup allows an employee to submit expenses claims in Google Docs and Spreadsheets, and attach the claims form as well as the supporting receipts. His or her manager, also using Google Docs and Spreadsheets, then approves the expenses claims and they are retrieved by the mashup and used to reimburse the employee through PayPal.

Salary and expense claims

Most online payment applications relate to buying something off the Internet so sometimes we tend to forget purchase and sale is not the only payment-related transaction. One of the most common payment transactions is the salary, which is a periodic payment paid by the employer to an employee and specified in an employment contract.

Another form of payment particularly common in the corporate world is the expenses claim. Expenses claims are claims for reimbursement of expenses incurred during the course of an employee's duties. Claim reimbursement payments are also paid periodically.

This mashup describes how an online payment system like PayPal can be used for these payment types and how a typical expense claims process can be automated through Google Docs and Spreadsheets and integrated into the payment process.

Requirements overview

The expense claims web mashup plugin enhances an HR management application by extending the expense claims capabilities through a well-known interface. Most salaried workers who claim expenses are familiar with the process of expense claims, which normally involves filling up forms and attaching evidence receipts. These claim submissions are then routed to their managers who in turn approve or reject them accordingly. Approved claims are vetted and archived for audit purposes, while the reimbursement payment is done at the end of the month.

Design

This mashup is slightly different from most of the other mashups in this book because the user interface in this mashup is minimal. The main bulk of processing is within a rake script that runs periodically.

This is the flow of the mashup:

1. The employee creates and fills up an expense claim spreadsheet in Google Docs and Spreadsheets.

2. He or she also attaches the expense evidence (i.e. expense receipts) into a word processor document in Google Docs and Spreadsheets.

3. The employee then shares these two documents with his or her manager for approval.

4. Upon receiving the shared documents, the manager will approve or reject the expense claim. Rejection is out of scope in this mashup, and in most cases verbally disputed and out of most systems.

5. If the manager approves the claim, he or she will place it into an `approved-claims` folder.

6. At regular intervals (once a week or once a moth) a rake script will be automatically run to retrieve all the claim documents in the `approved-claims` folder.

7. The script parses the spreadsheets to retrieve the claim details and amount and stores the evidence in a word processor document in the database.

8. Using the claim amounts the script creates a set of claims payments in PayPal.

9. After the expense claims spreadsheet is parsed, it is removed from the manager and placed into his or her trashbin.

10. At the end of the month, another rake script runs to send the salary and claims payments to all the employees.

We will be creating a Payment class for this mashup. This class represents a payment to the employee. The information in this class will be used to trigger the actual payment of funds through PayPal. There are two types of payments; one is the monthly salary and the other is the monthly expense claim reimbursement. In our mashup we will subclass Payment into a Salary and Claim class respectively and use a Single-Table Inheritance design built-in with Rails. Each expense claim would normally come with a few claims items bundled into one, so a Claim object will in turn contain one or more Claim Item objects.

The employee is not mapped in the system but we will need a Manager class to manage the manager's accounts.

Mashup APIs on the menu

The two main mashup APIs we will be using in this chapter are PayPal and Google. For Google we will be using four different mashup APIs within Google, all of which falls under the Google Data APIs family.

PayPal

PayPal is an Internet-based financial services company that provides payment and money transfer services through the Internet. PayPal also offers products for online merchants to accept payment over the Internet.

Mass Payment

The API we will be using in PayPal is the Mass Payment API. The Mass Payment API is an API that allows you to send payments to up to 250 recipients with a single API call. However, unlike the other payment APIs in PayPal, the sender pays for the transaction. The current transaction fee for Mass Payment is 2% per payment, with a maximum of $1.00 per payment.

The Mass Payment API is available in Website Payment Pro through either the Name-Value Pair (NVP) APIs or the SOAP APIs. In this chapter we will be using the Ruby-PayPal library that wraps around the NVP APIs. More details on the PayPal NVP library can be found in Chapter 7.

PayPal Sandbox

The PayPal Sandbox is a self-contained environment in which developers can prototype and test PayPal applications. The Sandbox simulates almost every function available in the actual PayPal environment. We will be using the Sandbox to simulate our salary and expense claims mashup. Details on how to acquire an account in the PayPal Sandbox are found in Chapter 7.

Google

Google is an Internet-based company that provides a number of useful online services, many of which are also accessible through mashup APIs. In this mashup we will be using four different Google APIs:

- Google Account Authentication APIs
- Google Data APIs
- Google Document List Data APIs
- Google Spreadsheet Data APIs

Google Account Authentication

This set of APIs allows third-party applications to authenticate to Google APIs. There are currently two ways of authenticating a third-party application:

1. Using the ClientLogin API (which is mostly for desktop applications, and for which you need to have access to the user's login credentials)
2. Using the AuthSub API (which is for web applications and for which you are not required to have the user's login credentials)

In this mashup we will be using the ClientLogin API because we are running it from a rake script.

Google Data APIs

The Google Data APIs provide a simple, standard protocol for reading and writing data to and from Google services. Google Data API uses the XML-based Atom 1.0 and RSS 2.0 syndication formats as well as the Atom Publishing Protocol.

To get data from the service, you need to send an HTTP `Get` request to the service. To update data, you send an HTTP `Put` request and to delete data you send an HTTP `Delete` request. Data that is returned is in either a RSS or Atom feed.

The Google Data API is the basis on which we use the other two sets of Google APIs in this mashup — the Google Document Data List APIs and the Google Spreadsheet Data APIs.

Google Document Data List APIs

The Google Documents List Data API allows third-party applications to access documents stored in Google Docs using Google Data API feeds. For our purposes we will use the Google Documents List Data API to search for spreadsheets in the approved-claims folder, as well as to retrieve the word processor document as a PDF document.

Google Spreadsheet Data APIs

The Google Spreadsheets Data API allows third-party applications to view and update spreadsheets in Google spreadsheet using Google Data API feeds. For this mashup we will be using this API to get data off the expense claim spreadsheet and populate a payment database.

Ruby-PayPal library

The Ruby-PayPal library (`http://rubyforge.org/projects/ruby-paypal`) is a lightweight wrapper library around the PayPal NVP APIs. It provides basic validation support for input into PayPal NVP APIs to reduce processing time if the input is erroneous. It also provides interpretation to the response from PayPal and an easy interface for Ruby developers.

To install it, type the following at a command prompt:

```
$gem install ruby-paypal
```

In Chapter 7, we used it for Direct Payment for accepting credit card payment from cardholders. In this chapter we will use it for Mass Payment to reimburse expenses claimed by employees.

Acts_as_state_machine plugin

While not strictly necessary for this mashup, we will also be using the `acts_as_state_machine` plugin to make the Payment class behave as a state machine. This useful plugin relieves us of writing a lot of code to simulate the state changes in Payment objects.

To install the plugin, go to the `$RAILS_ROOT` folder and run this command at the console:

```
$./script/plugin install
http://elitists.textdriven.com/svn/plugins/acts_as_state_machine/trunk/
```

This copies the plugin into your `$RAILS_ROOT/vendor/plugin` folder and you're ready to go.

XmlSimple

XmlSimple (`http://xml-simple.rubyforge.org/`) is a Ruby API that allows XML formatted data to be easily read and written to. It is a Ruby translation of the Perl module XML::Simple and is written on top of REXML, an XML parser that is included in the Ruby distribution.

To install XmlSimple, run this at the command line:

```
$gem install xml-simple
```

As in Chapter 5, we will use XmlSimple to read in an XML response (in this case an ATOM feed) that is sent by the API and convert the XML into a nested hash.

What we will be doing

The following section describes the steps we will be taking to create the mashup. The basic steps are:

1. Create a Rails application
2. Set up the database
3. Create the Payment and Claim Item scaffolds
4. Modify Payment and create its subclasses
5. Create the Google API access library
6. Create the Manager class and its controller and views
7. Create the expense claims parsing rake script
8. Create the mass payment rake script
9. Modify the Payment and Claim Item controllers

Creating a Rails application

We begin this mashup as before by creating the usual Rails application.

`$rails Chapter8`

This will create a new Ruby on Rails application. We will not be using most of its interface but will be running the rake scripts located in the $RAILS_ROOT/lib/tasks folder. Running the scripts should be automated at a regular interval.

Setting up the database

Next, we will set up the database for this chapter with a data migration script. I assume that you have already created a database and set up the database access correctly. First, create the migration script using the built-in generator by running the following at the command line:

`$./script/generate migration create_payments`

This will create a file 001_create_payments.rb in the db/migrate folder:

```
class CreatePayments < ActiveRecord::Migration
  def self.up
    create_table :payments do |t|
      t.column 'type', :string, :default =>
            'salary' # either salary or claims
      t.column 'name', :string
      t.column 'description', :string
      t.column 'email', :string
      t.column 'amount', :float
      t.column 'state', :string, :default =>
            'pending' # states are pending, suspended and paid
      t.column 'expense_evidence', :binary, :limit => 10.megabytes
      t.column 'created_on', :datetime
      t.column 'updated_on', :datetime
    end
    create_table :claim_items do |t|
      t.column 'claim_id', :integer
      t.column 'expense_date', :date
      t.column 'project', :string
      t.column 'item', :string
      t.column 'remarks', :string
      t.column 'created_on', :datetime
      t.column 'amount', :float
    end
  end
```

```
    def self.down
      drop_table :payments
      drop_table :claim_items
    end
  end
```

Note that the `payments` table contains data for both `Salary` and `Claim` as we're using the single table inheritance design. Also note that the `claim_items` table's foreign key is `claim_id` and not `payment_id`. We also placed a binary field in the `payments` table to store the data for the word processor document.

Now that you have the migration script, run `migrate` to create the tables:

$rake db:migrate

Creating the Payment and Claim Item scaffolds

Next, create the Payment and Claim scaffolds with the following command:

$./script/generate scaffold Payment

and:

$./script/generate scaffold ClaimItem

This will generate the necessary files that we will modify for later usage.

Modifying Payment and creatomg subclasses

We will use the `acts_as_state_machine` plugin to make `Payment` a state machine. Modify the `payment.rb` file in the `$RAILS_ROOT/app/models` folder.

```
class Payment < ActiveRecord::Base
  acts_as_state_machine :initial => :pending
  state :pending, :enter => :add_to_account_payable
  state :paid, :enter => :log_payment
  state :suspended
  event :pay do
    transitions :from => :pending, :to => :paid
  end
  event :suspend do
    transitions :from => :pending, :to => :suspended
  end
  event :unsuspend do
```

```
      transitions :from => :suspended, :to => :pending
    end
    def add_to_account_payable
      # hook up with accounts system to record expense in account payable
    end
    def log_payment
      # hook up with accounts system to log actual payment
    end
  end
```

This maps to a Payment object that it created and initialized to the pending state. Each event maps to a method that transitions the state of the object. For example by calling:

```
payment.pay!
```

The event `pay` is triggered and this transitions the payment from the `pending` state to the `paid` state. In turn, as the `paid` state is entered, the `log_payment` method is called to log this payment to the account payable in the company's accounting system.

Then, subclass the Payment class into Salary and Claim classes. Both classes need to be created as separate files in the `$RAILS_ROOT/app/models` folder:

```
class Salary < Payment
end
```

and:

```
class Claim < Payment has_many :claim_items
end
```

Creating the Google API access library

We have the models now but unlike in the previous chapters, the next step is not to create the views but to populate the database. To do this, we will first parse the expense claims in Google Docs and Spreadsheets. We will need to create a library that accesses Google Data and extracts the necessary information for us.

Create a library file named `gdata.rb` in the `$RAILS_ROOT/lib` folder:

```
require 'net/http'
require 'net/https'
require 'open-uri'
require 'xmlsimple'
GOOGLE_CLIENT_LOGIN_URL = 'www.google.com/accounts/ClientLogin'
GOOGLE_DOCS_URL = 'docs.google.com'
GOOGLE_SPREADSHEETS_URL = 'spreadsheets.google.com'
```

```ruby
SPREADSHEET_CATEGORY = {"term"=>"http://schemas.google.com/docs/
2007#spreadsheet",
  "scheme"=>"http://schemas.google.com/g/2005#kind",
  "label"=>"spreadsheet"}
# convenience module to use HTTP (mainly used for login)
module Net
  class HTTPS < HTTP
    def initialize(address, port = nil)
      super(address, port)
      self.use_ssl = true
    end
  end
end
class GData
  def login(email, password)
    @user_id = email
    gdoc_params = { 'Email' => email,
      'Passwd' => password,
      'source' => 'saush-gdocs-01',
      'accountType' => 'HOSTED_OR_GOOGLE',
      'service' => 'writely'
    }
    gss_params = { 'Email' => email,
      'Passwd' => password,
      'source' => 'saush-gss-01',
      'accountType' => 'HOSTED_OR_GOOGLE',
      'service' => 'wise'
    }
    gdoc_response = Net::HTTPS.post_form(
      URI.parse("https://#{GOOGLE_CLIENT_LOGIN_URL}"),
      gdoc_params)
    gdoc_response.error! unless gdoc_response.kind_of?
      Net::HTTPSuccess
    @gdoc_token = gdoc_response.body.split(/=/).last
    gss_response = Net::HTTPS.post_form(
      URI.parse("https://#{GOOGLE_CLIENT_LOGIN_URL}"),
      gss_params)
    gss_response.error! unless gss_response.kind_of?
      Net::HTTPSuccess
    @gss_token = gss_response.body.split(/=/).last
  end
  # Get a Google Docs feed
  def gdoc_feed(feed)
    results = ''
```

```
      open("http://" + GOOGLE_DOCS_URL + feed, 'Authorization' =>
          "GoogleLogin auth=#{@gdoc_token}") { |s|
        results = XmlSimple::xml_in(s.read, 'force_array' => false)
      }
      return results
    end
    # Get a Google Spreadsheets feed
    def gss_feed(feed)
      results = ''
      open("http://" + GOOGLE_SPREADSHEETS_URL + feed, 'Authorization'
          => "GoogleLogin auth=#{@gss_token}") { |s|
        results = XmlSimple::xml_in(s.read, 'force_array' => false)
      }
      return results
    end
    # returns all spreadsheets in a given folder
    # returns an array of GSpreadsheet objects
def spreadsheets_in_folder(folder)
    feed = gdoc_feed("/feeds/documents/private/full/-
          /%7Bhttp:%2F%2Fschemas.google.com%2Fdocs%2F2007%2Ffolders%
          2F#{@user_id}%7D#{folder}")
    spreadsheets = []
    spreadsheet_data = []
    if feed['totalResults'].to_i > 1 then
      spreadsheet_data = spreadsheet_data + feed['entry']
    else
      spreadsheet_data = spreadsheet_data << feed['entry']
    end
    spreadsheet_data.each { |doc|
      if doc['category'].include? SPREADSHEET_CATEGORY then
        ss = Spreadsheet.new
        ss.title = doc['title']['content']
        ss.author = doc['author']['name']
        ss.spreadsheet_id = doc['id']
        doc['link'].each { |link|
          case link['rel']
          when "http://schemas.google.com/spreadsheets/
              2006#worksheetsfeed"
            # hack to overcome bug in Google Spreadsheets http://
              code.google.com/p/gdata-issues/issues/detail?id=321
            wks_link =  link['href'].sub "trix.", ""
            ss.worksheets = get_worksheets_from(wks_link)
          when "alternate"
            ss.link = link['href']
          when "edit"
```

```ruby
            ss.edit_link = link['href']
          end
        }
        ss.updated_on = doc['updated']
        spreadsheets << ss
      end
    }
    return spreadsheets
  end
  # get a list of worksheets in this spreadsheet
  def get_worksheets_from(worksheetfeed)
    uri = URI.parse worksheetfeed
    worksheets = []
    feed = gss_feed(uri.path)
    if feed['totalResults'].to_i > 1 then
      feed['entry'].each {|ws|
        worksheets << populate_worksheet(ws)
      }
    else
      worksheets << populate_worksheet(feed['entry'])
    end
    return worksheets
  end
  # populate a Worksheet object from a feed
  def populate_worksheet(data)
    ws = Worksheet.new
    ws.title = data['title']['content']
    ws.row_count = data['rowCount']
    ws.col_count = data['colCount']
    ws.worksheet_id = data['id']
    data['link'].each { |link|
      case link['rel']
      when "http://schemas.google.com/spreadsheets/2006#listfeed"
        ws.rows = get_rows(link['href'])
      when "edit"
        ws.edit_link = link['href']
      end
    }
    return ws
  end
  # get row data from list feed
  def get_rows(listfeed)
    uri = URI.parse listfeed
    rows = []
```

```
    feed = gss_feed(uri.path)
    if feed['totalResults'].to_i > 1 then
      feed['entry'].each { |row|
        rows << Row.new.merge(row)
      }
    elsif  feed['totalResults'].to_i == 1 then
      rows << Row.new.merge(feed['entry'])
    end
    return rows
  end
  def get_pdf_document(docid)
    results = ''
    url = "http://docs.google.com/MiscCommands?command=saveasdoc&exp
         ortformat=pdf&docID=#{docid}"
    open(url, 'Authorization' => "GoogleLogin auth=#{@gdoc_token}")
{ |s|
      results = s.read
    }
    return results
  end
  # delete the spreadsheet
  def delete(spreadsheet)
    url = URI.parse(spreadsheet.edit_link)
    res = Net::HTTP.new(url.host, url.port).start {|http| http.
         delete(url.path, 'Authorization' => "GoogleLogin auth=#{@
         gdoc_token}") }
    case res
    when Net::HTTPSuccess, Net::HTTPRedirection
      return true
    else
      return false
    end
  end
end
# Models a Google spreadsheet
class Spreadsheet
  attr_accessor :title, :author, :spreadsheet_id,
                :worksheets, :link, :edit_link,
                :updated_on
end
# Models a worksheet in a spreadsheet under Google Spreadsheets
  class Worksheet
  attr_accessor :title, :row_count, :col_count,
                :worksheet_id, :rows, :edit_link
end
```

```ruby
# Models a row in a worksheet, in a spreadsheet under Google
# Spreadsheets
class Row < Hash
  def method_missing(m,*a)
    if m.to_s.upcase =~ /=$/
      self[$`] = a[0]
    elsif a.empty?
      self[m.to_s]
    else
      raise NoMethodError, "#{m}"
    end
  end
end
```

This is a pretty long library but it is the heart of the code that extracts information from the Google spreadsheet so we will work through it step by step.

Before we begin, you should know that Google Docs and Spreadsheets are actually a few applications rolled into one, namely the Docs, Spreadsheets, and Presentations applications. For this mashup we will focus only on the Docs and Spreadsheets applications. Both Docs and Spreadsheets are accessed through different URLs and different APIs though there is some interchangeability through the Google Data APIs.

First, we create a convenience module to access HTTPS as the login to Google APIs is through HTTPS only. Next, we create the main GData class, which houses all the Google data parsing methods. The first method we need though, is the login method:

```ruby
def login(email, pwd)
    @user_id = email
    gdoc_params = { 'Email' => email,
      'Passwd' => pwd,
      'source' => 'saush-gdocs-01',
      'accountType' => 'HOSTED_OR_GOOGLE',
      'service' => 'writely'
    }
    gss_params = { 'Email' => email,
      'Passwd' => pwd,
      'source' => 'saush-gss-01',
      'accountType' => 'HOSTED_OR_GOOGLE',
      'service' => 'wise'
    }
    gdoc_response = Net::HTTPS.post_form(URI.parse("https://
                #{GOOGLE_URL}/accounts/ClientLogin"), gdoc_params)
```

```
gdoc_response.error! unless gdoc_response.kind_of? Net::
    HTTPSuccess
@gdoc_token = gdoc_response.body.split(/=/).last
gss_response = Net::HTTPS.post_form(URI.parse("https://#{GOOGLE_
    URL}/accounts/ClientLogin"), gss_params)
gss_response.error! unless gss_response.kind_of? Net::
    HTTPSuccess
@gss_token = gss_response.body.split(/=/).last
end
```

This method allows us to log in through Google Account Authentication APIs to access the Google Document Data List and the Google Spreadsheet Data APIs. In this mashup we will be using the ClientLogin API. This means that we will be sending an HTTP Post request to `https://www.google.com/accounts/ClientLogin` with the following required parameters, requesting an authentication token.

Parameter	Description
accountType	This is the type of account to be authenticated. Possible values are:
	• GOOGLE (authenticate as a Google account)
	• HOSTED (authenticate as a hosted account i.e. accounts hosted on Google)
	• HOSTED_OR_GOOGLE (authenticate first as a hosted account; if attempt fails, authenticate as a Google account)
	For our mashup we will be using HOSTED_OR_GOOGLE.
Email	The user's full email address.
Passwd	The user's password.
Service	Name of the Google service that is requested. For Google Docs the service name is `writely`; for Google Spreadsheets the service name is `wise`.
Source	This is a string identifying our application, for logging purposes.

The response from Google comes in a form like this:

```
HTTP/1.0 200 OK
Server: GFE/1.3
Content-Type: text/plain
SID=DQAAAGgA...7Zg8CTN
LSID=DQAAAGsA...1k8BBbG
Auth=DQAAAGgA...dk3fA5N
```

Google will return either an HTTP 200 response, if login succeeded, or an HTTP 403 response, if login failed. If successful, we parse the response to get the token string (from `Auth`), which we need in our subsequent API calls. Note that we have to log in in twice, once into Google Docs and another time into Google Spreadsheets because we cannot use the same token for both applications.

Armed with the token we can now call the Google Document List and Spreadsheet APIs. First, we need to be able to get the feeds. Google Docs and Google Spreadsheets have different URLs for their feeds so we need to have a method for each:

```
def gdoc_feed(feed)
    results = ''
    open("http://" + GOOGLE_DOCS_URL + feed, 'Authorization' =>
        "GoogleLogin auth=#{@gdoc_token}") { |s|
      results = XmlSimple::xml_in(s.read, 'force_array' => false)
    }
    return results
end
def gss_feed(feed)
    results = ''
    open("http://" + GOOGLE_SPREADSHEETS_URL + feed, 'Authorization'
        => "GoogleLogin auth=#{@gss_token}") { |s|
      results = XmlSimple::xml_in(s.read, 'force_array' => false)
    }
    return results
end
```

We use Open URI here to get the feed and parse it through XmlSimple as in Chapter 7. The returned results are an array of hashes with the information, which we will parse into the various container objects. Note that we need to pass in an `Authorization` value with the Google login token in the header.

Before we examine the feed, let's go through the container objects that we will be storing the spreadsheet information in. The first one is the `Spreadsheet` class:

```
class Spreadsheet
  attr_accessor :title, :author, :spreadsheet_id,
                :worksheets, :link, :edit_link,
                :updated_on
  end
```

This class models a Google Spreadsheet document. Each spreadsheet contains one or more worksheets, so `worksheets` is an array of `Worksheet` objects. The `link` is the URL to the spreadsheet while the `edit_link` is the URL of the feed should we need to modify the spreadsheet or delete it. We will be using this in a while. Next we look at the `Worksheet` class, which models a worksheet in the Google spreadsheet document:

```
class Worksheet
    attr_accessor :title, :row_count, :col_count,
                    :worksheet_id, :rows, :edit_link
  end
```

This is very similar to the `Spreadsheet` class but this time, it contains an array of rows instead. Finally we take a look at the `Row` class, which models a row in the worksheet:

```
class Row < Hash
    def method_missing(m, *a)
      if m.to_s.upcase =~ /=$/
        self[$`] = a[0]
      elsif a.empty?
        self[m.to_s]
      else
        raise NoMethodError, "#{m}"
      end
    end
  end
```

The `Row` class extends `Hash` and doesn't have any attributes. Instead it overrides the `method_missing` method to redirect any method calls to the internal hash with the method name as the key to the hash. Let's look at why we do this as we inspect the feeds more closely.

Take this spreadsheet for example:

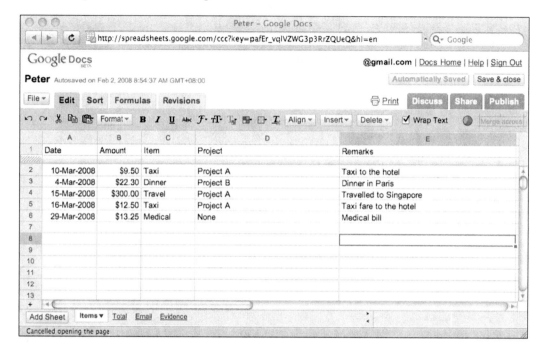

This produces an ATOM feed that looks like this:

```
<entry>
<id>http://docs.google.com/feeds/documents/private/full/
    spreadsheet%3ApafEr_vqlVZWG3p3RrZQUeQ</id>
    <updated>2008-02-02T00:54:37.383Z</updated>
    <category scheme="http://schemas.google.com/docs/2007/folders/
                    somemail@gmail.com" term="approved-claims"
                    label="approved-claims"/>
    <category scheme="http://schemas.google.com/g/2005#kind"
                term="http://schemas.google.com/docs/2007#spreadsheet"
                label="spreadsheet"/>
    <title type="text">Peter</title>
    <content type="text/html" src="http://spreadsheets.google.com/fm?f
            mcmd=102&amp;key=pafEr_vqlVZWG3p3RrZQUeQ"/>
    <link rel="alternate" type="text/html" href="http://spreadsheets.
            google.com/ccc?key=pafEr_vqlVZWG3p3RrZQUeQ"/>
    <link rel="http://schemas.google.com/spreadsheets/
            2006#worksheetsfeed" type="application/atom+xml"
            href="http://spreadsheets.google.com/feeds/worksheets/
            pafEr_vqlVZWG3p3RrZQUeQ/private/full"/>
    <link rel="self" type="application/atom+xml" href="http://
            docs.google.com/feeds/documents/private/full/
```

```
            spreadsheet%3ApafEr_vqlVZWG3p3RrZQUeQ"/>
    <link rel="edit" type="application/atom+xml" href="http://
           docs.google.com/feeds/documents/private/full/
           spreadsheet%3ApafEr_vqlVZWG3p3RrZQUeQ/fc5gdcuf"/>
    <author>
      <name>sausheong</name>
      <email>username@gmail.com</email>
    </author>
  </entry>
```

This is a spreadsheet feed that is returned when we search for spreadsheets or ask
for spreadsheet listings. Notice that it is placed within an `<entry>` element. Two
links we are interested in is the worksheet feed link and the edit link. We use the
worksheet feed link to get to the worksheet feed, while we will need the edit link
later to delete the spreadsheet after parsing it.

To parse this feed, we run it through XmlSimple. This returns a hash following the
structure above:

```
{"category"=>
    [{"term"=>"approved-claims",
      "scheme"=>"http://schemas.google.com/docs/2007/folders/
                 somemail@gmail.com",
      "label"=>"approved-claims"}, {"term"=>"http://schemas.google.
                 com/docs/2007#spreadsheet",
      "scheme"=>"http://schemas.google.com/g/2005#kind",
      "label"=>"spreadsheet"}],
  "title"=>{"type"=>"text", "content"=>"Peter"},
  "author"=>{"name"=>"sausheong", "email"=>"somemail@gmail.com"},
  "id"=>"http://docs.google.com/feeds/documents/private/full/
        spreadsheet%3ApafEr_vqlVZWG3p3RrZQUeQ",
  "content"=> {"src"=>"http://spreadsheets.google.com/
               fm?fmcmd=102&key=pafEr_vqlVZWG3p3RrZQUeQ",
               "type"=>"text/html"},
  "link"=> [{"href"=>"http://spreadsheets.google.com/ccc?key=pafEr_
            vqlVZWG3p3RrZQUeQ",
  "rel"=>"alternate",
  "type"=>"text/html"},
    {"href"=>"http://spreadsheets.google.com/feeds/worksheets/pafEr_
    vqlVZWG3p3RrZQUeQ/private/full", "rel"=>"http://schemas.google.
    com/spreadsheets/2006#worksheetsfeed",
    "type"=>"application/atom+xml"},
    {"href"=>"http://docs.google.com/feeds/documents/private/full/
    spreadsheet%3ApafEr_vqlVZWG3p3RrZQUeQ",
    "rel"=>"self",
    "type"=>"application/atom+xml"},
    {"href"=>"http://docs.google.com/feeds/documents/private/full/
    spreadsheet%3ApafEr_vqlVZWG3p3RrZQUeQ/fc5gdcuf",
```

```
    "rel"=>"edit",
    "type"=>"application/atom+xml"}],
  "updated"=>"2008-02-02T00:54:37.383Z"}
```

This code shows how XmlSimple translates the feed into hashes and arrays of hashes. For example, to get to the worksheet feed, we would check `hash['link']['rel']` to find out which element contains the worksheet feed and refer to `hash['link']['href']` as the worksheet feed.

Next, we want to get to the worksheet feed.

```
<?xml version="1.0" encoding="UTF-8"?>
<feed xmlns="http://www.w3.org/2005/Atom" xmlns:openSearch=
          "http://a9.com/-/spec/opensearchrss/1.0/" xmlns:gs=
          "http://schemas.google.com/spreadsheets/2006">
<id>http://spreadsheets.google.com/feeds/worksheets/
   pafEr_vqlVZWG3p3RrZQUeQ/private/full</id>
  <updated>2008-02-02T00:54:37.383Z</updated>
  <category scheme="http://schemas.google.com/spreadsheets/2006"
    term="http://schemas.google.com/spreadsheets/2006#worksheet"/>
  <title type="text">Peter</title>
  <link rel="alternate" type="text/html" href="http://spreadsheets.
    google.com/ccc?key=pafEr_vqlVZWG3p3RrZQUeQ"/>
  <link rel="http://schemas.google.com/g/2005#feed" type="application/
    atom+xml" href="http://spreadsheets.google.com/feeds/worksheets/
    pafEr_vqlVZWG3p3RrZQUeQ/private/full"/>
  <link rel="http://schemas.google.com/g/2005#post" type="application/
    atom+xml" href="http://spreadsheets.google.com/feeds/worksheets/
    pafEr_vqlVZWG3p3RrZQUeQ/private/full"/>
  <link rel="self" type="application/atom+xml" href="http://
    spreadsheets.google.com/feeds/worksheets/pafEr_vqlVZWG3p3RrZQUeQ/
    private/full"/>
  <author>
    <name>sausheong</name>
    <email>somemail@gmail.com</email>
  </author>
  <openSearch:totalResults>4</openSearch:totalResults>
  <openSearch:startIndex>1</openSearch:startIndex>
  <entry> <id>http://spreadsheets.google.com/feeds/worksheets/
    pafEr_vqlVZWG3p3RrZQUeQ/private/full/od6</id>
    <updated>2008-02-02T00:54:37.383Z</updated>
    <category scheme="http://schemas.google.com/spreadsheets/2006"
        term="http://schemas.google.com/spreadsheets/2006#worksheet"/>
    <title type="text">Items</title>
    <content type="text">Items</content>
    <link rel="http://schemas.google.com/spreadsheets/2006#listfeed"
        type="application/atom+xml" href="http://spreadsheets.google.
```

```
        com/feeds/list/pafEr_vqlVZWG3p3RrZQUeQ/od6/private/full"/>
    <link rel="http://schemas.google.com/spreadsheets/2006#cellsfeed"
          type="application/atom+xml" href="http://spreadsheets.google.
          com/feeds/cells/pafEr_vqlVZWG3p3RrZQUeQ/od6/private/full"/>
    <link rel="self" type="application/atom+xml" href="http://
        spreadsheets.google.com/feeds/worksheets/
        pafEr_vqlVZWG3p3RrZQUeQ/private/full/od6"/>
    <link rel="edit" type="application/atom+xml" href="http://
        spreadsheets.google.com/feeds/worksheets/
        pafEr_vqlVZWG3p3RrZQUeQ/private/full/od6/bu1jir0swo"/>
    <gs:rowCount>100</gs:rowCount>
    <gs:colCount>20</gs:colCount>
  </entry>
</feed>
```

This is a worksheet feed containing all the worksheets in the particular spreadsheet (only the first worksheet is shown). Each worksheet is contained within an <entry> element. The link we're interested here is the list feed. The list feed is a feed of the contents of the worksheet shown in rows. The worksheet also has a cell feed, which shows the contents of the worksheet by individual cells. However, for this mashup we will be using the list feed only. As before, we get the URL to the list feed, which returns an ATOM feed containing the rows in the worksheet. Each row again is represented within an <entry> element.

```
<entry> <id>http://spreadsheets.google.com/feeds/list/
        pafEr_vqlVZWG3p3RrZQUeQ/od6/private/full/cokwr</id>
    <updated>2008-02-02T00:54:37.383Z</updated>
    <category scheme="http://schemas.google.com/spreadsheets/2006"
            term="http://schemas.google.com/spreadsheets/2006#list"/>
    <title type="text">3/10/2008</title>
    <content type="text">amount: $9.50, item: Taxi, project: Project
            A, remarks: Taxi to the hotel</content>
    <link rel="self" type="application/atom+xml" href="http://
        spreadsheets.google.com/feeds/list/pafEr_vqlVZWG3p3RrZQUeQ/
        od6/private/full/cokwr"/>
    <link rel="edit" type="application/atom+xml" href="http://
        spreadsheets.google.com/feeds/list/pafEr_vqlVZWG3p3RrZQUeQ/
        od6/private/full/cokwr/gf6ji7n3f2d53"/>
    <gsx:date>3/10/2008</gsx:date>
    <gsx:amount>$9.50</gsx:amount>
    <gsx:item>Taxi</gsx:item>
    <gsx:project>Project A</gsx:project>
    <gsx:remarks>Taxi to the hotel</gsx:remarks>
</entry>
```

By running this through XmlSimple, we get the rows from the worksheet, each row looking like this:

```
{"remarks"=>"Taxi to the hotel",
    "category"=>{"term"=>"http://schemas.google.com/spreadsheets/
                2006#list",
 "scheme"=>"http://schemas.google.com/spreadsheets/2006"},
    "title"=>{"type"=>"text", "content"=>"3/10/2008"},
    "project"=>"Project A",
    "date"=>"3/10/2008",
    "id"=>"http://spreadsheets.google.com/feeds/list/pafEr_
        vqlVZWG3p3RrZQUeQ/od6/private/full/cokwr",
    "amount"=>"$9.50",
    "content"=>
     {"type"=>"text",
      "content"=>
       "amount: $9.50, item: Taxi, project: Project A, remarks: Taxi
                to the hotel"},
    "item"=>"Taxi",
    "link"=>
     [{"href"=>"http://spreadsheets.google.com/feeds/list/pafEr_
             vqlVZWG3p3RrZQUeQ/od6/private/full/cokwr",
       "rel"=>"self",
       "type"=>"application/atom+xml"},
      {"href"=>"http://spreadsheets.google.com/feeds/list/pafEr_
             vqlVZWG3p3RrZQUeQ/od6/private/full/cokwr/gf6ji7n3f2d53",
       "rel"=>"edit",
       "type"=>"application/atom+xml"}],
    "updated"=>"2008-02-02T00:54:37.383Z"}
```

As you can see, this hash contains data that is accessible by calling a method with the name of the first row of the column. In the sample earlier, the row that is mapped is row 2 in the spreadsheet shown in the screenshot above. You can see that calling `hash['remarks']` will return the value of the row for the corresponding `remarks` column. It is now clear why the `Row` class is a subclass of `Hash` with an overridden `method_missing`. Calling a properly populated Row object with the name of the column will return the row value.

With all the groundwork on the feeds, let's look at the code that will populate the Spreadsheet, Worksheet, and Row objects. First, we need to get all the spreadsheets from the `approved-claims` folder, and we have an appropriately named `spreadsheets_in_folder` method to do this:

```
def spreadsheets_in_folder(folder)
    feed = gdoc_feed("/feeds/documents/private/full/-
            /%7Bhttp:%2F%2Fschemas.google.com%2Fdocs%2F2007%2Ffolders
            %2F#{@user_id}%7D#{folder}")
    spreadsheets = []
    spreadsheet_data = []
```

```ruby
  if feed['totalResults'].to_i > 1 then
    spreadsheet_data = spreadsheet_data + feed['entry']
  else
    spreadsheet_data = spreadsheet_data << feed['entry']
  end
  spreadsheet_data.each { |doc|
    if doc['category'].include? SPREADSHEET_CATEGORY then
      ss = Spreadsheet.new
      ss.title = doc['title']['content']
      ss.author = doc['author']['name']
      ss.spreadsheet_id = doc['id']
      doc['link'].each { |link|
        case link['rel']
        when "http://schemas.google.com/spreadsheets/
            2006#worksheetsfeed"
          # hack to overcome bug in Google Spreadsheets http://
            code.google.com/p/gdata-issues/issues/detail?id=321
          wks_link =  link['href'].sub "trix.", ""
          ss.worksheets = get_worksheets_from(wks_link)
        when "alternate"
          ss.link = link['href']
        when "edit"
          ss.edit_link = link['href']
        end
      }
      ss.updated_on = doc['updated']
      spreadsheets << ss
    end
  }
  return spreadsheets
end
```

With the previous background, it is now easy to understand the code. Note that we're using the Google Document List Data API here. We parse the feed `/feeds/ documents/private/full/-/%7Bhttp:%2F%2Fschemas.google.com%2Fdocs%2F20 07%2Ffolders%2F<user's Google email ID>%7D<folder to search>` to return a feed containing all documents in the folder. Next, for each document we check if the document is a spreadsheet and populate a newly created spreadsheet accordingly. At the time of writing there exists a bug in Google Spreadsheet Data API that adds a string 'trix.' to the spreadsheet link, so we need to work around to remove it. To populate the array of worksheets, we call another method `get_worksheets_from`, parsing the corrected worksheet feed.

```ruby
def get_worksheets_from(worksheetfeed)
    uri = URI.parse worksheetfeed
    worksheets = []
    feed = gss_feed(uri.path)
    puts '-- end worksheet --'
    if feed['totalResults'].to_i > 1 then
```

```
        feed['entry'].each {|ws|
          worksheets << populate_worksheet(ws)
        }
      else
        worksheets << populate_worksheet(feed['entry'])
      end
      return worksheets
    end
```

`get_worksheets_from` parses the feed and calls another method, `populate_worksheet` to work through the worksheet content.

```
    def populate_worksheet(data)
        ws = Worksheet.new
        ws.title = data['title']['content']
        ws.row_count = data['rowCount']
        ws.col_count = data['colCount']
        ws.worksheet_id = data['id']
        data['link'].each { |link|
          case link['rel']
          when "http://schemas.google.com/spreadsheets/2006#listfeed"
            ws.rows = get_rows(link['href'])
          when "edit"
            ws.edit_link = link['href']
          end
        }
        return ws
    end
```

`populate_worksheet` works through the worksheet content and creates a new worksheet for each worksheet in the spreadsheet. This method in turn calls `get_rows` to create and populate the Row objects.

```
    def get_rows(listfeed)
      uri = URI.parse listfeed
      rows = []
      feed = gss_feed(uri.path)
      if feed['totalResults'].to_i > 1 then
        feed['entry'].each { |row|
          rows << Row.new.merge(row)
        }
      elsif feed['totalResults'].to_i == 1 then
        rows << Row.new.merge(feed['entry'])
      end
      return rows
    end
```

Now that we can get a properly populated Spreadsheet document, let's finish up with the rest of the library methods.

After we parse the expense claim spreadsheet, we need to remove the spreadsheet from the `approved-claims` folder so that it won't be parsed again in the next scheduled run. To do this, we will use the Document Data List API again in a `delete` method:

```
def delete(spreadsheet)
    url = URI.parse(spreadsheet.edit_link)
    res = Net::HTTP.new(url.host, url.port).start {|http| http.
        delete(url.path, 'Authorization' => "GoogleLogin auth=#{@
        gdoc_token}") }
    case res
    when Net::HTTPSuccess, Net::HTTPRedirection
      return true
    else
      return false
    end
end
```

This is a simple method. We get the spreadsheet's edit link and send an HTTP `Delete` request to the URL, using the authentication token. This will remove the spreadsheet from the application and place it in the trash bin. The expense claim spreadsheet is not deleted until the manager empties the trash bin.

The final method we will be creating in our Google library is a method that retrieves a word processor document from Google Docs and saves it in PDF format.

```
def get_pdf_document(docid)
    results = ''
    url = "http://docs.google.com/MiscCommands?command=saveasdoc&exp
        ortformat=pdf&docID=#{docid}"
    open(url, 'Authorization' => "GoogleLogin auth=#{@gdoc_token}")
  {
    |s| results = s.read
  }
    return results
end
```

This time we use Open URI again to send an HTTP request to an undocumented (as of now) URL that allows us to save the document in various formats. The returned result is a string containing the data in the PDF document.

Creating the Manager class and its controller and views

As an intermediate step, we need to create a simple Manager class that represents the manager. We will use the Manager to store and retrieve a set of managers who manage the employees.

Create a migration file for the managers:

```
$./script/generate migration create_managers
```

This will generate a `002_create_managers.rb` migration script in the `$RAILS_ROOT/db/migrate` folder. Modify it to look like this:

```
class CreateManagers < ActiveRecord::Migration
  def self.up
    create_table :managers do |t|
      t.column 'name', :string
      t.column 'google_username', :string
      t.column 'google_password', :string
      t.column 'created_on', :datetime
    end
  end
  def self.down
    drop_table :managers
  end
end
```

Then run the migration to create the database tables.

```
$rake db:migrate
```

Next, create the necessary scaffolding for the Manager class:

```
$./script/generate scaffold Manager
```

This is all we need to do for now, except to enter a few manager records.

Creating the expense claims parsing rake script

With our Google library now complete, let's turn to creating the script that parses through the expense claims spreadsheets on Google Docs and Spreadsheets. Create a rake script named `check_claims.rake` in the `$RAILS_ROOT/lib/tasks` folder:

```
require 'GData'
namespace :chapter8 do
  desc "Activated regularly by AT or cronjob to process expense
```

```
claims"
  task(:check_claims => :environment) do
    Manager.find(:all).each { |manager|
      puts "Processing claims for manager [#{manager.name}]"
      gdata = GData.new
      gdata.login manager.google_username, manager.google_password
      spreadsheets = gdata.spreadsheets_in_folder 'approved-claims'
      spreadsheets.each { |spreadsheet|
        puts "Processing [ #{spreadsheet.title} ]"
        claim = Claim.new
        claim.name = spreadsheet.title
        spreadsheet.worksheets.each { |worksheet|
          case worksheet.title
          when 'Items'
            worksheet.rows.each {|row|
              item = ClaimItem.new
              item.expense_date = row.date
              item.project = row.project
              item.remarks = row.remarks if row.remarks
              item.amount = row.amount.delete('$').to_f
              item.item = row.item
              claim.claim_items << item
            }
          when 'Total'
            claim.amount =
                      worksheet.rows[0].totalamount.delete('$').to_f
          when 'Email'
            claim.email = worksheet.rows[0].email
          when 'Evidence'
            doc_id = ''
URI.parse(worksheet.rows[0].evidencedocument).query.split('&').each
{|p| doc_id = p.split('=')[1] if p.include? 'docid=' }
            claim.expense_evidence = gdata.get_pdf_document(doc_id)
          else
            raise 'Unknown worksheet found'
          end
        }
        claim.save
        puts "Expense claims ($#{claim.amount}) entered into system."
        if gdata.delete(spreadsheet) then
          puts "Moved claims spreadsheet to trashbin"
        end
      }
    }
  end
end
```

This script is quite straightforward. It starts off with getting all the managers entered into the mashup, and iterates through them to check on their approved expense claims. First, it gets all the spreadsheets in the `approved-claims` folder and creates a Claim object for each claims spreadsheet.

Next, it works through each worksheet in each spreadsheet. When it finds the `Items` worksheet, it will store each of the claim items in this worksheet into a claim details object, which is subsequently attached to the Claim object. When it finds an `Evidence` worksheet, it will look for the URL of the word processor document in Google Docs and extract it as a PDF then save it into a binary field in the Claim object. This document will be used later for auditing the expense claims.

Finally after the spreadsheet it parsed, the claim object is persisted into the database and the claims spreadsheet in Google Spreadsheets is moved to the trash bin.

This script should be run on a regular basis, either executed through a Windows task scheduler or a cron job in Unix. The frequency of the execution depends mostly on the work patterns of employees submitting claims. Since this is a monthly expense claims reimbursement, the script should be run at least once a month.

Creating the mass payment rake script

The previous section described how to extract the expense claims data. This section will describe how we will use this data to reimburse the employees for their expenses. The main mechanism is a rake script, which is run at the end of the salary month, just after the salary payment. This means that the script is normally run once a month.

Create a rake script named `masspay.rake` in the `$RAILS_ROOT/lib/tasks` folder:

```ruby
require 'rubygems'
require 'ruby-paypal'
namespace :chapter8 do
  desc "Activated regularly by AT or cronjob to process payments"
  task(:masspay => :environment) do
    payments = Payment.find_all_by_state('pending')
    pending_payments = []
    payments.each { |payment|
      puts "Paying [#{payment.name}]"
      pay = PayPalPayment.new
      pay.email = payment.email
      pay.unique_id = "claim_#{Time.now.to_i}"
      pay.note = 'Reimbursement for expense claim'
      pay.amount = payment.amount
      payment.pay!
      pending_payments << pay
```

```
        }
        paypal = Paypal.new('PAYPAL PRO ACCOUNT USERNAME',
                            'PAYPAL ACCOUNT PASSWORD',
                            'PAYPAL API SIGNATURE')
        if paypal.do_mass_payment(pending_payments, "Payment sent #{Time.
                now}").ack == "Success"
          puts "Successfully processed #{pending_payments.size} payments"
        else
          raise "Error in payment processing, please check the error logs"
        end
      end
    end
```

Notice that we're using the Ruby-PayPal gem here. The logic in the script is simple as well. It finds all pending payment records in the database and iterates through each one of them and creates an array of `PayPalPayment` objects. This array is then sent to the `Paypal` object for mass payment.

This results in payment to the employees who have their expense claims approved and successfully recorded in the mashup. The payment record in the database is then set to `Paid` and will not be run in the subsequent months.

Modifying the Payment and Claim Item controllers

Finally after the models have been created and data populated into the database, it's time to see how it looks with a simple user interface. We already have the models; we just need to tweak the scaffold-generated controllers a bit to meet our needs. Modify the `list` method in `claim_items_controller.rb` file in the `$RAILS_ROOT/app/controllers` folder to display the expense claim details of a specific claim only:

```
def list
    @claim_item_pages, @claim_items = paginate :claim_items, :per_page
        => 10, :conditions => ['claim_id = ?', params[:id]]
end
```

Also change the `payments_controller.rb` file in the `RAILS_ROOT/app/controllers` folder and add in an `expense_evidence` method to display the expense evidence in Adobe Acrobat (PDF) format:

```
def expense_evidence
    payment = Payment.find(params[:id])
    send_data(payment.expense_evidence,
            :type => "application/pdf",
            :disposition => "inline",
            :filename => "#{payment.name}_evidence.pdf")
end
```

This method will use the document (stored in a binary format) in the payment table and show it as an inline PDF document.

Correspondingly modify the `list.rhtml` view in `RAILS_ROOT/app/views/payments` to show the extra actions.

```
<h1>Salary and Expense Payments</h1>
<table>
  <tr>
  <th>Date</th>
   <th>Type</th>
   <th>Name</th>
   <th>Status</th>
   <th>Email</th>
   <th>Amount</th>
   <th>Actions</th>
  </tr>
    <% for payment in @payments %>
  <tr>
    <td><%=h payment.created_on.strftime '%d/%m/%Y' %></td>
    <td><%=h payment.type %></td>
    <td><%=h payment.name %></td>
    <td><%=h payment.state %></td>
    <td><%=h payment.email %></td>
    <td><%=h number_to_currency payment.amount %></td>
  <td>
    <%= link_to 'Show', :action => 'show', :id => payment %> |
    <%= link_to 'Edit', :action => 'edit', :id => payment %> |
    <%= link_to 'Del', { :action => 'destroy', :id => payment },
        :confirm => 'Are you sure?', :method => :post %> |
    <%= link_to 'Evidence', :action => 'expense_evidence',
        :id => payment %> |
    <%= link_to 'Details', :controller => 'claim_items',
        :id => payment if payment.kind_of? Claim %>
  </td>
  </tr>
<% end %>
</table>
<%= link_to 'Previous page', { :page => @payment_pages.current.
    previous } if @payment_pages.current.previous %>
<%= link_to 'Next page', { :page => @payment_pages.current.next } if @
    payment_pages.current.next %>
<br />
<%= link_to 'New payment', :action => 'new' %>
```

Now we have everything. To show you more clearly how it all works, let's go through the process by screenshots.

How it works all together

We start off with the employee. If it is the first time he or she is claiming for expense reimbursement, he or she can upload a spreadsheet template (Excel or any other spreadsheet document format supported by Google Docs and Spreadsheets) by the Finance department. There is a template in the source code material. Otherwise he or she just needs to duplicate an existing expense claims spreadsheet. This is how the spreadsheet should look:

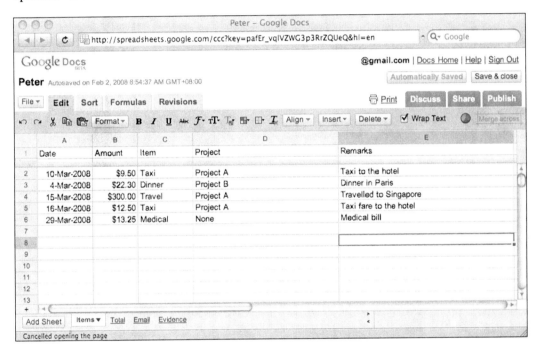

He or she also needs to scan his or her expense receipts and attach them to a word processor document.

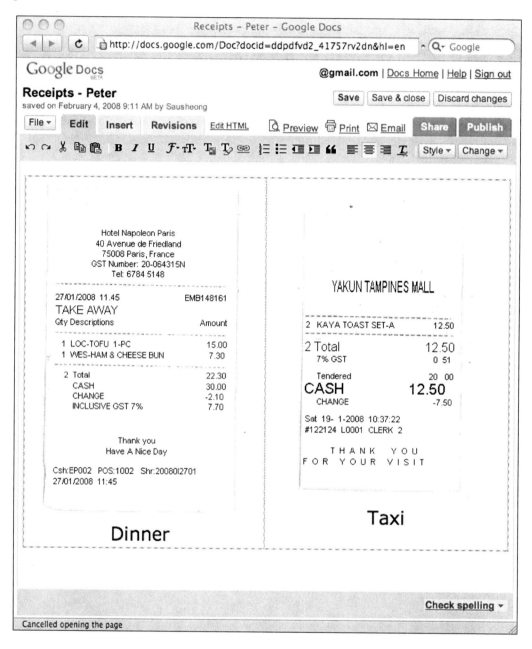

He or she links up the claims spreadsheet with the receipts document through the Evidence worksheet in the claims spreadsheet.

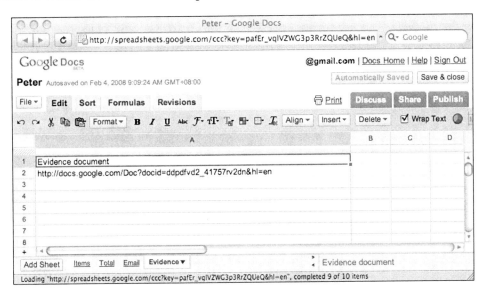

When ready to submit his claims to his or her manager for approval, he or she shares both documents with his or her manager. (The manager needs to have set up an account through the application—`http://localhost:3000/managers/new`).

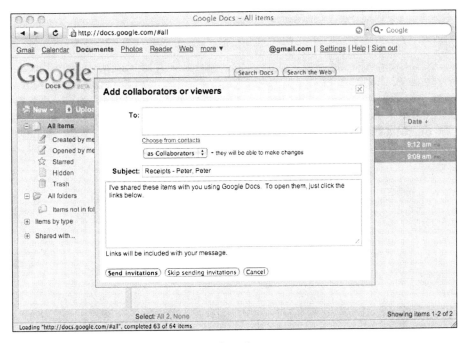

When his or her manager sees the expense claims, he or she can open up both documents to review and change the expense claims as necessary. Any changes will be reflected back to the employee so he or she knows what has been approved. When the manager is ready to approve the claims, he or she will place the claims spreadsheet and receipt document into a folder named `approved-claims` together with all the other approved expense claims documents.

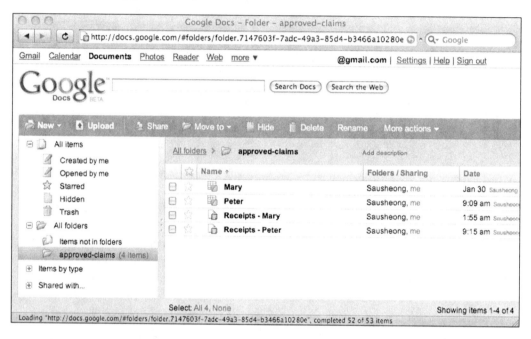

At scheduled intervals, the check-claims rake script will be run to extract these documents from the manager's approved-claims folder and save them as claims payments into the database. After the data is extracted, the claims spreadsheet is moved into the manager's trash bin, which the manager can empty at a later time while the original claims spreadsheet still remains with the employee.

The Finance person can also review the claims and audit the expense receipts from the mashup.

Clicking on the Evidence link will retrieve and display the PDF document and clicking on the Details link will show the details of the claims.

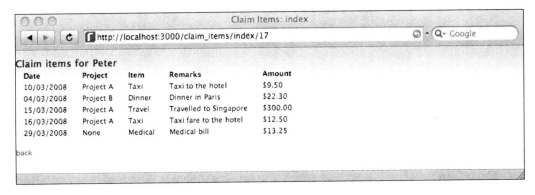

At the end of the month, the mass payment rake script is run and the employee is paid through PayPal. This is the history of the payment that was paid out of the company's account (which includes two employees in this example):

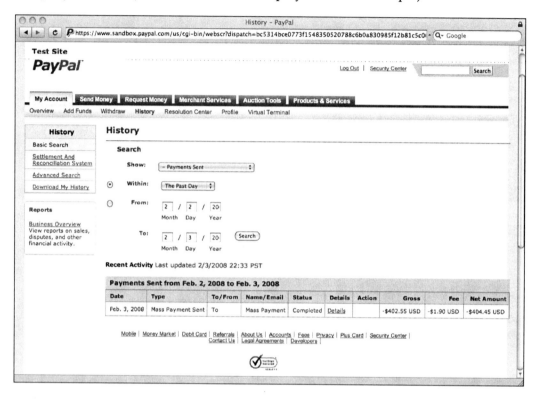

This is the history of the payment that is received by the employee:

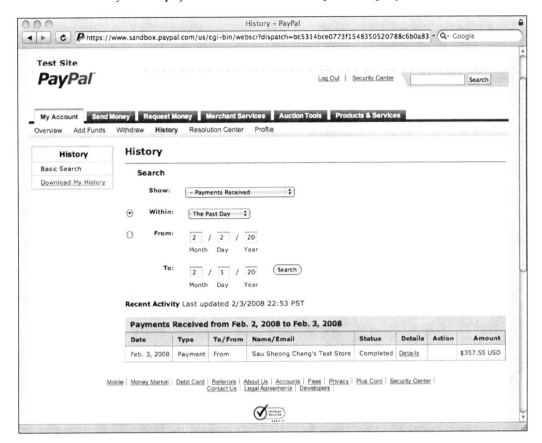

Summary

We have created a simple expense claims mashup using Google Docs and Spreadsheet and PayPal. We allowed the employee to submit expense claims through a spreadsheet and a word processor document with attached scans of expense receipts. The expense claim is then approved by his or her immediate manager and placed into an approved-claims folder. At periodic intervals, we use a script to extract the contents of the claims spreadsheet and archive the receipts documents into a PDF format and save them into the mashup database. At the end of the month, we use the information in the database to send mass payments to all employees through PayPal.

Index

Packt Open Source Project Royalties

When we sell a book written on an Open Source project, we pay a royalty directly to that project. Therefore by purchasing Ruby on Rails Web Mashup Projects, Packt will have given some of the money received to the Ruby on Rails Project.

In the long term, we see ourselves and you—customers and readers of our books—as part of the Open Source ecosystem, providing sustainable revenue for the projects we publish on. Our aim at Packt is to establish publishing royalties as an essential part of the service and support a business model that sustains Open Source.

If you're working with an Open Source project that you would like us to publish on, and subsequently pay royalties to, please get in touch with us.

Writing for Packt

We welcome all inquiries from people who are interested in authoring. Book proposals should be sent to authors@packtpub.com. If your book idea is still at an early stage and you would like to discuss it first before writing a formal book proposal, contact us; one of our commissioning editors will get in touch with you.

We're not just looking for published authors; if you have strong technical skills but no writing experience, our experienced editors can help you develop a writing career, or simply get some additional reward for your expertise.

About Packt Publishing

Packt, pronounced 'packed', published its first book "Mastering phpMyAdmin for Effective MySQL Management" in April 2004 and subsequently continued to specialize in publishing highly focused books on specific technologies and solutions.

Our books and publications share the experiences of your fellow IT professionals in adapting and customizing today's systems, applications, and frameworks. Our solution-based books give you the knowledge and power to customize the software and technologies you're using to get the job done. Packt books are more specific and less general than the IT books you have seen in the past. Our unique business model allows us to bring you more focused information, giving you more of what you need to know, and less of what you don't.

Packt is a modern, yet unique publishing company, which focuses on producing quality, cutting-edge books for communities of developers, administrators, and newbies alike. For more information, please visit our website: www.PacktPub.com.

Printed in the United Kingdom by
Lightning Source UK Ltd., Milton Keynes
139229UK00001B/118/P